It's Good Business

Ethics and Free Enterprise for the New Millennium

Robert C. Solomon

ROWMAN & LITTLEFIELD PUBLISHERS, INC.
Lanham • Boulder • New York • Oxford

ROWMAN & LITTLEFIELD PUBLISHERS, INC.

Published in the United States of America
by Rowman & Littlefield Publishers, Inc.
4720 Boston Way, Lanham, Maryland 20706

12 Hid's Copse Road
Cummor Hill, Oxford OX2 9JJ, England

British Library Cataloguing in Publication Information Available

Library of Congress Cataloging-in-Publication Data

Solomon, Robert C.
  It's good business : ethics and free enterprise for the new
millennium / Robert C. Solomon.
      p.   cm.
  Includes index.
  ISBN 0-8476-8804-6 (alk. paper)
  1. Business ethics. 2. Free enterprise   Moral and ethical
aspects. I. Title.
HF5387.S6253   1997
174'.4—dc21
                                                              97-31301
                                                              CIP

Printed in the United States of America

♾™ The paper used in this publication meets the minimum requirements of American
National Standard for Information Sciences—Permanence of Paper for Printed Library
Materials, ANSI Z39.48–1984.

*In memory of my father
Charles M. Solomon
A truly moral man
in a world that did
not always agree*

What good people they are. It is not at all bad being a businessman. There is a spirit of trust and cooperation here. Everyone jokes about such things, but if businessmen were not trusting of each other the country would collapse tomorrow....

Walker Percy, The Moviegoer

CONTENTS

Part Two: Motivation, Money, and Morals: Micro-Ethics

Part Three: In, Out, and Up the Organization: Molar Ethics

PREFACE

During the four decades I have been in business, I have found that the corporate world is filled with businessmen who want to do what is right, not with Scrooges who delight in exploiting widows and orphans. The vast majority of today's executives are ethical and honest. Yet sometimes we can become so occupied with fretting over our mathematical models, sales projections and quarterly earnings statements that it is difficult to keep in mind one of the most basic truths of successful business—in the long run, the best business decision is that which is founded on the most ethical judgments.

Donald V. Seibert (CEO and chairman, J. C. Penney Co.)

Business is an ethical activity. That is the premise of this book. The search for excellence, whatever else it may be, begins with ethics.

The world of business has become global. With globalization, business is not only more competitive, it increasingly depends on cooperation and intelligence. And, accordingly, it is becoming increasingly self-reflective.

In fact, the ethics of business and the moral code of our society are inseparable, sometimes indistinguishable. Our daily concern with efficiency, fair exchange, and the work ethic—getting what we pay for, earning our keep, being paid what we're worth—is the very heart of business ethics. Our emphasis on negotiation, our respect for promises and contracts, are ethical lessons basic to business. And, most important, our respect for individual differences and our concern for the material well-being of all—or what Adam Smith called the "wealth of the nation"—are the ultimate promises of a democratic business society. Our founding fathers were businessmen, not saints or military heroes. The business person considers himself—now herself, too—to be a "pillar of the community." Our universities, our government, our charities, and even our churches are run by business people.

Yet "business ethics" is still a matter of controversy. Public opinion is clearly antagonistic to business. Corporations large and small are attacked as amoral and unethical. Business people are depicted in popular television programs, one Media Institute study suggested, as "crooks and clowns." In two hundred episodes of fifty top network series, businessmen were portrayed 67 percent of the time "in a negative manner—as criminals, fools, or greedy or malevolent egotists—while only 25 percent are shown in a positive light." In a study of 863 sitcoms, dramas, and made-for-TV movies on the four U.S. networks, 29.2 percent of 514 criminals portrayed were business people, more than any other occupation, including career criminals (U.S. Media Research Center, 1997).

Some of the blame for this unflattering portrait lies with business people themselves. Business schools, business thinking, and especially

---

CROOKS AND CLOWNS ON TV

See the dastard. Hiss at him. See the dolt. Hoot at him. They're both businessmen, TV variety.

In the skimpy fare served up as network entertainment night after night, the business world is peopled mostly by ne'er-do-wells and nincompoops. Likely as not, businessmen and women are portrayed on the tube as schemers and lawbreakers, *à la* J. R. Ewing, or else they're bubbleheads bumbling about and mouthing off for laughs, in the manner of Archie Bunker.

Such are the gleanings of a study by the Media Institute in Washington, first of its kind ever done, looking into the way television depicts people in business. The study found that two out of every three businessmen on television come across as foolish, greedy, or evil. In the prime time view, over half of all corporate chiefs commit illegal acts, ranging from fraud to murder. Some 45% of all business activities are shown as illicit. Only 3% of TV business people behave in ways that are socially and economically productive. . . . In TV's vision of business, ethics are about as rare as rowboats in the Sahara.

From an advertisement for United Technologies

the language of business contribute to the popular perception of business as a vulgar and "dog-eat-dog" activity marked by obsession with markets, numbers, and personal success. There is still too much talk about doing "whatever it takes" to get ahead, to meet a quota or a deadline, to beat the competition. There is still too much of a sense that you can and should do "whatever you can get away with."

Business at its best, by contrast, is the conscientious production and promotion of not only quality goods and services but a better life for everyone—one's customers, one's employees, the surrounding community, and society in general. It should be a source of pride, not only profits. It is or can be a life of integrity and helping others, as well as doing well oneself. And ethics is not a burden or a business disadvantage but the very ground rules of business as such and the key to business success. There can be no business without trust and cooperation; no free enterprise, in short, without ethics.

When business people think in "dog-eat-dog" and purely self-interested terms of business, they mislead themselves, create the very conditions they describe, and provoke public antagonism, inviting government regulation. That is another reason why business ethics has become a practical problem for business as well as a popular topic in the media, in politics, and in the universities.

In decades past, ethics policies have been seen as mere window dressing, "PR," a nice embellishment for those companies that could afford them. Times have changed. In November 1991, the U.S. government introduced "draconian" new sentencing guidelines for corporate misbehavior. These guidelines allow prosecutors to demand enormous, even ruinous, fines from offending companies. They also encourage the companies to develop substantial ethics and compliance programs in order to reduce these fines. The guidelines take a "carrot-and-stick" approach to corporate compliance. The stick is a combination of fines and threats of further damages, including prison terms for guilty executives. The carrot is the promise that the law will look kindly on those companies that have developed internal mechanisms of education, self-examination, and self-correction.

In a recent discussion of the sentencing guidelines and the new order of business, Georgetown University ethicist Tom Donaldson warned of the possibility of fines of $290 million "and more." The U.S. attorney for the Southern District of New York, Otto G. Obermaier, threatened multiple penalties; not only fines but orders for restitution, civil suits, and legal costs. An executive ex-con described how he ended up in Lewisburg Federal Prison Camp for six months, and he noted omi-

> Public policy and social issues are no longer adjuncts of business planning and management. They are in the mainstream of it.
>
> Reginald H. Jones (former CEO, General Electric)

nously that although he might have changed things (or quit) at the beginning of his otherwise successful career, his eventual violations were the result of "nondecisions," not "like the decision to rob a store." It was "just the way things were done," he lamented, built into the culture of the company and his industry. A litigation expert subsequently described the various ways that a corporation and its top executives can be held criminally liable for activities that they may not have even known about.

On the other hand, ethics, or what I will call "the strategic ethical response," emerges not as the result of such threats alone but out of the conviction and the cultivation of attitudes that perceive the ethical solution to be the only solution. James Burke, one of this book's heroes and the chairman of Johnson & Johnson at the time of the Tylenol crisis, has said, "There were no alternatives, . . . none," to the option of pulling every bottle from the shelves (at a cost of $150 million). Johnson & Johnson instituted an ethical code over a long period of time, getting input from every manager in the company (a process Burke admits was "tedious"). But he insightfully comments that the tragedy "institutionalized" those standards, which got tested in the most severely imaginable way. The result: Johnson & Johnson got back the business it briefly lost. It gained a reputation "second to none in the world," and it became the most upbeat business ethics example to date.

For the past twenty years or so, I have been consulting and conducting seminars for a wide variety of corporations and business institutions. During that period, I have found that the subject of business ethics has been transformed from a dull joke ("must be a very short program") to the center of attention. Executives have come to realize that their brilliance in business does not automatically translate into a feeling of comfort in dealing with the hard cases of business ethics, and their personal moral character does not always have the dominance or even the influence one would like it to have in the context of a high-pressured business decision. Many executives, understandably, have never been trained to think conceptually and abstractly, but such thinking has become as essential to good business as good business sense itself. The new world of business is being defined by just such thinking and reflection, by an understanding of not only business but of the deep significance of business life and the nature and obligations of the free-enterprise system as such.

My experience in teaching and talking business ethics is the basis of this book, and in that experience, I have found, again and again, that

- The more successful the company, the more attention it pays to its code of ethics; also, the higher one climbs in the corporate hierarchy, the more there is an emphasis on and a sophistication about ethics.
- Conversely, the cynical view that ethics is irrelevant to business and not concerned with the bottom line seems to be prevalent in businesses on the brink and among people who are locked into middle-management jobs that no longer satisfy them.

The most successful people and companies are those that take ethics seriously. This is not surprising, since ethical attitudes largely determine how one treats employees, suppliers, stockholders, and consumers as well as how one treats competitors and other members of the community. Inevitably, this affects how one is treated in return. Ethical managers and ethical businesses tend to be more trusted and better treated and to suffer less resentment, inefficiency, litigation, and government interference. Ethics is just good business.

It is often thought that a book on business ethics ought to be a recipe book of moral dos and don'ts. In fact, there are very few recipes in this book. Does anyone really need to be told that cheating is wrong, that pollution is undesirable, or that it is a good thing to hire qualified

---

THE ETHICS OF SELF-PRESERVATION

The ethics movement couldn't be more timely. Given the looming threat of layoffs and enormous pressure to turn a profit these days, managers are sometimes understandably tempted to engage in a bit of dodgy behavior. "People are so desperate to keep their jobs that they act inappropriately," says Michael Josephson, who heads the Joseph & Edna Josephson Institute of Ethics in Marina Del Rey, California.

—*Business Week*, September 23, 1991

minority workers and managers? Ethical problems arise not because their solutions (or preventives) are not obvious but because ethical thinking is simply neglected. Ethical problems tend to be difficult not because of a confusion about right and wrong but rather, as the American philosopher John Dewey said, because they are choices between right and right. Ethics, accordingly, cannot be a sequence of recipes, techniques, test cases, formulas, or prescriptions. It is rather an attitude, a matter of good judgment, a way of looking at business questions, an invitation to open our eyes and enlarge our vision. The best way to improve on the bottom line is always to look beyond it.

RCS
Austin, Texas
March 1993

ACKNOWLEDGMENTS

Many people have helped me develop these views, and I especially want to thank Clancy Martin, David Sherman, and Janet McCracken at the University of Texas and Jenene Allison of WWordwwizardry. I want to thank Quincy Lee of San Antonio for his support and encouragement and my colleagues in the business school at the university for the opportunity to work with their excellent students. Thanks too to John Rose and Alasdair MacCormick, deans of the University of Melbourne and University of Auckland business schools, respectively, and thanks to my editors and publishers for letting me adapt some of the chapters from my textbook, *Above the Bottom Line* (2nd edition), for a very different role in this book. My thanks again to Kristine Hanson, who got me interested in business and business ethics in the first place, and the good people I have worked with at Chase Manhattan Bank, IBM, AT&T, NCR, and elsewhere. I owe a special, eternally unpayable debt to my father, who brought me up to think this way. It is to his memory that the book is dedicated.

INTRODUCTION

In the past decade or so, we have watched the free-enterprise system through some startling events and circumstances. We can now forget about old Marxist warnings about the supposedly iron laws of history, the inevitable revolution of the working class, and the collapse of so-called "capitalism" under its own weight. We can safely smile at the once-terrifying memory of Red Menace Comrade-in-Chief Nikita Khrushchev predicting with his bumpkin certainty that Communism would "bury" us. But with the collapse of so-called "communism" and the consequent discrediting of socialism throughout Eastern Europe, the late Union of Soviet Socialist Republics and the end of the cold war, something else of great importance is happening, though with much less fanfare and self-congratulation. Deprived of a global antagonist, we defenders of free enterprise have been forced to look inward, to ask ourselves hard questions that go beyond the usual slogans about freedom, prosperity, and the evils of communism. The problems, the possibilities, and the preconditions of what we call "the free-enterprise system" have themselves been called into question. And as we watch the nations of Eastern Europe and the former USSR struggle to transform themselves into market economies, we begin to appreciate how deep those questions, how profound those problems, how varied those possibilities and how deep and hard-earned those preconditions must be. The free-enterprise system is not a miracle and not "magic" but a very human institution. It is based on a foundation of ethics and expectations that are by no means merely "human nature" but must be cultivated—the idea that work is meaningful, even satisfying and rewarding; the idea of a good day's work for a good

1

FREE ENTERPRISE?

Tigers in Russia, an endangered species. Under totalitarian communism, ironically, they were protected. Under the tenuous new democracy and nervous turn to the free market, on the other hand, the attitude seems to be that everything is for sale. The remaining wild population of Siberian tigers (perhaps less than 200) may soon be destroyed forever. (The going price of a black market Siberian tiger skin is about $4,000. A tiger gall bladder, believed to have medicinal properties, is $400.)

(*Newsweek*, January 1993)

---

day's pay; the idea that serving and satisfying other people is the basis for one's own reward; the idea that you get what you pay for. These are platitudes to us, but difficult or barely comprehensible truths to those in societies struggling to make a market. The newly elected president of the new Czech Republic, Václav Havel, instructed his people that they have to get rid of "bad old habits." First of all, he told them, "you have to learn to trust one another." How easily we forget what we have always taken for granted!

Of course, our new appreciation for the conditions of capitalism and the ethics of free enterprise has not been inspired by the loss of a habitual enemy alone. During the same period, we have watched our one-time adversaries, Germany and Japan, become industrial giants. They have come to dominate two industries that once seemed to be essentially American—automobiles and electronics—and the United States has slipped from being the largest exporting country in the world to being the largest importing country in the world, and the largest debtor nation as well. What has become all too clear is that there is no single kind of economy called "capitalism," that the free-enterprise system is not the special province of any one country, and free enterprise can be made to fit into very different social and cultural systems, with different values and objectives and different obligations and responsibilities. And yet they all share what has become a global market. They also share the same shrinking and endangered planet, and they all share as well in "the human condition." We have as much to learn from the successes as from the failures of others, but most of all, perhaps, from our own failings and failures. The half-*trillion*-dollar Savings and Loan debacle and an epidemic of downsizing taught us a lesson of one sort or another, mere caution for some but a whole new way to look at business for others. "Get-rich-quick" is not the bottom line of the free-enterprise system, and as the financial economy becomes more and more a casino, where cleverness rather than contributions are rewarded, that freedom soon becomes "anything goes" rather than "may the best enterprise win." As John Maynard Keynes wrote some seventy years ago, "Speculators may do no harm on a steady stream of enterprise. But the position is serious when enterprise becomes a bubble on a whirlpool of speculation." The point of free enterprise is to build a better society. The well-being of billions of people, and not just the interests of a few favored players, is what the business world is all about. In the wake of the past decade, our own shortcomings have forced us to look at ourselves and what we have done, beyond the glib slogans and the pseudo-Adam Smithian cant about "the invisible hand." The new question is, how can we do it differently now?

There is one aspect of ethics in business to which I want to give scant attention, and those are the scandals that rocked Wall Street and other dubious doings on and off Wall Street in the past decade. I much prefer emphasizing what businesses do right and how they prosper, not how they do wrong and get their comeuppance. This is not to deny, of course, the existence of insider-trading scandals, embarrassing bankruptcies, environmental catastrophes, the jailing of several of some of the most respected men on Wall Street, some extremely hostile corporate acquisitions and straightforward extortions with more than enough high-level backstabbing to push several tell-tale business books to the top of the best-seller list and some businesses off the "Best Companies" list (or out of the market altogether). More recently, the incredible success of Japan has been marred by similar scandals, accusations about corruption in government, ties to organized crime, and a secret compensation scandal involving the four largest securities companies, with the resignation of one of the most powerful businessmen in Tokyo. Much has been made of the differences between America and Japan, but of equal or perhaps greater fascination are our shared successes and similarities, our mutual efforts to establish business ethics at the heart of the business ethos, to promote concern for the environment, and a sense of social responsibility as well as a kinder, gentler attitude toward employees—as well as our embarrassing failures to do so.

As for the scandals, on the one hand our fascination with these capers has been just another manifestation of our seemingly tireless soap-opera voyeurism, one more set of no doubt well-earned calamities besetting the rich and powerful. The only difference might seem to be that these have been publicized in the *Wall Street Journal* rather than the supermarket tabloids. On the other hand, such scandals have undermined many people's faith in the market and confidence in our best corporations, not to mention the capitalist ideal itself—the almost religious idea that getting as rich as humanly possible is not only an individual's God-given right but it is in the interest of all. We are learning to appreciate the restraint that is necessary in the free-enterprise system; the importance of personal and corporate character and cooperation that are necessary to make a free market work. We are learning that without ethics and a sense of the common good, there is no freedom, and very little productive enterprise.

While these changes have been, by turns, edifying and traumatic, they do not resemble anything like the "future shock" that Alvin Toffler and John Naisbitt and other futurologists have been promoting. They do not require new and dramatic remedies, whatever the names they bear this month. Indeed, what seems most surprising about the free-enterprise economy, according to its own precepts, is its own stability despite its inevitable ups and downs; its dogged persistence over time, representing, perhaps, a deep-set proclivity in human nature to bargain and exchange, to produce and share one's production for mutual benefit and for something in return; but also presenting itself as a cultural achievement that has proven itself despite its doubters and its admitted deficiencies. On a micro-level, of course, markets are always changing, just as technology is always changing, and one must often be flexible enough to meet those new markets and take advantage of new technology. But, looking at the big picture, the fundamentals of business remain remarkably the same—the importance of producing or providing a good product or service, paying attention to the customer, dealing in good faith, maintaining a good reputation, playing fair, and working together as part of a larger community. With all of the emphasis on change, we have ignored the "logos" that underlies that change, just as, with so much emphasis on scandals, we have ignored what goes right about business, taking the free market and its "magic" for granted. That underlying logos, in a word, is ethics.

The coming of the new millennium brings with it a healthy and refreshing self-examination, reflection on the principles and preconditions of a truly free market, debate about the presuppositions and meaning of prosperity and the obligations that go along with it. The economic wizards have discredited themselves, and even the economists are turning back to the language of "values," "quality," and "cooperation." Ethics has replaced economics as the first language of business, and the current self-examination, reflection, and debate are healthy alternatives to the narrow-minded focus on "the market." It is people that count, first of all. Profits and products, corporations and markets, are secondary and subservient. The writing is on the wall, or, rather, it is in the bookstores, by the ton. The new word in business is "caring," caring in particular for the impact of one's actions on other people. The new concern is for "quality," where quality means doing what business has always tried to do and had to do, producing good products, treating people decently, working for something more meaningful than merely "making money," getting involved in your business and listening to your employees and your customers. Admittedly, some writers have gotten overly enthusiastic recently and declared even "love" to be the primary management and corporate tool, but far better "love" than the virtues of Attila the Hun and the ideology of buy, loot, and burn. Such authors have captured something that was grotesquely omitted from most management and business books until recently—the importance of human relationships, mutual dependencies, personal needs, human psychology, and human values.

Fewer and fewer pinheads these days are willing to say, in public at least, that it is only profits that count, that business is just a means of "making money," that the "the only social responsibility of a business is to increase its profits." Twenty years ago it was considered inappropriate, or worse, to mention the word "ethics" in a business meeting. Today, there are few major corporations that do not have extensive programs in ethics, that do not have a code of ethics, that do not insist on ethics as one of their basic products. It is now generally recognized (indeed the word itself has become an already-tired piece of compulsory business jargon) that every corporation has its stakeholders—not only stockholders but employees, consumers, vendors, and the surrounding community—to which it is obliged and must be responsible. Concern for the environment has become *de rigeur,* and whether or not a corporation designates a portion of its yearly giving to the

---

"Beautiful credit! The foundation of modern society. Who shall say that this is not the age of mutual trust, of unlimited reliance on human promises?"

—*Mark Twain, 1873*

Environmental Defense Fund or the Sierra Club, it is no doubt keenly aware that being green is a good way to bring in the green. Good ethics is good business, and if that little slogan still strikes some ears as cynical or philosophically confused, the general acceptance of such sage advice indicates that we are indeed past that pathetic period in which all ethical choices were couched in the "no win" dichotomy of self-sacrifice versus mere survival. Now we know that free enterprise succeeds only insofar as it satisfies a society's needs, and among those needs are general prosperity; a clean environment; and a healthy, aesthetically, and spiritually rewarding social world.

Part One

ETHICS AND BUSINESS: BUSINESS AS ETHICS

THE ONE-MINUTE MORALIST

Once there was a bright young businessman who was looking for an ethical manager.

He wanted to work for one. He wanted to become one.

His search had taken him over many years to the far corners of the business world.

He visited small businesses and large corporations.

He spoke with used-car dealers, chief executive officers of Fortune 500 companies, management-science professors, vice presidents for strategic planning, and one-minute managers.

He visited every kind of office, big and small, carpeted and tiled, some with breathtaking views, some without any view at all.

He heard a full spectrum of ethical views.

But he wasn't pleased with what he heard.

On the one hand, virtually everyone he met seemed frank, friendly, and courteous, adamant about honesty even to the point of moral indignation. People were respectful of one another, concerned about their employees, and loyal to their own superiors. They paid their debts and resented the lawsuits in which they considered themselves the innocent party, victims of misunderstanding and antibusiness sentiment. They complained about regulation and the implied distrust of their integrity. They proudly asserted that they were producing quality products or services that truly did satisfy consumer demand, making the world a better—even if only a very slightly better—place in which to live.

Their superiors were proud of their trustworthiness.

Their subordinates were confident of their fairness.

But, on the other hand, when they were asked for their views about ethics and business, what all of these people had to say was startling, to say the least.

The answers varied only slightly.

"You have to understand that it's a jungle out there!"

"Listen, I'm a survivor."

"If I don't do it, the other guy will."

"You've got to be realistic in this business."

"Profits—that's what it's all about. You do whatever you have to."

And when our bright young businessman brought up the topic of business ethics, he invariably heard:

"There aren't any ethics in business"; or . . .

"Business Ethics—the shortest book in the world."

The latter usually with a grin.

At the same time, however, many executives shook their heads sadly and expressed the private wish that it were otherwise.

He met a few unscrupulous businessmen who admitted cutting corners, who had made a profit and were proud of it.

He met others who had cut corners and were caught. "This is a cutthroat world," they insisted, often contradicting this immediately by complaining about the injustice of being singled out themselves.

He met several self-proclaimed "ethical managers" who insisted that everyone who worked for them—and of course they themselves—had to be Perfectly Virtuous, to the letter of the Moral Law.

These managers' subordinates generally despised them, and their departments were rife with resentment. More than one employee complained about autocratic management and dogmatic ineffectiveness; a philosophical assistant manager pointed out the difference between morality and moralizing. Almost everyone pointed out that the principles that were so precisely printed out in both memos and plaques above their desks were usually impossible to apply to any real ethical issues. Their primary effect was rather to cast a gray shadow of suspected hypocrisy over everyday business life.

Our bright young businessman was discouraged. He could not understand why the conscientious, sociable, civilized, thoroughly ethical flesh-and-blood managers he met in the office talked in their off moments like the most cynical prophets of corporate Darwinism.

The flesh-and-blood managers complained that the public did not appreciate them.

The cynical prophets joked, "There are no ethics in business," and then wondered why people didn't trust them.

Our bright young businessman was perplexed: Could there be ethics in the real business world? he wondered. Were compromises and cut corners inevitable? he asked. Did the untrammeled pursuit of virtue have to be either hypocrisy or damaging to the bottom line, as he now feared?

And then he met the One-Minute Moralist.

The bright young businessman presented the One-Minute Moralist with his dilemma. The One-Minute Moralist answered him without hesitation.

"You don't understand ethics," he said. "And you don't understand business either.

"You set up an absurd dichotomy between ethical absolutism and the so-called real world, and then you wonder how ethics can possibly be at home in business, and whether business can function without cutting corners and making uneasy compromises. But cutting corners presumes that there are sharply delineated corners. And talking so uneasily of compromise (that is, compromising one's moral principles rather than compromising with other people) seems to assume that ethics consists of engraved principles rather than relations between people who (more or less) share values and interests.

"But ethics isn't a set of absolute principles, divorced from and imposed on everyday life. Ethics is a way of life, a seemingly delicate but in fact very strong tissue of endless adjustments and compromises. It is the awareness that one is an intrinsic part of a social order, in which the interests of others and one's own interests are inevitably intertwined. And what is business, you should ask, if not precisely that awareness of what other people want and need, and how you yourself can prosper by providing it? Businesses great and small prosper because they respond to people, and fail when they do not respond. To talk about being 'totally ethical' and about 'uneasy compromises' is to misunderstand ethics. Ethics is the art of mutually agreeable tentative compromise. Insisting on absolute principles is, if I may be ironic, unethical.

"Business, on the other hand, has nothing to do with jungles, survivalism, and Darwin, whatever the mechanisms of the market may be. The 'profit motive' is an offensive fabrication by people who were out to attack business, which has curiously—and self-destructively—been adopted by business people themselves. Business isn't a single-minded pursuit of profits; it is an *ethos,* a way of life. It is a way of life that is at its very foundation ethical. What is more central to business—any kind of business—than taking contracts seriously, paying one's debts, and coming to mutual agreements about what is a fair exchange?

Ethics isn't superimposed on business. Business is itself an ethics, defined by ethics, made possible by ethics. Two hundred years ago, Benjamin Franklin insisted that business is the pursuit of virtue. If you find yourself wondering or doubting whether virtue is possible in business, I suggest you reexamine your ideas about business.

"If you want to talk about hypocrisy, by the way, it is not just to be found in such bloated phrases as 'the untrammeled pursuit of virtue.' There is just as much hypocrisy in the macho, mock-heroic insistence that business is a tough-minded, amoral struggle for survival and profits rather than a staid and established ethical enterprise.

"Now you've had your Minute. When you think about business and ethics, don't worry about whether one is possible along with the other. In America, at least, nothing is more ethical than good business."

SOME OPENING CASES

1. Your company builds whatsits, whose primary component is the rorem. As long as you can remember, you have bought your rorems from Old George, who has come to depend on your business for his very survival. But now a large-scale competitor produces rorems much more efficiently than Old George, which is reflected in a price that is lower by almost 20 percent. Is your standing relationship with Old George and his dependence on you any consideration whatever? What do you do? Do you have any obligation to Old George?

2. You are in charge of new-product development at Company A in the midst of a fierce competition for the development of a new and more efficient gizmo. The research department has come up with a workable model, and the engineering department is just now in the midst of "getting the bugs out." One of your main competitors, Company B, has obviously fallen behind and offers you a lucrative position, more than commensurate with your present duties and at

almost double the salary. Your current employer insists that he cannot possibly match the offer but does give you a 20 percent raise, "to show our appreciation."

Should you feel free to accept the competing offer from Company B?

If you do accept it, should you feel free to develop for Company B the gizmo designed by Company A?

3. You are a worker in an automobile factory and you become convinced that the hood latch on the new-model Crocodiliac is insufficiently secure and may well pop open at high speeds in a small number of cars, probably causing an accident or, at the least, considerable damage to the car itself. You go to your supervisor and insist that the latch be redesigned, but you are told that production is too far under way; the cost would be formidable and the delay intolerable. You go to the president of the firm and get the same response. What should you do?

4. Your company sells pharmaceutical products in a developing country, in which one of your products, Wellness Plus, promises to provide an effective cure for a common infantile illness. But you find, much to your horror, that the product is being systematically misused, with sometimes serious medical consequences, by people who are mostly illiterate and have no medical supervision. At the same time, the product is selling like hotcakes. What should you do?

5. Palomine, Inc., stock is selling well below its real value. Your company has lots of cash. Your overture to Palomine, Inc., is flatly rejected; its managers fear for their jobs, and they insist—correctly— that the stockholders are basically satisfied with their small but reasonable return and that the company is making and marketing its products efficiently enough, given the nature of the business. Under what conditions would you consider an "unfriendly" takeover justified? Under what conditions would such a takeover *not* be justified, even if it could in fact be accomplished and the profits to your own company considerable?

6. Your company markets a line of inexpensive clothing manufactured in a developing country. A human rights group discovers abysmal working conditions in your foreign factories, conditions that would never be tolerated at home: children working dangerous machinery for long hours without respite, practically chained to machines churning out clothes for Americans. The ensuing barrage of consumer protests tarnishes your brand name, perhaps irreparably. On the other hand, managers at these factories and some respected sociologists point out

that the income these children bring home to their impoverished families means the difference between eating and starving. The country is so poor that children who don't have the chance to work in clothing factories may have to steal food instead. What should you recommend?

7. Your Fashion Jean Co. could save almost 30 percent on labor costs by moving your main manufacturing plant from El Paso, Texas, across the river to Juarez, Mexico. Should you do so?

8. Your bank has a standing policy of firing almost half of its new employees at the end of their first six months. "It makes them more competitive." "It weeds out the slow learners." What effect do you think this has on their efficiency? What effect on their morale and their attitudes toward the bank? Is such a policy ethical?

9. Is it ever right to lie?

10. In a mostly black community, your work force includes only 9 percent black workers, although most of the jobs can be learned in a matter of a few weeks. Do you have an obligation to hire more black workers? Is it "good business" to do so?

11. A minority employee hired in an affirmative-action program is not working up to expectations, in part because of cultural differences and a lack of familiarity with the corporate world. Does the company have an obligation to give him special consideration and extra on-the-job training?

12. You've got the cash, and the local art museum asks you for a substantial donation. The tax breaks are significant but not so considerable that there is any advantage to giving the money away rather than investing it. You can (and do) always give money as an individual citizen—but this is company money that is in question. Is there any good reason why a corporation in business for profits should give to culture or charity? Are there good reasons why it should not do so?

13. You're strapped for cash and need a federal "bail-out." What, if anything, should you expect to owe in return, besides the borrowed money itself?

14. You are running a midsize high-tech company. You have developed a new product—an easy Internet access program—which you anticipate will generate some 80 percent of your company's income for the next four years. Your expected 12 percent increase in revenues turns out to be less than six percent, however, and you have to cut back in the company. Where do you start doing this?

15. You run a large steel company, but you're not making any money making steel. You fight and win large concessions from your work force. The stockholders are impatient for dividends. There's a juicy oil

company up for grabs down the road. What are your obligations to the workers, who, in effect, have provided you with the money with which you are considering your purchase? Their concessions, needless to say, were aimed at keeping the company working and their keeping their jobs.

16. Rumors around the office have it that one of your employees, a reserved young woman, has been "bothered" by her supervisor, an outgoing young man who has a well-known habit of physically expressing himself with slaps on the back and an occasional hug (for male and female colleagues alike). No one has seen him misbehave with this woman or abuse her in any way (even including his usual slaps and hugs), but there is an "feeling" around the office that won't go away. The young woman herself has said nothing to you. What are your responsibilities as the manager of the department?

17. You have a plant in Sierra Vista, Arizona, in which half of your temporary employees are suspected of having illegally entered the country. They fill essential slots in your operations, work well and cheaply, and you could not readily replace them. What are your obligations, legal, moral, and personal, to the workers, the business, the community, the United States?

18. A young man in your employ took two weeks off "for illness," but a picture in the local paper happens to show him at the shopping mall during one of his supposedly "sick" days. He is a good employee, a hard worker, and he has been under a lot of pressure lately. How do you handle the situation? What considerations are most impressive, as far as you are concerned, in deciding whether or not to fire him?

19. You have a manufacturing plant in Conway, Arkansas, which has a very high level of productivity and, as far as you can see, excellent employee morale. Your benefits are above the industry standard, pay is good, and social activities (including both workers and management) are encouraged. Some of the employees decide, however, that they would like to form a union, and they invite a national labor organizer to speak to all of the employees. How do you feel about this? How do you handle the situation? What, above all, should you *not* do?

20. You are the CEO of a large oil company and one of your ships breaks up near an isolated but beautiful coastline in the North Atlantic. It turns out that there was, indisputably, a navigation miscalculation and the pilot is judged to be at fault. What are your obligations and responsibilities, and to whom? In what sense (if any) are *you* responsible for the mishap? What should you do about it?

21. One of your best customers objects when he is assigned a minority woman as his contact person for dealing with your firm. What do you do?

WHY ETHICS?

Seminars in business ethics are typically sandwiched in between sessions on financial analysis and production planning. Not unreasonably, business people expect similarly hard-headed, decisive, pragmatic, issue-oriented, goal-directed, job-defined, bottom-line-minded, and imminently useful information. Not surprisingly, then, our seminars almost always begin with and are periodically brought back around to such practical questions as "What does this have to do with my job?" or "Will understanding ethics help me do my job better?"

Such questions deserve and demand three immediate, practical answers.

1. Ethical errors end careers more quickly and more definitively than any other mistake in judgment or accounting.

To err is human, perhaps, but to be caught lying, cheating, stealing, or reneging on contracts is not easily forgotten or forgiven in the business world. And for good reason: Such actions undermine the ethical foundation on which the business world thrives. Almost everyone can have compassion for someone caught in an ethical dilemma. No one can excuse immorality.

For every glaring case of known unethical conduct that goes unpunished, a dozen once-promising careers silently hit a dead end or quietly go down the tubes. On relatively rare occasions, an unhappy executive or employee is singled out and forced to pay public penance for conduct that everyone knows—he or she and the attorney will loudly protest—"goes on all the time." But much more often, unethical behavior, though unearthed, will go unannounced; indeed, the executive or employee in question will keep his or her job and may not even find out that he or she has been found out—may never even realize the unethical nature of his or her behavior. A career will just go nowhere. Responsibilities will remain routine, promotions elusive.

What makes such career calamities so pathetic is that they are not the product of greed or immorality or wickedness. They are the result of ethical naiveté.

- They happen because an employee unthinkingly "did what he was told to do"—and became the scapegoat as well.
- They happen because a casual public comment was ill considered and had clearly unethical implications—though nothing of the kind may have been intended.
- They happen because a middle manager, pressed from above for results, tragically believed the adolescent clichés that pervade the mid-regions of the business world, such as "In business, you do whatever you have to do to survive." (It is both revealing and instructive that although we often hear such sentiments expressed in seminars for middle managers, we virtually never hear them in similar seminars for upper-level executives.)
- They happen because upper management wasn't clear about standards, priorities, and limits, or wasn't reasonable in its expectations, or wasn't available for appeal at the critical moment.
- They happen because an anonymous employee or middle manager hidden in the complexity of a large organization foolishly believed that such safe anonymity would continue, whatever his or her behavior.
- They happen, most of all, because a person in business is typically trained and pressured to "think business," without regard for the larger context in which business decisions are made and legitimized.

Unethical thinking isn't just "bad business"; it is an invitation to disaster in business, however rarely (it might sometimes seem) unethical behavior is actually found out and punished. And the new sentencing guidelines make the cost—and liabilities—of ethical laxity potentially ruinous for the entire company.

2. *Ethics provides the broader framework within which business life must be understood.*

There may be a few people for whom business is all of life, for whom family and friendship are irrelevant, for whom money means only more

---

THE CARROT OR THE STICK?

With all the greed, hubris, and corruption now being showcased world-wide, perhaps it's heartening that a growing number of U.S. corporations are embracing in-house ethics programs. In fact, the Center for Business Ethics at Bentley College in Waltham, Mass., recently found that 45 percent of the 1,000 largest U.S. companies now have ethics programs or workshops, up from 35 percent five years ago. Is some kind of reformist fervor taking hold of corporate America?

Well, not exactly. While many of these programs are doubtless sincere attempts to deter wrongdoing, companies now have a hefty incentive to quickly start an ethics program. Aside from the obvious public relations value in maintaining a commitment to ethics, companies have a wary eye on [tough] new U.S. sentencing guidelines that [took] effect November 1, 1991.

—*Business Week*, 1991

---

investment potential and has nothing to do with respect or status or enjoying the good life. But most successful executives understand that *business is part of life.* Corporations are part of a society that consists of something more than a market. Executives and employees do not disappear into their jobs as if into a well, only to reappear in "real life" at the end of the business day.

Successful managers, we now all know, stay close to their subordinates—and not just as subordinates. The best corporations in their "search for excellence" begin and remain close to their customers, and not just in their narrowest role as consumers. Money may be a scorecard, a measure of status and accomplishment, but it is not the ultimate end. Business success, like happiness, often comes most readily to those who do not aim at it directly.

Executives are most effective and successful when they retain their "real life" view of themselves, their position, and the human world outside as well as inside the corporation. Business ethics, ultimately, is just business in its larger human context.

A corporation's responsibilities include how the whole business is conducted every day. It must be a thoughtful institution which rises above the bottom line to consider the impact of its action on all, from shareholders to the society at large. Its business activities must make business sense.

Andrew Siglér, The Business Roundtable,
New York Times, February 1981

3. Nothing is more dangerous to a business—or to business in general— than a tarnished public image.

In a 1995 Harris Poll (*Business Week,* March 13) only 19 percent of those surveyed had "a great deal of confidence" in big businesses. (The highest degree of confidence, 42 percent, was reserved for small businesses.) Two years later, another poll revealed a similar deficiency in the public image of business: while most (75 percent) of the executives surveyed deemed that they do a "pretty good" job, only half of the general public gave them such a high grade. Whether or not such doubt seriously affects sales, it indisputably hurts the bottom line in a dozen other hurtful ways—not least among them the pressure for government regulation. The fact is that a tarnished image has direct consequences, for sales, for profits, for morale, for the day-to-day running of the business. Distrust of an industry ("big oil," "the insurance racket") can hurt every company, and distrust of an individual company can quickly drive it to bankruptcy.

The editors of the *Review* tried to find the reason for the "falling image of private enterprise" and the flawed image of the men and women who devote their lives to business. They surveyed the chief executives of some of the nation's large corporations, asking for their opinions about what had happened and what could be done. As one would expect, there was vast disagreement on causes—from blaming the press to blaming the universities to expressing the view that since Watergate, all people and institutions in power are inevitably suffering from a more general loss of confidence. But what all of the respondents agreed about was the need to correct the image of business and free enterprise as essentially antagonistic or indifferent to the public good and morality. That correction, in turn, depends on the ability of business people to speak out for themselves, to express in their own terms the ethics and economics of their work without depending on the press to do it for them. Indeed, business ethics is not so much a subject matter as an alternative language in which business people must articulate their own awareness and aims of the work that they do. (The alternative assumption: "If they won't even tell us what they're doing, they must be doing something wrong.")

While businessmen were minding their own business, intellectuals were busy developing a powerful case against capitalism. This cause went largely unanswered and eventually bore fruit in the form of regulatory and other government policies to which the business community was unhappily forced to pay attention.

Norman Podhoretz, "The New Defenders,"
Harvard Business Review, 1981

CONFESSIONS

	Business Executives Reporting
Have you ever taken home work supplies	74%
used company phones for personal long distance calls	78%
overstated deductions on tax forms	35%
driven while drunk	80%
smoked marijuana	17%
used cocaine	2%

Gallup survey in the *Wall Street Journal*, 1984

THE IMPORTANCE OF PEOPLE

A company's ability to foster employee morale and loyalty, attract talented people and so on, are drawing growing scrutiny in some quarters of Wall Street.

A study by Ernst & Young's Center for Business Innovation shows investor decisions are a surprising 35 percent driven by non-financial factors. One people issue, a company's "ability to attract and retain" talented employees, ranks fifth among 39 such factors investors use in picking stocks, right behind strategy execution.

Why the interest in people issues? The workplace climate has taken a questionable turn, for one thing. An annual survey of 3,300 employees by Towers Perrin, management consultants, shows a rise in employee feelings of disenfranchisement. In an era of supposed participatory management the poll shows an increase to 30 percent from 255 in [1996] in employees who say their bosses ignore their interests when making decisions that affect them.

—*Wall Street Journal*, March 19, 1997

THE MYTH OF AMORAL BUSINESS

> *Nature . . . is what we are put on this earth to rise above.*
>
> *Katharine Hepburn in* The African Queen

Business people have not always been their own best friends. John D. Rockefeller once boasted that he was quite willing to pay a man an annual salary of a million dollars, if the man had certain qualities:

> [He] must know how to glide over every moral restraint with almost childlike disregard . . . [and have], besides other positive qualities, no scruples whatsoever, and [be] ready to kill off thousands of victims—without a murmur.
>
> Robert Warshow, *Jay Gould* (1928)

Such talk is unusually ruthless, but it exemplifies horribly a myth that has often clouded business thinking—what University of Kansas business ethicist Richard de George calls the "myth of amoral business." According to the myth, business and ethics don't mix. People in business are concerned with profits, with producing goods and services, with buying and selling. They may not be immoral, but they are amoral—that is, not concerned with morals. Moralizing is out of place in business. Indeed, even good acts are to be praised not in moral terms but only in the cost/benefit language of "good business."

The myth of amoral business has a macho, mock-heroic corollary that makes ethical paralysis almost inevitable. It is the dog-eat-dog rhetoric of the Darwinian jungle—"survival of the fittest." In fact, almost everybody and most companies manage to survive without being the "fittest." The anxiety of switching jobs, of not getting promotions, of losing an investment, or of going bankrupt, however upsetting, is rarely a "matter of life and death." In *The Right Stuff*, Tom Wolfe sympathetically quotes the wife of one of the Air Force test pilots. She mentions a friend's complaint about her husband's dog-eat-dog existence on Madison Avenue and reflects, "What if her husband went into a meeting with a one-in-four chance of survival?"

If the myth of amoral business and its Darwinian corollary were nothing but a way of talking on the way to the office, it would not be worth attention or criticism. But the fact is that it does enter into business thinking, and often at exactly the critical moment when an ethical decision is to be made. Worse, the amoral rhetoric of business quickly feeds public suspicion of business and easily becomes part of the condemnation of business. A handful of scandals and accidents that might otherwise be viewed as the unfortunate by-products of any enterprise become "proof" of what the business people themselves have been saying all along—that there is no interest in ethics in business, only the pursuit of profits.

What has become apparent is that there is too much theoretical agreement between those who attack business and those who practice it. It is as if both business people and their harshest critics agree that business is amoral and self-serving, but whereas the critics say so in the persuasive language of justice and fairness, business people damn themselves in the language of "cost effectiveness," thus demonstrating in linguistic form if not in content just the accusation being leveled against them.

Business people who do not talk about ethics often complain a great deal about "regulation" without realizing that the two are intimately connected. Legal regulation is the natural response of both society and government to the practice of amorality, however nobly that practice is couched in the rhetoric of "free enterprise." If a business scandal or tragedy is quickly and convincingly chastized by business people, there is neither time nor pressure for regulation. But when scandal and tragedy are at the same time surrounded by ethical neglect or silence or, worse, yet another appeal to "the market" as the long-term corrective, government regulation becomes inevitable. In case anyone still wants to ask why ethics should be relevant to the bottom line, one might simply reply that regulation is the price business pays for bad ethical strategy.

A PERSONAL ETHICAL AUDIT (CONFIDENTIAL)

Do you believe that
   "it's a jungle out there"?

   _____   _____
    yes   no

   "free enterprise is the best way to ensure fairness as well as general prosperity"?

   _____   _____
    yes   no

   "most leaders of American businesses are morally upstanding"?

   _____   _____
    yes   no

   "business needs government regulation to keep it honest and in the public interest"

   _____   _____
    yes   no

   "most people in business cut corners or cheat a little"?

   _____   _____
    yes   no

Does your job
   satisfy you?

   _____   _____
    yes   no

   let you feel that you are doing something "worthwhile"?

   _____   _____
    yes   no

ever make you feel cheap, dishonest, used, abused, or distressed?

_____   _____
 yes   no

make you feel proud of yourself?

_____   _____
 yes   no

make you feel proud of your company?

_____   _____
 yes   no

Have you ever done something that you consider seriously wrong on your job?

_____   _____
 yes   no

considered doing something seriously wrong on your job?

_____   _____
 yes   no

found a subordinate doing something seriously wrong on the job?

_____   _____
 yes   no

discovered your boss doing something seriously wrong on the job?

_____   _____
 yes   no

THE EASY WAY

It is far simpler for managers to discuss the ethics of not doing business in South Africa than it is for them to confront the effects of their own behavior on the ethical conduct of the young men and women of the organizations they lead.

Wortman and Missirian, "Whatever Happened to Ethics?"

Survey Question	Percent who agree	
	1990	*1980*
1. Most people will tell a lie if they can gain from it.	66	60
2. People claim to have standards of honesty and morality but few stick to them when money is at stake.	67	62
3. People pretend to care more about one another than they really do.	58	58
4. An unselfish person is taken advantage of in today's world.	55	53
5. Most people are just out for themselves.	51	46
6. People inwardly dislike putting themselves out to help people.	54	46
7. Most people are not really honest by nature.	40	34

From *Business and Society Review*

FANTASIES OF BLACK AND WHITE: IN DEFENSE OF COLORS

In a recent book, *Business Ethics: The State of the Art,* Ezra Bowen, a distinguished senior writer at *Time* magazine, proclaims that "the fact is that ethics comes in two decorator colors, black and white." "Gray," he adds, "is the color we impose, or hide beneath, to rationalize indecision or failed standards." Black and white, good and evil: It is a fantasy that we would all like to entertain—with ourselves on the side of the good, of course. But the awesome fact of our moral lives is the pervasiveness of shades of gray; or rather, the multicolored rainbow that includes the whole spectrum of moral coloration, mixed affections and loyalties, contrasting duties and obligations, varied and often overlapping responsibilities, dangerous attractions and embarrassments, clear and moral imperatives and vague or even obscure feelings of obligation. There are, to be sure, certain crises that strike us at the time as ethical, an offer that seems too good to refuse despite the fact that it requires a betrayal of loyalty or a serious compromise of standards or integrity; and in retrospect (one would hope) these do indeed appear to be what they were, choices between the ethical and the unethical.

But most of our moral quandaries are in fact ethical dilemmas, not right versus wrong or good versus bad but, as John Dewey said, right versus right, good versus good, and each with its trade-offs and downside. Ethical behavior may sometimes come down to the choice between good and evil, but, for anyone who would bother reading Bowen's book, the choices are usually much more difficult than that. They require good judgment and careful consideration, not just sound moral upbringing. They involve what business ethicist Joanne Ciulla calls ''moral imagination,'' the creation of alternative options and compromises. They involve consultation and negotiation, consensus rather than dogmatic moral dictates from on high.

Of course, none of this is to say that ethics is in every case a matter of negotiation, or that there is no good and evil. It is just to warn us away from the temptation and the fantasy of thinking that ethics is easy, that ethical behavior is in every case a matter of moral heroism or sainthood. In most cases, ''doing the right thing'' is not a matter of black and white but a matter of moral character, good judgment, and a willingness to talk with others involved. Indeed, one of the factors that we have found most problematic in business ethics is the false belief held by many people that an ethical dilemma is a mark against them, a blot on their character or the way they are doing their job. Instead of talking about it, therefore, they try to cover it up—or get rid of it as quickly as possible. That is where the trouble really starts, whether it is in the office of an assistant manager or the CEO of the company. In fact, moral dilemmas and tough choices are just another part of every position with any responsibility, and therefore, virtually every job whatever. And as business goes global, we can expect the new world of business to become all the more colorful.

COMPLIANCE, CONTRIBUTIONS, AND CONSEQUENCES: THE MEANING OF INTEGRITY

Writing in the *Wall Street Journal,* Irving Kristol commented:

> Once again, modern business is paying the price for conceiving of itself as representing an abstract species of "economic man," rather than as men and women engaged in a fully human activity. It is this self-delusion that has helped so significantly to create the divorce between the business communities and academic-intellectual communities—a divorce that leaves the business community so defenseless when ideas (about morality or anything else) are used unscrupulously as weapons against it.

Business ethics is not an attack on business but rather its first line of defense. Adam Smith knew this well enough: Business has prospered because business has dramatically improved the quality of life for all of us. Moreover, the emphasis on freedom and individuality in a business society has done more than any conceivable socialist revolution to break down traditional inequities in power and wealth, even if it inevitably creates some inequities of its own. Business ethics begins with consumer demand and productivity, with the freedom to engage in business as one wishes, and with the hope that one can better one's life considerably through one's own hard work and intelligence. These are the values of business ethics, and the whole point of business ethics is to define and defend the basic goals of prosperity, freedom, fairness, and individual dignity.

Many critics of business are trained in the rhetoric of ethics, but most business people are not. Those in business naturally prefer to stick with what they know and sidestep the ethical issues—which is ruinous. It is one thing to know that product Z costs 14 cents to make and retails for $1.59, that raising the price to $1.79 would increase profits and not dampen demand, that cheaper materials or foreign labor could lower the cost of manufacturing to 9 cents, although sales would eventually diminish as consumer expectations went unsatisfied. But it is something more to think about the quality of product Z, the contribution it makes to American life (even if only by way of amusement or novelty), and one's responsibilities toward loyal workers. Not incidentally, these ethical virtues may be essential to the bottom line as well.

Business ethics is nothing less than the full awareness of what one is doing, its consequences and complications. Thinking about ethics in business is no more than acknowledging that one has taken these into account and is willing to be responsible for them. It is being aware of

1. the need for *compliance* with the rules, including the laws of the land, the principles of morality, the customs and expectations of the community, the policies of the company, and such general concerns as fairness;
2. the *contributions* business can make to society, through the value and quality of one's products or services, by way of the jobs one provides for workers and managers, through the prosperity and usefulness of one's activities to the surounding community;
3. concern for the *consequences* of business activity, both inside and outside the company, both intended and unintended, including the reputation of one's own company and industry, long term as well as short term.

These are the "three Cs" of business ethics, and I will refer to them again and again throughout this book.

Part of the problem for business ethics is the image of business as "big" business, as a world of impersonal corporations in which the individual is submerged and ethics is inevitably sacrificed to bureaucratic objectives. To set the image straight, therefore, let us remind ourselves of a single vital statistic: Half of American business is family business; 50 percent of the GNP; 50 percent of the employees. Some of these family businesses are among the Fortune 500. Others are Mom and Pop groceries and Sally and Lou's Restaurant. But it is essential to remember that however much our focus may be on corporations and corporate life, business in America is not a monolithic, inhuman enterprise. As the great French philosopher Rousseau once said of society, we might say of American business life—that its origins are in the family, that its "natural" model *is* the family. Business is ultimately about relationships between people—our compliance with the rules we all form together, our contributions to the well-being of others as well as to our own, the consequences of our activities, for good and otherwise. There is nothing amoral or unethical about it.

The single term that sums up and ties together these critical components of business ethics is *integrity*. This is a term that appears in

CHANGING THE SOCIAL CONTRACT

The terms of the contract between industry and society are changing.
. . . Now we are being asked to serve a wider range of human values and
to accept an obligation to members of the public with whom we have no
commercial transactions.

Henry Ford II

many corporate slogans and mission statements, but its realization is a
bit harder to discern. Indeed, all too many people in business still think
that integrity, like "honor"—its close kin—is a rare luxury and usually
unaffordable in the rough-and-tumble of corporate life. To other managers and executives, it suggests stubbornness and inflexibility, a
refusal to be a "team player." But integrity is the very essence of
ethics and it lies at the very heart of business. The very word suggests
"wholeness" (like an "integer" in mathematics, a "whole number").
But insofar as one's identity in business is not that of an isolated player
but rather as a member of a larger social unit—a corporation, a
department, a community—wholeness includes rather than excludes
other people and one's social roles. Integrity is the integration of one's
personal and social values, the morality one was raised to follow and
the corporate values one was hired to promote. Ideally, these form a
seamless mesh, and one's work and career provide an expression and
a stage on which to realize what one values most highly. At the worst,
one finds one's deeply held values at odds with what one is paid and
expected to do, and the result is a moral dilemma, and sometimes a
tragedy. In that case, integrity may dictate violating one trust or role
in order to answer to some "higher" value.

Luckily, such outright fragmentation and contradiction of values is
relatively rare, but a partial split between one's most important personally held values and the tasks that one sometimes finds oneself facing
is a common part of the corporate experience—and not only of the
corporate experience. A person's integrity on the job typically requires
him or her to follow the rules and practices that define that job, rather
than allow oneself to be swayed by distractions and contrary temptations. And yet, critical encounters sometimes require a show of integrity that is indeed antithetical to one's assigned role and duties. Thus
the word has (at least) two very different meanings, one of them
encouraging conformity, the other urging a belligerent independence.

But the important point is that your integrity *defines who you are*. And this, of course, applies to whole corporations as well as to individuals. Compliance with morality and the law is not merely an obligation to external authority; it *is* you. Contributions to the community and the larger society are not merely the external consequences of your behavior; they define what you are. And in the face of tragedy or impending disaster—such as CEO James Burke and Johnson & Johnson faced in the Tylenol poisonings—that is when your personal and corporate integrity really come up for measure.

ETHICS AND THE LAW

Free enterprise does not mean "anything goes." The freedom of the market obviously has its limitations, for both the individual and the corporation. Even Nobel economist, free-market champion Milton Friedman readily admits that business is constrained by "the law and ethical customs" in its pursuit of profits. "Freedom" does not mean "all is allowed." The free market depends on respect for people as well as for private property (and not just one's own), respect for contracts, and respect for the rules of fair play. It demands restraint from brute force and coercion and it forbids fraud. Without such respect and restraint, the free market would not be free; in fact, it could not operate as a "market" at all. Ideally, every participant in the market, like every player in a friendly football game, could be assumed to agree with some basic rules and respect the integrity of the game. Unfortunately, a free market that is open (by its very nature) to all producers and participants cannot make this assumption. Therefore the market, if it is to be free, requires protection from rule breakers, those who would take advantage of its freedoms and commit fraud or extortion. It requires rules and sanctions, and this is not a restriction of freedom but the protection of it.

In short, the market and its participants must be constrained by *law*. It is the law that ultimately decides and defends the legitimacy of contracts, and prohibits theft, force, and fraud. The first obligation of any business and every business person, and the most obvious meaning of *compliance*, is to obey the law. Without law, there would be no business, and business law thus becomes central to the study of business life. But this is not to say that law is all there is to ethics, or that compliance ultimately comes down to business law. In our friendly football game, there are all sorts of mutual understandings and expectations that need not be spelled out in the rules of the game. So, too, in business there are all sorts of mutual understandings and expectations that may not be spelled out in the law.

The most important of these is mutual *trust*. This does not mean that in business it is obligatory to trust everyone. That would be downright stupid. But it does mean that when a cautious business person confides in you (somewhat paradoxically), that he or she "never trusts anyone," that is without doubt an exaggeration, a perverse way of saying that he or she is very cautious in business dealings. Trust, in fact a remarkably high level of trust, is built into most business dealings, from "Self-Serve" stations where you pay for your gas after you've already put it in your tank to international agreements among giant multinational corporations. Of course, the law is usually there to back up such agreements, but it is a misunderstanding of both law and ethics to suppose that the law as such is the crucial element here. Indeed, if a business person or corporation makes a practice of just remaining on "this side of the law," narrowly avoiding indictments and lawsuits, it is virtually certain that he, she, or it is unethical. Talking an elderly person out of his or her life savings to make a risky investment (and taking a substantial brokerage fee off the top) may be perfectly legal but it is repulsively unethical. The law circumscribes the limits of tolerable behavior, but it does not define ethics as such.

It is often said, "You cannot legislate morality." But this is not so much a plea for tolerance as it is a deep insight into the nature of the law. Respect and obedience for law first have to be embodied in practice, in the way people actually behave. The law can successfully circumscribe and sanction only that which is already accepted—no matter how grudgingly—by the people and practices it governs. Law may present the ground rules of business behavior but ethics provides the atmosphere, the very air that business breathes. If the *ethos* of the business world were not already securely in place, no number of laws or sanctions could shape a world of mere mutual chicanery into a free-enterprise system.

The preponderance of law relating to business, of course, takes the form of *regulation*. It is a matter of some curiosity and concern that "regulation" is considered a "dirty word" by most people in business. Regulation is decried as contrary to the free market and destructive of competitiveness. Regulation is said to "tie the hands" of business. And, of course, there are an absurd number of regulations and an even more annoying amount of red tape and paperwork involved in compliance (or rather, proof of compliance) in virtually every industry. It is important, however, to appreciate the value of regulation as well as its abuses and limitations.

Many regulations are archaic, residues of a problem long resolved or a period of past abuses. Some of them are simply stupid and the product of a partisan political opportunity. Too much regulation signifies lack of trust in business, in the integrity of business people, in the intelligence of consumers, in the efficiency of the market itself to make a success of good quality and punish poor quality. Too much regulation is a residue of the old intrusiveness of government (the origins of the traditional free-market cry, *laissez faire,* "leave us alone"). Too much regulation is still reminiscent of the authoritarianism of the medieval guild ("exactly 1,408 weaves per fabric"). In general, it is probably fair to say that most business is overregulated, which has the unfortunate consequence of shifting the emphasis on the preconditions of the free market away from self-restraint and respect for the rules of fair play and the public good to mere compliance with the law. There is no argument against the proposition that the best regulation is self-regulation, but the simple facts of business life show that this ideal solution is not the only one. Regulation is often necessary, and often beneficial to the industries regulated as well.

The ultimate purpose of regulation is to protect the market as such; to guarantee the conditions within which an industry can thrive and survive, and, of course, to protect the public good, to provide safeguards for those consumers who could not possibly assess the dangers of some of the products they use (for example, pharmaceuticals and various household chemicals). Regulation is essential to business and it is or should be aimed at the public well-being, whatever the private motives of certain politicians or special interests may be. There will always be regulations, but it should never be thought that these take the place of self-restraint or obviate the need for corporate ethics and integrity within the organization. *Compliance* means, first of all, compliance with the demands of ethics and morality, and compliance with the law is, in this sense, only secondary.

THE LIMITS OF ETHICS: BUSINESS SCUM

The most powerful argument for ethics in business is success. Ethical businesses are successful businesses; excellence is also ethical. But ethics is no guarantee of success. To say so on our part would be—unethical. The fact is that there are, as we all know, business scum—those shifty, snatch-a-buck operations that give business a bad name. And some of them, ethics be damned, are profitable.

Brake Breakers, Inc., is a small franchise in the Midwest that specializes in brake, suspension, and wheel repairs. Company policy includes hiring men with little education and working them long hours at a single semiskilled job. Wages are accordingly minimal, and employee turnover is more often a matter of burnout than of leaving for another job. (This saves a lot on fringe benefits and pensions; no one has ever collected on them.)

Foremost among the employees' skills, however, is the delivery of a prepackaged sermon designed to convince all but the most cautious customer that the $149.25 brake-rebuilding special is far preferable to the mere replacement of the brake shoes, which is all that is usually required (and often all that is actually done).

Managers are rewarded on the basis of the success of these little speeches by their employees. Their job is first and foremost to make sure that the minimum is never enough—not hard given the level of mechanical know-how of most of the customers. But even with the $149.25 special, extra costs are almost always included, sometimes for some other (unnecessary) part but more often than not because of the "unexpected difficulty" of this particular repair. When a customer

---

CUSTOMERS WHO COMPLAIN

[A]ccording to a Burke [Customer Satisfaction Associates] telephone survey of 1,179 randomly selected department-store shoppers . . . grousers are likely to remain loyal even after the incidents that displease them. Complainers are . . . likely to be older, frequent shoppers. In contrast, the most "vulnerable" customers are infrequent shoppers under age 35. Older people are also more likely to expect results, which may be part of the reason why they are willing to make the effort in the first place. Nearly half of older complainers but just one in five younger complainers expect stores to resolve problems satisfactorily. . . . Many of the people who say they would complain might not carry through. . . . Some don't want to spend the time, and others feel the time will be wasted. This makes the actual complaining customer a rare and special person indeed.

—*American Demographics,* May 1996

---

insists on the minimum repair, it is up to the manager to see to it that more absolutely necessary work is "discovered" in the middle of the job. (This is called the "step method.") Few customers are in a position to do more than complain and curse for the moment, but no one ever expects them to come back anyway.

Managers are expected to keep actual costs down. Used parts are sold in place of new parts. (Sometimes, the car's original part is cleaned or polished and simply reinstalled.) A few miles down the road, who can tell?

Within the company, employees are reminded daily, "There are fifty people waiting for your job." Everyone is hired with the promise, "Within three years, you can work up to a managerial position." In fact, managers are always hired from outside—typically friends of the boss. (It is understood that they will supplement their salaries by skimming within the shop.) Managerial turnover, accordingly, is low. Brake Breakers is not the sort of company that can afford to have a disgruntled manager quit in disgust, although any charges he might bring against the company could dependably be turned against him as well.

Brake Breakers, Inc., is everyone's stereotypical image of unethical business in action. Its people sell a shoddy product to customers who don't need it, and they don't always sell what they say they are selling. Employees are treated like serfs, and accounting procedures at every level of the company are, to put it politely, suspect. The customer is virtually never satisfied, but it is the nature of the business that people who need brake repairs need them fast and do not know what has to be done or how much it should cost. They are ripe for the taking, and they are taken. The price is still low enough and the job near enough adequate that no one sues. The "lifetime guarantee" isn't worth the paper it's printed on, but it is a fact about brake jobs that there is only so much that can go wrong, and a disgruntled customer usually doesn't bother coming back anyway. It's a perfect setup. At least half of the profits, even on a modest system of objective ethical accounting, are obtained by cheating the customer and the employees.

How does Brake Breakers, Inc., stack up according to our three Cs of business ethics? Not very well.

Compliance: Minimal; just enough to avoid legal penalties and major lawsuits but far below the level of concern for ethics that we all expect of every business.

Contributions: Well, they do fix brakes, even if some of them aren't broken. But a dozen more dependable businesses—both national franchises and local service stations—would do a better job with less flimflam. To provide a service is not in itself a contribution. We also want to know if it is a service that would otherwise be performed as well and as cheaply by other firms.

Consequences: Disgruntled customers, hesitation among motorists to have their brakes checked when they ought to, occasional accidents, a notoriously bad reputation for car repair shops in general (hurting those that do good, honest work), and an exemplary case of unethical business to turn consumers and congressional investigators against business in general.

It is too often supposed that the business of business ethics is to prove to the management of such unethical enterprises as Brake Breakers, Inc., that crime does not pay. That is too much to ask for.

GNATS AND CAMELS

To strike harder at the petty pickpocket than at the prominent and unabashed person who, in a large and impressive way, sells out his constituents, his followers, his depositors, his stockholders, his subscribers, or his customers is to strain at a gnat and swallow a camel.

Edward Ross, *Sin and Society*

- Show them, perhaps, that they are setting themselves up for lawsuits.

  In fact, it just hasn't happened.
- Show them, then, that they are losing customers.

  In fact, it is a business with a regular supply of customers, no repeat customers in any case and little dependence on word of mouth. (In fact, they depend on the absence of word of mouth, since people are often too ashamed at having been "taken" to tell their friends about it.)
- Show them how well Midas and Meineke have been doing because of their reputation for dependability,

  But, the manager at Brake Breakers tells us with a laugh, "We ain't Midas."
- Argue, then, that unethical business practices cannot possibly pay off in the long run.

"In the long run," the amused manager tells us, unknowingly echoing the economist John Maynard Keynes, "we're all dead."

The fact—sad, perhaps—is that unethical business, like crime, sometimes pays. In any system based on trust, a few deceivers will prosper. There is no guarantee that ethics is good for the bottom line. There is no guarantee that those who do wrong will get caught or feel guilty. There is no guarantee—in business or elsewhere—that the wicked will suffer and the virtuous will be rewarded (at least, not in this life). But, that said, we can nonetheless insist without apology that

---

Even thieves are able to justify their work. A veteran, a very professional thief who lives in New Jersey, reasons, "What I do is good for everybody. First of all I create work. I hire men to deliver the cars, work on the numbers, paint them, give them paper, maybe drive them out of state, find customers. That's good for the economy. Then I'm helping people to get what they could never afford otherwise. A fellow wants a Cadillac but he can't afford it. . . . I save him as much as $2000. Now he's happy. But so is the guy who lost his car. He gets a nice new Cadillac from the insurance company. The Cadillac company—they're happy too because they sell another Cadillac. The only people who don't do so good is the insurance company, but they're so big that nobody cares personally. They got a budget for this sort of thing anyway. . . . Come on now—who am I really hurting?"

New York Times, 1971

good ethics is good business. Where immorality is so easily identified, we can be sure that morality is the general rule, not merely an accessory or an exception. The *point* of doing business is to do well by providing the best service or product at a reasonable cost. Those businesses that exploit the *possibility* of getting away with less are merely parasitic on the overwhelming number of businesses that are doing what they are supposed to.

HOW DO YOU KNOW WHEN YOU'VE DONE SOMETHING WRONG?

_____ lose sleep

_____ drink too much

_____ take drugs

_____ feel guilty

_____ become irritable and suspicious

_____ can't relax

_____ wish you could live your life over again (or at least that one little part of it)

_____ don't enjoy things you usually enjoy

_____ fear getting caught

_____ terrified of memos and mail; afraid to pick up the paper

_____ can't look people in the eye

_____ feel embarrassed with friends, family

_____ get defensive, argumentative

_____ become unusually belligerent in stating opinions (politics, sports, etc.)

_____ need to go to confession (to psychiatrist, etc.)

_____ obsessively contemplate possible consequences

_____ keep kicking self (in fact or in mind)

_____ keep thinking of excuses and finding scapegoats

_____ doesn't bother you at all*

*We're all in trouble.

PRACTICES MAKE PERFECT:
A BETTER WAY TO LOOK AT BUSINESS

> *A practice is any association of definitely patterned
> human behavior wherein the description and mean-
> ing of kinds of behavior involved and the kinds of
> expectations involved are dependent upon those
> rules which define the practice.*
> John Rawls *(professor of philosophy,*
> *Harvard University)*

Business is not a scramble for profits and survival. It is a way of life,
an established and proven *practice* whose prosperity and survival
depends on the participation of its practitioners. Business ethics is not
ethics applied to business. It is the foundation of business. Business
life thrives on competition, but it survives on the basis of its ethics.

Business is first of all a cooperative enterprise with firmly fixed rules
and expectations. A view from the visitor's gallery down to the floor
of the New York Stock Exchange may not look very much like a
cooperative enterprise with fixed rules and expectations, but beneath
the apparent chaos is a carefully orchestrated set of agreements and
rituals without which the Exchange could not operate at all. There can
be no bogus orders, and bid ranges are carefully controlled. The use
of information is restricted, but traders trade information as well as
securities. The rules of the exchange, contrary to superficial appearances, are uncompromising. Break them and you're off the floor for
good. Right there at the busy heart of capitalism, there is no question
that *business is a practice,* and people in business are *professionals.*

In business ethics, it is often profitable to compare business with a
game. Games are also practices. Baseball, for instance, is a practice.
It has its own language, its own gestures with their own meanings, its
own way of giving significance to activities that, apart from the game,
might very well mean nothing at all. (Imagine a person who suddenly
runs and slides into a canvas bag filled with sand on the sidewalk,
declaring himself "safe" as he does so.) The practice is defined by
certain sorts of behavior—"pitching" the ball in a certain way (if, that
is, the practice designates you as the "pitcher"), trying to hit the ball

---

"FOUL!"

Business should be less reluctant to cry "foul" when a foul has indeed been committed.

Robert S. Marker (management consultant and former CEO, McCann-Erickson Worldwide)

---

with a certain well-defined implement (the "bat"), running a certain sequence of "bases" in a certain order subject to certain complex restrictions (one of which is that one not be "tagged" by another person holding the ball). Anyone who has tried to explain what is happening in a baseball game to a visitor from another country with a different "national pastime" can attest to the complexity of these rules and definitions, though most Americans feel quite familiar with them and can focus their attention—as players or as spectators—on such simple-sounding concerns as "Who's up?" and "Who's on first?"

Business is like baseball in that it is a practice. A day at the stock exchange makes it quite clear just how many rituals, rules, and restrictions are involved in every buy-and-sell transaction. The implements of doing business (like "base," "bat," and "ball" in baseball) are also defined within business. What constitutes a contract and fulfillment of a contract is an essential part of the language of business—and often of the contract itself. Consider the not uncommon misunderstanding when a statement of casual intention is misconstrued as a promise (or when "I love you" is mistaken for a statement of commitment instead of an imprudent outburst of passion). The business world is far more open to extra "players" and to alternative courses of action than is baseball, but within the institutions that make up the practice of business, roles and alternatives are clearly specified—as "jobs" and "positions," as obligations and options. Strategic ethics begins by emphasizing business as a practice with strict rules and expectations that acceptable players honor implicitly—*or they are out of the game.* To throw out players who cheat is as important to a healthy enterprise as is the inevitable exit of players who can't play well. Bad business is much more damaging to business than are badly run businesses.

Business, like baseball, is defined by its rules. Some of these have to do with the nature of contracts. Many have to do with *fairness* in dealing with employees, customers, and government agents (hence, the existence of such policing bodies as the IRS, the SEC, the FDA, etc.). Indeed, the notion of fairness in exchanges is more central to business than to any other practice—whether in terms of work and salary, price and product, or public services and subsidies. Without fairness as the central expectation, there are few people who would enter into the market at all. (Consider the chill on the market following dramatic "insider trading" cases.) Without the recognition of fair play, the phrase "free enterprise" would be something of a joke. The rules of business, accordingly, have mainly to do with fairness. Some of these rules ensure that the market will remain open to everyone. Some of the rules protect those who are not players in the practice but whose health, jobs, or careers are affected by it. Some of the rules have to do with serving the needs or wishes of the community (the law of supply and demand can be interpreted not only as an economic mechanism but as an ethical imperative). Some have to do with "impact"—the effects of a business on its surrounding communities and environment. If business has no effects on the surrounding community but was rather a self-enclosed game, there would be no more public cry for business ethics than for "hopscotch ethics" (which is not to say that there is no ethics to hopscotch).

It is within this description of a practice that we can also define the terms "virtue" and "vice" in business ethics. Some virtues and vices go far beyond the bounds of business, of course; they are matters of morality (honesty, for instance). But in business ethics there are virtues and vices that are particular to business and to certain business roles. Close accounting and "watching every penny" are virtues in a shipping clerk but not in someone who is entertaining a client. Keeping a polite distance is a virtue in a stockholder but not in a general manager. Tenaciousness may be a virtue in a salesman but not in a consultant. Outspokenness may be a virtue in a board member but not in the assistant to the president. Being tough-minded is a virtue in some managerial roles but not in others.

In general, we can say this: A virtue sustains and improves a practice. A virtue in business is an ethical trait that makes business in general possible, and this necessarily includes such virtues as respect for contracts as well as concern for product quality, consumer satisfaction, and the bottom line. A vice, on the other hand, degrades and undermines the practice. Shady dealing and reneging on contracts are vices and unethical not because of an absolute moral law but because they undermine the very practice that makes doing business possible.

Thinking about business as a practice and business people as profes-

THE BEST DEFENSE

There is nothing more valuable to me as a professional man than my reputation for being someone who is honest and fair in his dealings. And so we've developed a defensive sort of code: a set of rules that don't allow me to accept gifts from a client, that don't allow me to make investments in client companies, that don't allow me to enter into business with people that are even officers of corporations. By and large, we live by those rules. Is it hard? Of course it is. . . . Nevertheless, I think all these burdens are worth bearing because the rewards of participating in this profession are greater than the costs.

Kenneth P. Johnson (vice president, Coopers & Lybrand)

sionals gives us a set of persuasive responses to the Brake Breakers case:

1. Business in general depends on the acceptance of rules and expectations, on mutual trust and a sense of fairness, even if—as in any such practice—a few unscrupulous participants can take advantage of that trust and betray that concerns for fairness.
2. Brake Breakers, Inc., can continue to prosper in their scummy ways only so long as they remain relatively insignificant, with a small enough market share not to bring down the wrath of major competitors and sufficiently little publicity not to inspire a class-action suit. Unethical behavior may bring profits, but only limited profits.
3. It is clearly in the interest of business in general and other firms in that particular industry to warn consumers about Brake Breakers, even to put them out of business. The success and strength of a profession and its independence from externally imposed regulations depends on the internal "policing" of unethical behavior. Doctors have never doubted this; lawyers are learning. But so long as business thinks of itself as unregulated competition where "anything goes" rather than as a profession to be protected from abuse, this vital policing for survival will go unattended, or it will be attended to by the government.
4. The practice of business is a small world. Fly-by-Night Enterprises Ltd. and Brake Breakers, Inc., may succeed for a while, but, in general, people catch on—fast. Irate customers tell their

friends—and their lawyers. They also get even. They sue, for triple damages. They write the newspapers or *60 Minutes*. They drop a note to the IRS, or they call the Better Business Bureau. The banker's kid who was cheated on the job complains to his father the month before the lease has to be renewed. Or the victim happens to be a litigious lawyer with time on his hands. But the effects of unethical business practices are not always so obvious as a dip in the bottom line or a subpoena waiting at the office. They are often slow and insidious, the bottom of a career eaten out from under, or a company that is doing "OK" but could and should be doing much better. There are no guarantees that unethical behavior will be punished, but the odds are pretty impressive.

5. In any profession, it's hard to get clean again. Suppliers tighten their terms; priority status disappears. The hardheaded business-man is supposed to say "Who cares?" But if so, there are few hardheaded businessmen, only a small number of bottom-line-minded sociopaths. Character is who you are, the thing you are trying to prove by making money in the first place. One of the classic movie lines is "My money's as good as anyone else's." Perhaps. But are *you* as good? That isn't just a matter of money.

Why should Brake Breakers, Inc., get ethical? Let's ask another question: How would you feel about yourself if you spent your working days as a manager of Brake Breakers? What would you tell your kids?

THE QUESTION OF QUALITY

The whole point of the free-enterprise system, according to Adam Smith, is the production of quality goods at reasonable prices. The pursuit of profit may be the motive, but the justification of business is the quality (and the quality of life) it produces. Quality is also good business, and one does not have to look very far into the shift of the market in automobiles or electronics over the past two decades to appreciate the power of quality. And this means quality all the way through the production process. High-quality ideas halfheartedly manufactured and serviced do not produce quality products. Thus quality refers not only to products but to the entire production process, from innovation to salesmanship and servicing, from top management to the workroom floor. Quality "control" is not nearly as important as planning for quality from the outset. One might remove one flawed microchip from a million, but it is the quality of the other 999,999 that must be planned for. We fight too often about "who will clean up (or take the blame for) the mess" and concern ourselves too little with preventing the mess in the first place.

"Quality" has become something of a "buzzword," however; another marketing term with more dazzle than substance, rather than a definition of purpose. Like "excellence" (its close kin), it implies good value without any particular substance or commitment. But both practically and philosophically, it is a word of great significance and indicates a sense of mission, a commitment beyond profit potential and the bottom line. It is a word that synthesizes the demands of the marketplace and the demands of ethics. In business life, this assumption—so basic that it is rarely even discussed as such—is that quality "sells" and is the key to success. And this is true within the corporation as well as in the marketplace as such.

Two decades ago, when Japanese industry became the model for many American industries, the idea of "quality circles" became popular and, with varied success, was tried in various companies. The idea was right, without question. Instead of or in spite of the military hierarchy that ruled most corporations (and, make no mistake, this was the rule in most Japanese corporations as well), all decision making regarding production and even innovation not only invited but demanded input from everyone involved in the project. Where it worked, it made a marvelous difference, but more often than not, quality circles promoted at best a facade of empowerment, inspiring cynicism rather than enthusiasm. Democracy, for all its virtues, promises a messy decision-making process, and the unsorted combination of democratic discussion and the old top-down authoritarianism made for some unsettling confrontations. At their worst, quality circles became one more ploy for union busting and abuse of the employees. As so often, the word "quality" (coupled at the time with an uncritical emulation

NONE OF THE ABOVE

When you think of U.S. manufacturers with top-quality standards, which one company comes to mind? That's the question posed to 250 American executives by Grant Thornton, the accounting firm. While the companies listed below came up most often, the most frequent response was "none."

1. IBM
2. Ford
3. Motorola
4. Hewlett-Packard
5. General Motors
6. Xerox
7. Cadillac
8. General Electric
9. 3M
10. Apple Computer

From *Business and Society Review*

of the Japanese) dictated policy, rather than the concern for quality as such.

More recently, we have been treated to a banquet of "total quality management," the rage of the 1980s. Again, the idea was right, and the importance of quality goes uncontested, but behind the implementation were hidden some unflattering truths. The concept itself can be traced back to W. Edward Deming, who, ironically, taught management techniques to the Japanese after World War II. After 1960, when the Japanese found themselves facing a potentially disastrous confrontation between industry and their own workers, an integrated, harmonious system of workers, management, and their mutual interests really did seem to be a miracle. Of course, Japanese culture was particularly conducive to the kinds of commitment and dedication to a shared mission that Deming had endorsed. Why it is, on the other hand, that American industry so long tolerated and encouraged antagonism and an adversarial stance regarding its own labor force is something of a sociological mystery and a business disaster. (In England, it is much less of a mystery but even more of a disaster.)

In 1980, Deming's teachings came home to the United States under the name "total quality management." As so often, the name is misleading and the concept often abused. What it means, when you come right down to it, is nothing but the age-old recipe for good business: look to and listen to your customers, take care of and listen to your employees, let those who do the work identify the problems, don't get trapped by your own numbers, and *know what you are doing*, at every level. Total quality management is not magic and it is not new, and it involves no deep philosophical insights. What it does involve, as does this book, is the reminder of what we should have remembered all along. It involves the undoing of a number of dangerous and destructive myths, many of them misinterpreted from Adam Smith's classic defense of the free-market system. The product might be a means to profit but it is not only that. Quality is an end in itself, and with it, usually, come increased profits as well. The motive of business might be profit but the test of success is general prosperity and well-being. The market may be competitive but underlying that competition is cooperation and a sense of the general community. And if labor, too, tends to become a commodity of the market, the only true source of value, ultimately, is the worth of a person, his or her time and labor. And that is no communist talking; it is pure and genuine Adam Smith.

Total quality management is management that knows what it is doing, that sees beyond the "bottom line" to the people and processes that go into success. It is not yet another "magic bullet" of management techniques, able to solve all our problems and leap tall corporate headquarters at a single bound. It is not enough for a few wizards at the top to understand what is going on and what is intended. The corporation (and any other human institution) is ultimately an organized and organic whole, and the "mind" of its activities is everywhere, embodied in the company and in every one of its people. Assembly-line work is in this sense no different from middle management or, for that matter, the work of professionals in accounting or the legal department. It is all an organic part of the overall process and, in an important sense, the "brains" of the operation. Who knows better than an assembly worker where the inefficiencies are and where the mistakes are most often made; and who knows better than a middle manager where to locate the unhappiness and frustration—as well as the sources of hope and satisfaction—in the bureaucracy he or she serves. People need to be listened to, not just as a matter of personal respect (no small matter when it comes to inspiring loyalty, dedication, and good workmanship) but as an essential part of perfecting the processes upon which the success and survival of the company and, ultimately, the whole industry depends.

In short, business isn't just a job. It's a challenge, a goal, a mission. Management doesn't just "manage"; it inspires and encourages. Employees aren't to be kept in line; they are made to aspire, to strive, to share in success. Karl Marx warned, years ago (in some of his "youthful" essays), that the great personal danger of the capitalist economy was the "alienation" of labor, the reduction of the worker to a mere means, without a stake or appreciation, without any sense of personal pride in the product he or she helped to produce. Total quality management, when all is said and done, is just the proper response to Marx and Marxism. Free-market pundits may make themselves and their viewers feel better by pummeling communism and declaring the fact that "we won!" But the free market itself succeeds by correcting the very real faults that Marx sometimes identified.

THE QUESTION OF QUANTITY: IS BIG SO BAD?

> *The public be damned! I'm working for my stockholders.*
>
> William Vanderbilt

"What's good for General Bullmoose is good for the U.S.A.," roared an old Al Capp character. The readers loved it, and they hated the general. He represented the arrogance of Big Business. He plotted and schemed and put the country at his mercy. He was the personification of the omnivorous, omnipotent, untamed giant corporation.

Suspicion of big business is one of the great American traditions. The American business hero is the individual entrepreneur; the villain is the giant corporation. Ralph Nader didn't invent that villain. He had only to summon up—once again—that good old American tradition.

But suspicion is not the same as moral censure. The righteous American discomfort with large and impersonal institutions (universities, churches, hospitals, and government just as much as corporations) too easily slips into a wrongful assumption that any large and powerful company is in itself unethical and unnecessary. In fact, 496 of the Fortune 500 companies are not involved in any scandals, payoffs, or public extortion in any given year, a much less newsworthy fact than the four that are so involved. And in some industries, at least, enormousness is a necessity, not for the sake of monopoly but for the sake of efficiency and effectiveness. We might feel less threatened by Adam Smith's nation of small shopkeepers, but that is a world long gone. Ours is a world of international conglomerates, where size becomes a key factor not only in the success but also in the ethics of business life.

Size and power obviously make a difference in ethics. A small decision by a giant corporation can affect thousands, perhaps millions of people. If General Motors HQ in Detroit decides to close a small, rundown plant outside Atlanta, it can destroy an entire community. If Exxon makes a small change in its oil-drilling policies, the entire life of the nation can be altered. Brake Breakers can cause a few accidents or a dent in one's wallet. An unethical baker can cause a few stomach cramps. But ITT or Exxon can bring about a revolution, a national crisis, a change in the way the world works. With increased size and power there is exponentially increased impact. So, too, comes increased social responsibility.

Our argument against Brake Breakers, Inc., was essentially that a company with such dubious practices and reputation could survive only so long as it was not too successful, for with increased success would come the wrath of angry consumers and of higher-quality competitors. But this idea—that unethical businesses must always be anonymous exceptions rather than the visible rule—needs to be reinterpreted when we are talking about some of the most powerful institutions on earth. A corporation that can afford to spend hundreds of millions of dollars on lobbying and legal costs is obviously not as vulnerable to competitive pressures and consumer complaints as a small, fly-by-night outfit operating in the shadows. It is this enormous power that rightly worries business critics, and it therefore becomes one of the most difficult problems of business ethics.

Why do we assume that big is bad?

First, of course, there is that traditional American sense of individualism and the corresponding prejudice against impersonal institutions.

This will, no doubt, continue to be the ethical key to American life and to business, too. But it has very little to do with business ethics and perhaps even less to do with the shape that international business has already taken in the world. The notion of the megolithic corporation is currently being challenged by the German concept of *Mittelstand*: the small or mid-size company, of generally 100–500 employees, which focuses on a very specific product and market. These small, product-specific companies are enjoying amazing success in Europe, and the idea—which incorporates the financial stability of larger companies, the flexibility and adaptability of smaller ones, and the high degree of specialization of the sciences—is expected to make rapid inroads into American and Japanese business, in both their markets and their corporate structures.

Second, size and power mean impact, and the very idea that a single company can have so much control over us and possibly cause so much damage terrifies most people. But the answer to this fear is not to have a nation of impotent industries capable of competing (with enormous government protection) only with each other, if they can compete at all. The answer is to make sure that the corporations, their management, and owners continue to see themselves as particularly powerful citizens, with the interests and responsibilities appropriate to that role; and to make sure that there are countervailing forces on corporations by way of the public interest. There has been a lot of talk about consumer rights lately, but not much about consumer responsibilities. If we "vote with our dollars," as Milton Friedman is so fond of saying, then it must be said that most voters don't seem to know that they are at the polls.

Third, the existence of giant corporations seems to go against the free-market assumption that competition is essential to business, monopoly detrimental. But there can be brutal competition among giants. The only pharmacy in town may have a near-absolute monopoly. What's more, many modern products require the enormousness of our largest corporations for their very existence. For all of our celebration of the individual inventor and the adventurous entrepreneur, there is no reason to think that much of modern technology could survive and improve without the muscle of giant corporations. And competition, we no longer need to remind ourselves, is not limited to companies; it can be even more vigorous among countries. It is not evident that Apple, Inc., can take on Japan, Inc., or that any one country can any longer take on the whole of the world.

Size and power can and should be evaluated according to ethical

BIG IS PASSÉ?

If I had to go way out on a limb, I would say that large corporations as we have known them will not exist in 30 years' time. They won't be able to sustain their position. They won't be able to hold on to their people; everyone will know too many other people who have gone out on their own and made a fair amount of money. So all the good people are going to be spinning off.

. . . You get the highest productivity, morale, and performance from a small work force. A few corporations like Hewlett-Packard have recognized that. In fact the evidence seems to point to between 50 and 100 people as the most efficient work unit. If that is true, and if the economy is moving in that direction, then if you are running IBM, the biggest 10-year challenge you face is how to break IBM into the 10,000 little units of 100 people, with an entrepreneurial stake. IBM will survive in some mode, but I think it will be very different from what we know right now.

Allan Kennedy, co-author, *Corporate Cultures*

criteria. There is nothing intrinsically wrong with size and power; nor are size and power their own justification. Might does not make right—in business or in any other enterprise. There is unwarranted size; there is illegitimate power. There is no warrant for attacking bigness as such, but neither is bigness a God-given right (as John Rockefeller used to claim). The right to be big must itself be earned, established, as in every other ethical context, by the three Cs:

COMPLIANCE. Does the giant corporation break any laws? Does it manipulate the law? Does it comply with morality and local customs? Is there anything *wrong* with the giant corporation, or is it just a suspicion of bigness?

CONTRIBUTIONS. How does the size of the corporation benefit society? Can it compete better with other firms (including international firms) than it could if it were smaller—and what are the consequent benefits for the consumer? Does it provide more and perhaps better jobs than several smaller companies? Can it more readily afford expensive research-and-development projects, making possible new and possibly valuable products that would otherwise remain unaffordable? Can it maintain a distribution chain superior to those of smaller companies? What nonbusiness projects and institutions are supported by the corporation—in the arts, in education, in the community? How much—and how well—does the corporation define the mores of the community, or of the nation?

CONSEQUENCES. Does the giant corporation in fact reduce competition? Is it beyond public control? Is the inevitable impact of its every action on society for the most part beneficial—or at least harmless? (*Every* action with consequences is going to have *some* negative consequences; the question is always the *balance* of good and harm.) Does the size and power of the corporation threaten other values? Local customs? Does it set a dangerous precedent, even if it is itself without noticeably harmful consequences?

All in all, the answers to these questions have been satisfactory; otherwise big business would not survive, despite its power. It is not by sheer power alone that the Fortune 500 companies survive. They comply with law, morality, and custom; contribute to the well-being of society; and do far more good than harm. Indeed, they must do so, for there are no institutions in our society more visible, and potentially more vulnerable, than the giant corporations. But the fact that the public perceives these companies as impersonal and amoral only shows once again that, for corporate survival as well as for the public interest, ethics—both in reality and in appearance—is nowhere more vital or necessary. Large corporations, like the biggest kid on the block, must always be wary of looking like a bully. A little kid can get away with an awful lot, but "Butch" has only to raise his fist in defense to earn a moral denunciation. Hertz had to endure a lot from Avis (when the latter was "number two") before it could claim the right to fight back, and IBM had to continue eyeing Apple with that restrained and frustrated annoyance that is the ethical price of power.

Prejudices aside, Mom and Pop's grocery store is no more intrinsically moral than IBM. The same questions and temptations arise; the same errors are made. It is easier to discover whether you have been cheated or not at the grocery store, of course. You have only to count your change, squeeze the melon, weigh the meat again. It is not so easy to measure such personal virtues as honesty in a corporation with several hundred thousand employees. But size is a factor that often magnifies vices and sometimes dwarfs virtues. After IBM spent a decade under fire for alleged antitrust violations, the federal government finally admitted that it was IBM's size and power alone that motivated the suit, for the marketing strategies that caused the commotion were in fact no more unethical than those used by a dozen other computer companies. But the consequences of the activities of a giant corporation are always so pervasive and powerful that, unlike similar actions by a smaller company, virtually everything it does becomes an ethical issue—which is not to say that what it does is unethical.

It is one of the more telling symptoms of the new decade that IBM—and automotive giant GM as well—are in states of crisis. IBM has split itself into increasingly autonomous subcorporations, the value of its stock has halved in a year, and it faces a protracted struggle to regain its long-esteemed place in the industry. But if there is a lesson to be learned here—and certainly there are many—it is not that "big is bad" but that any corporation, whatever its size, is minuscule compared to the market as a whole. To survive and thrive it needs to remain limber and attuned—to its customers, to the needs of the community, to the needs of its own employees, and to an increasingly competitive world market. The question is one of biodynamics rather than size as such, and if the much-maligned dinosaurs had survived whatever the global catastrophe that killed them, they would no doubt have a good deal to teach us about the advantages and disadvantages of size. But they would also have to learn from the mammals (and some of the insects) about the superior advantages of cooperation. There may be nothing wrong with bigness, but without cooperation in the world today, we may all be out of business.

STRATEGIC ETHICS

At the conclusion of the congressional hearings following the much-publicized Lockheed bribery scandals in Japan, Carl Kotchian of Lockheed summarized the indictment against his company—and against much of American business—in a simple, inelegant, disastrous statement:

If, in a situation where high government officials have influence on
matters pertinent to a private company, money is requested as payoffs
for those officials, can that private foreign company, which wants its
products to be bought at all costs, realistically decline the request on the
grounds that it is not a good thing from the ethical point of view?

This was, to put it mildly, precisely the wrong response. It failed to
serve as a justification or even as an excuse; instead, it supported what
the harshest critics of business had been saying all along: that business
is essentially antagonistic to ethics. Such statements are not uncommon in the sometimes antagonistic "interface" between business and
the rest of society, but they are uniformly disastrous. In their language
if not in their intention, they neglect the ethical point of view if they
do not explicitly exclude it. Kotchian's reply harmed his company's
reputation when a more considered statement might have pointed out
the ethical ambiguity of the situation. He also earned himself an
unenviable place in textbooks—not in business but in business ethics—
as a glaring example of what is wrong with business.

What is strategic ethics? The combination of ethics and strategy is
sure to raise some protests immediately; indeed, many moralists would
call it cynical. But it seems cynical only because of the myth of amoral
business, because of the idea that business and ethics are discrete if
not antagonistic, that the ethical response is typically bad for business
and that the necessities of business are often unethical. If one assumes
that business is intrinsically amoral, that profit and personal gain are
its only legitimate motives, then the idea that a business response
would take ethical propriety into consideration as a matter of strategy
does indeed seem suspicious. And if it is assumed that business and
ethics are antagonistic, then when business solicits ethics on its behalf,
the public naturally expects deceit, hypocrisy, or fraud. It is because
these assumptions are so widely shared that the typical response to
well-intended speeches by business people is contempt rather than
praise—"they're only worried about their public image"—as if business people thought of their public image only when they had something to hide. In fact, concern for one's public image is at the heart of
ethics, and public image is a reflection of, not a front for, ethical
policies.

Strategic ethics begins, in short, with the realization that ethics is
not just good; it's good business, too.

A second example of an unstrategic, ethically ill-considered, and
damaging corporate response hit the newspapers and outraged Con-

gress and the public in May 1983. Chrysler Corporation had performed its miracle—made possible by $1.5 billion in federal loan guarantees. In the midst of the applause that greeted its announcement that it would begin paying off its debt, a company spokesman added that the company should not have to honor its agreement to sell the government several million shares of Chrysler stock at a now-bargain price (less than half the market value). The outrage was not limited to Congress and the newspapers; the president of the American Business Conference was quoted in *Newsweek* (May 23, 1983) as saying of the request "[It was] extremely unfortunate, bordering on disgrace. . . . It damages the credibility of the entire business community." Chrysler, despite the genius of its strategic planning, had not sufficiently considered its ethical strategy. The company was forced into a humiliating retreat, harming its hard-earned reputation—and clouding the very sensitive issue of government loans and subsidies for hard-pressed corporations—with a single, ill-considered comment.

Perhaps the most spectacularly successful example of strategic ethical thinking in recent years was Johnson & Johnson's remarkable reaction to and recovery from the Tylenol crisis of 1982. A small number of bottles of "Extra Strength" Tylenol had been tampered with, the contents of some capsules replaced with deadly cyanide. A number of people died. Apparently without hesitation, J&J chairman James Burke ordered the recall of millions of dollars' worth of untainted Tylenol, causing an enormous loss to the company. There were ad campaigns, rewards for apprehension of the murderer, and hotlines for help, and there was visible corporate concern throughout the tragedy. Johnson & Johnson, which could easily have been ruined, actually elevated and reaffirmed its reputation as a reliable and trustworthy enterprise.

As natural as that response might seem to some people now, it is clear that many companies faced with a similar crisis would not have made that decision. They would have stalled for time to "investigate." They would then have launched an immediate advertising campaign to convince the public that the tampering was confined to a single shipment. They might have waited to see if in fact the fatalities would continue.

In the Tylenol case, J&J might have offered to examine samples of Tylenol already purchased, emphasizing that still-sealed packages could not have been poisoned. They could have offered simply to exchange bottles of "Extra Strength" Tylenol capsules for other Johnson & Johnson products, including regular Tylenol and Tylenol tablets, which had not been found to be tainted. These strategies might have minimized the danger and had a less disastrous effect on the bottom line.

Looking at the tragedy in isolation, one might come to the conclusion that Chairman Burke overreacted and made a too-dramatic decision. In fact, a chairman looking only at the immediate damage to the company and its market would not decide to do what Burke did. The enormous cost in terms of industry reputation, longer-term sales, and inevitable government regulation would become evident only later on.

Burke's strategy, however, was an ethical strategy. In his review of the circumstances surrounding the tragedy, the recall, and the successful reintroduction of Tylenol, he emphasized not the usual agonizing decisions but the eighteen-month period just prior to the tragedy, when executives at every level of the corporation were called upon to review the company code of ethics. That underlying sense of purpose established a framework for thinking about and dealing with the tragedy that was more successful than any mere marketing strategy. The result was not only the survival of the company with optimistic prognoses for the future but a healthy increase in public respect and confidence both in the company and in the industry as a whole. A product that was declared "dead" by virtually every industry expert a year ago is today once again one of the best-selling over-the-counter pain relievers. One can easily imagine what would have happened if Johnson & Johnson had tried to minimize the danger, and had tried only to save itself from its immediate losses.

Tom Peters: "Ethics is not principally about headline issues. . . . How we work out the "little stuff" will determine our response to a Tylenol-sized crisis. When disaster strikes, it's far too late to seek out ethical touchstones."

A somewhat less heroic, because belated, but still an encouraging example of strategic ethics is Nestlé Corporation's leadership in announcing its compliance with the World Health Organization code concerning breast-milk substitutes marketed around the world. For nearly a decade, a number of international food companies had been under fire for supplying third-world mothers with infant formula, with tragic results. The mothers did not know how to use the formula. They used it when breast milk would have been preferable. Their own milk dried up, and they became dependent on the formula, which was not always available. They mixed the formula with polluted water. Many infants died. Nestlé, as the most visible and best known of the companies, was specifically and vigorously attacked and subjected to

TYLENOL: SUCCESS, TRAGEDY, SUCCESS AGAIN

Among American household names, it would be hard to find a consumer line more trusted than Johnson & Johnson. From Tylenol pain relievers to dental floss to baby oil, few bathroom medicine cabinets would seem well stocked without J&J health products. The name *Band-aid* itself is a trademark of the huge international conglomerate.

J&J officials attribute the firm's steady success to the implementation of a plain-spoken corporate philosophy statement known as "Our Credo." Thirty-five years before the trend-setting book *In Search of Excellence* cried out for companies to establish a clear set of values, Robert Wood Johnson, son of the founder, authored the J&J code in recognition of the fact that "the day has passed when business was a private matter—if it ever really was. In a business society, every act of business has social consequences."

Periodically updated, the credo outlines such ideals as high-quality goods, equal employment opportunity, safe working conditions, corporate charitable giving, and environmental responsibility. Ranked only as "our final" obligation is the need to earn a sound profit. "When we operate according to these principles," concludes the credo, "the stockholders should realize a fair return."

In the fall of 1982, a journalist from Chicago telephoned J&J executive offices. He wanted reaction to the stunning news that the company's leading product—Tylenol capsules—had apparently been contaminated with cyanide by a psychopath. J&J had no less than $100 million worth of Tylenol on the market at the time. The process of recalling so vast an output would cost a fortune.

The emergency served to test J&J's fidelity to the credo. Relying on the code's injunction that "our first responsibility" is to product users, a crisis committee of top executives decided to "go public" with a campaign to notify consumers of the status of the poisonings. Company officials held press conferences, appeared on leading interview programs, took out full-page ads in leading newspapers, established a toll-free consumer hotline (which received more than 30,000 calls), even lobbied in Washington to make product tampering a felony. And, of course, J&J withdrew Tylenol capsules from the market, pending the introduction a couple of months later of new packaging, sealed in three places, to resist tampering.

Observers generally lauded the company's swift action to remove the product and the open manner in which the emergency was handled. Wrote *The Washington Post:* "Though the hysteria and frustration generated by random murder have often obscured the company's actions, Johnson & Johnson has effectively demonstrated how a major company ought to handle a disaster."

The dominance of Tylenol in the market for over-the-counter analgesics has now been restored.

The Corporate Conscience, 1985, AMACOM

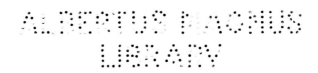

a substantial worldwide boycott of its products. Finally, in March 1982, Nestlé appointed an independent commission of its own, headed by former Senator Edmund Muskie, to make recommendations concerning the WHO code. Indeed, even the leader of the boycott, Douglas Johnson, proudly announced, "Nestlé has moved forward to become a model for the whole industry." "Nestlé QUIK sales are once again on the rise" (*Boston Globe,* January 2, 1984).

THE FORCES OF CHANGE: TEN ONGOING ETHICAL CHALLENGES

Without pressure, it is easy to take ethics for granted. In the absence of competition, there is no problem in being a fair competitor. When there were no women in management, there were no ethical pressures concerning their equality or their treatment. The new importance of business ethics has much to do with changes in America that put new pressures on business. Here are eight of them.

1. DISTRUST OF POWERFUL INSTITUTIONS. Long before Watergate, Americans distrusted large institutions—including big business. As corporations get more powerful, suspicion increases; small ethical questions tend to become scandals.
2. MORE WOMEN IN THE WORK FORCE. Perhaps the single most dramatic ethical change in American business is the number of women who are now earning their way to the top. It remains to be seen what changes this may mean in the way American corporations do business as the "glass ceiling" finally gives way.
3. DIVERSITY AND MULTICULTURALISM. Minority unemployment is not the only ethical concern facing business. Minority executives are ready for top positions, and, with women executives, they are challenging the "country club" traditions of many established boardrooms.

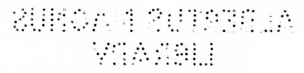

WORK VS. MOTHERHOOD

[T]he meeting of motherhood and workplace remains uneasy. The number of childbirth-related discrimination complaints filed with the Equal Employment Opportunity Commission has skyrocketed 40 percent in the past five years, from 3,000 women reporting in 1990 that they were unjustly fired, denied leave, or otherwise punished for having children, to 4,191 reporting the same in 1995. Part of this increase can be attributed to women's greater awareness of their rights, part of it to the sheer increase in numbers of employed women who have given birth—in 1994, 53 percent of all births were to women in the labor force versus 31 percent in 1976. Downsizing may play a role too. . . . Yet what's most disturbing about this trend, say experts, is that the new laws, coupled with a vigilant concern for the bottom line among employers, have simply forced companies to cover their tracks better. As a result, pregnancy and maternity discrimination claims are exceedingly difficult to prove.

—*Redbook*, July 1996

AFFIRMATIVE INACTION

Although women represented 46 percent of America's civilian labor force in 1994, they failed to reach even the 40 percent mark as managers in half of the industries studied. . . . Black women could be found in proportion to their representation in the working population—about 6 percent—in only one sector, the telephone industry.

—*Working Woman*, October 1995

[In 1997] Hispanic Business identified 249 Hispanic executives at the vice-president level and above at Fortune 1000 companies. That means Hispanics—while comprising 10 percent of the U.S. population—represent only 1.6 percent of the total 15,000 senior-level managers at these companies. Hispanic women fare much worse; they represent 16 percent of the Corporate Elite list and a mere 0.25 percent of all top-level Fortune 1000 executives.

—*Hispanic Business*, February 1997

FORTUNE'S EIGHT ATTRIBUTES OF REPUTATION

Quality of management
Quality of products/services
Innovativeness
Long-term investment value
Financial soundness
Ability to attract, develop, and keep talented people
Community and environmental responsibility
Use of corporate assets

---

4. HIGHER EDUCATION AND EXPECTATIONS. American workers and managers are typically high-school graduates, and as often as not college graduates, too. They have higher expectations, get bored more easily, and are unwilling to stick with a job that they don't find challenging.

5. OLDER SOCIETY. Questions about seniority and retirement have never been so pressing and they will get more pressing in the new millennium. Fairness and costs are the tangled issues.

6. FOREIGN COMPETITION. The days of easy economic dominance are past. International competition means new rules and new obligations at home, new ethical challenges abroad.

7. TIGHT TIMES. The days of generosity are over, too. The ranks of management are shrinking. Expectations and demands are higher, bringing new pressures and some unwelcome options.

8. CONSUMER AWARENESS. Ralph Nader didn't do it alone, but together with the press and *60 Minutes* and other television news magazine shows, the average American consumer is much more sensitive to questions of quality and methods of redress. This does not just mean that businesses must be more careful. It means that the standards themselves have actually changed.

9. POVERTY AND INEQUALITY. Where does business stand? What can business do? These are no longer merely "social" problems. Business is breeding increased inequality of incomes.

10. ITS OWN POWER. International business is now the most powerful force on the globe, more influential than governments and armies. Will it respond to its own importance with responsibility and sensitivity to issues other than its own search for markets, resources and profits?

THE STRATEGIC ETHICAL RESPONSE

Strategy is the key to good business. But when it comes to ethics, strategy is typically left behind and unplanned. Visceral reaction takes its place. Ethical dilemmas are the result of poor planning and a lack of ethical strategy. No competent executive would think of taking the company to the bargaining table without a clear sense of objectives, limits, and tactics. And yet some of the same executives lead their companies into the forum of public opinion with nothing but a grab bag of ethical platitudes. Even a seemingly spontaneous ethical response takes advance planning and presupposes a considered strategy, not only when a company is forced to respond to criticism, emergencies, and conflicts but also in response to good fortune and success.

Irving Kristol has complained in the *Wall Street Journal* that business people have never learned how to "think politically." He provides us with an apt illustration of poor public strategy by way of an ethically naive response. The case was the 1973 oil crisis, in which the large oil companies profited from what amounted to a heavy burden on the American people, not only causing widespread hardship but closing thousands of small businesses and putting hundreds of thousands of people out of work. However innocent these corporations may have been in bringing about the situation, they nevertheless found themselves in a position to reap huge profits at the expense of their fellow citizens. Consequently, they appeared as "profiteers" to the press and the public. Kristol advises that they would much better have shunned "like the plague" such "tainted money," if only because it threatened their very survival. (There was a major if ultimately ineffective public outcry to nationalize the oil companies as a result.) The oil companies argued that they would use these windfall profits for further exploration and development. They argued too that they did not bring about the crisis. But the question, Kristol argued, was not whether the oil companies would use those profits in further exploration or whether they caused the situation. (In fact, they spent a great deal of time and money unsuccessfully advertising their defense to the public.) In *Two Cheers for Capitalism* Kristol comments:

> Only immensely self-righteous men, who could not see themselves as others saw them, would think for a minute that such arguments might be

persuasive. Which is just another way of saying that, at a crucial moment
when it was necessary for the oil companies to "think politically," they
could not summon up either the will or the intellectual resources to do
so.

But it was not just a question of politics or persuasion; it was a matter,
as Kristol suggests, of faulty self-perception, a misconception of what
business can do and what it ought to do. It was a matter of choosing to
discuss economics when the topic of debate in the public forum was
ethics. It was a failure to understand the importance of a strategic
ethical response.

The strategic ethical response is nothing other than the best response
under the circumstances. But "best," of course, means something
more than the current number on the bottom line. Business is not a
simple game, one that can be measured and defined by the single goal
of immediate profitability. There is also the reputation of the company
and its long-term survival, the happiness and well-being of the individuals in it, and the integrity of the "game" itself. The oil companies
have now been "bad guys" for years, and if they have so far avoided
nationalization, they nevertheless will continue to face a public fight
for years to come, even when their policies are clearly in the public
interest.

The Johnson & Johnson response to the Tylenol tragedy, on the
other hand, is an excellent example of the strategic ethical response.
But such responses do not emerge spontaneously; Johnson & Johnson
had an established code of ethics that dictated—in advance—the
appropriate response to that dire emergency. It is highly unlikely that
any company, no matter how ethical, could easily come to such a
difficult decision under such tremendous pressure without such prior
ethical planning. On the other hand, Nestlé would be much better off
if they had supported the WHO code before they were pressured into
it.

Strategic ethical response is a matter of language as well as substance. The ethics of a company may come into question not because
something goes wrong but rather because some fool *says* something
stupid or thoughtless. The Chrysler spokesman who suggested that the
federal government forget its options cast a shadow on his otherwise
heroic company darker than that of any factory recall. A mechanical
defect is usually a correctable mistake. Reneging on one's debts is a
scandal, and scandals don't simply get "corrected."

A considered ethical response can move a business from the shadows into the limelight. Big business has not always been the focus of suspicion; it has also occupied the role of hero and friend of the common man. For an ideal example of ethical language in action in business, let us quote a master of the strategic ethical response. Here is Henry Ford in a letter to a stockholder:

> Business and industry are first and foremost a public service. We are organized to do as much good as we can everywhere for everybody concerned. I do not believe we should make such an awful profit on our cars. A reasonable profit is right, but not too much. So, it has been my policy to force the price of a car down as fast as production would permit and give the benefit to the users and laborers with resulting surprisingly enormous profits to ourselves.

Whether Ford's statement is self-serving, tongue-in-cheek, or insincere (those are usually undecidable matters and, in any case, not nearly so damaging as blatant amorality), it is the sort of response that disarms the opposition and turns corporations (and their officers) into heroes instead of public villains. Despite the traditional "populist" distrust of big business in America, Ford and his company were heroes in America for many decades. And former Ford executive Lee Iaccoca became a culture hero (even a presidential hopeful) as chairman of the resurrected Chrysler corporation.

SOME DANGEROUS PHRASES

"We've always done it that way."
"Too expensive."
"Not in the budget."
"Realistically . . ."
"In principle I agree, but . . ."
"Too much paperwork."
"It's not our policy."
"It is our policy . . ."
"This needs more study."
"They won't do anything about it anyway."
"They don't care."
"They don't want to know."
"We have enough complications already."
"There are no clear answers."
"That's just a matter of opinion."

THINKING ETHICS:
THE RULES OF THE GAME

> *. . . by thinking, nobody can ever get worse but will*
> *only get better.*
>
> Anne Frank, Diary of a Young Girl

Ethics is, first of all, a way of thinking.

Being ethical is also—of course—*doing* the right thing, but what one does is hardly separable from how one thinks. Most people in business who do wrong do so not because they are wicked but because they think they are trapped and do not even consider the ethical significance or implications of their actions.

What is thinking ethically? It is thinking in terms of *compliance* with the rules, implicit as well as explicit, thinking in terms of the *contributions* one can make as well as one's own possible gains, thinking in terms of avoiding harmful *consequences* to others as well as to oneself. Accordingly, here are eight crucial rules for ethical thinking in business.

Rule No. 1: Consider other people's well-being, including the well-being of nonparticipants.

In virtually every major religion this is the golden rule: "Do unto others as you would have them do unto you"; or, negatively, "Do not do unto others as you would not have them do unto you." Ideally, this might mean that one should try to maximize everyone's interests, but this is unreasonable. First of all, no one really expects that a businessman (or anyone else) would or should sacrifice his own interests for everyone else's. Second, it is impossible to take everyone into account; indeed, for any major transaction, the number of people who will be affected—some unpredictably—may run into the tens or hundreds of thousands. But we can readily accept a minimum version of this rule, which is to make a *contribution* where it is reasonable to do so and to avoid *consequences* that are harmful to others. There is nothing in the golden rule that demands that one deny one's own interests or make sacrifices to the public good. It says only that one must take into account human effects beyond one's own bottom line and weigh one's own gain against the losses of others.

Rule No. 2: Think as a member of the business community and not as an isolated individual.

Business has its own rules of propriety and fairness. These are not just matters of courtesy and protocol; they are the conditions that make business possible. Respect for contracts, paying one's debts, and selling decent products at a reasonable price are not only to one's own advantage; they are necessary for the very existence of the business community.

Rule No. 3: Obey, but do not depend solely on, the law.

It goes without saying, as a matter of prudence if not of morality, that businesses and business people ought to obey the law—the most obvious meaning of *compliance*. But what needs to be added is that ethical thinking is not limited to legal obedience. There is much unethical behavior that is not illegal, and the question of what is right is not always defined by the law. The fact is that many things that are not immoral or illegal are repulsive, disgusting, unfair, and unethical—belching aloud in elevators, throwing a disappointing dish at one's host at dinner, paying debts only after the "final notice" and the threat of a lawsuit arrives, fleecing the feebleminded, taking advantage of trust and good faith, selling faulty if not dangerous merchandise under the rubric "Buyer beware." Check the law—but don't stop there.

Rule No. 4: Think of yourself—and your company—as part of society, not just "the market."

Business people and businesses are citizens in society. They share the fabric of feelings that make up society and, in fact, contribute much of that feeling themselves. Business is not a closed community. It exists and thrives because it serves and does not harm society. It is sometimes suggested that business has its own ethical rules and that they are decidedly different from those of the larger society. Several years ago business writer Alfred Carr raised a major storm in the *Harvard Business Review* by arguing that business, like poker, had its own rules and that these were not to be confused with the moral rules of the larger society. The comparison with poker has its own problems, but, leaving those aside for now, we can see how such a view not only invites but *demands* the most rigorous regulation of business. Business is subject to the same ethical rules as everyone else because businessmen do *not* think of themselves as separate from society. A few years ago, the then chairman of the Ford Foundation put it bluntly: "Either we have a social fabric that embraces us all, or we're in real trouble." So too with ethics.

Rule No. 5: Obey moral rules.

The most obvious and unavoidable rule of ethical thinking and the most important single sense of *compliance*. There may be room for debate about whether a moral rule applies. There may be questions of interpretation. But there can be no excuse of ignorance ("Oh, I didn't know that one isn't supposed to lie and cheat") and there can be no unexcused exceptions ("Well, it would be all right to steal in *this* case"). The German philosopher Immanuel Kant called moral rules "categorical imperatives," meaning that they are absolute and unqualified commands for everyone, in every walk of life, without exception, even for harried executives. This is, perhaps, too extreme to be practical, but moral rules are the heart of ethics, and there can be no ethics—and no business—without them.

Rule No. 6: Think "objectively."

Ethics is not a science, but it does have one feature in common with science: The rules apply equally to everyone, and being able to be "disinterested"—that is, to think for a moment from other people's perspectives and from a larger viewpoint—is essential. Whether an action is *right* is a matter quite distinct from whether or not it is in *your* interest. For that matter, it is quite independent of your personal opinions as well.

Rule No. 7: Ask the question, "What sort of person would do such a thing?"

Our word "ethics" comes from the Greek word *ethos*, meaning "character." Accordingly, ethics is not just obedience to rules so much as it is the concern for your personal (and company) character—your reputation and "good name"—and, more important, how you feel about yourself. Peter Drucker summarizes the whole of business ethics as "being able to look at your face in the mirror in the morning."

Rule No. 8: Respect the customs and beliefs of others, but not at the expense of your own ethics.

The most difficult kind of ethical thinking that people in business have to do concerns not a conflict between ethics and profits but rather the conflict between two ethical systems. In general, it is an apt rule of thumb that one should follow the customs and ethics of the community. But suppose there is a conflict not only of mores but of morals, as in old apartheid policies of South Africa. Then the rule to obey (and support) one's own moral principles takes priority. What is even more difficult is what one should do when the moral issue is not clear and moral categories vary from culture to culture. A much-debated example is the question of giving money to expedite a transaction in many third-world countries. It is "bribery" in our system, "supporting public servants" in theirs. Bribery is illegal and unethical here because it contradicts our notion of a free and open market. But does the same apply in the third world, where business (and social life) have very different presuppositions? (This is the sort of response Kotchian, of Lockheed, should have given to his congressional examiners instead of the nonsense about a conflict between ethics and corporate self-interest.)

Ethical thinking is ultimately no more than considering oneself and one's company as citizens of the business community and of the larger society, with some concern for the well-being of others and—the mirror image of this—respect for oneself and one's character. Nothing in ethics excludes financially sound thinking, and there is nothing about ethics that requires sacrificing the bottom line. In both the long and the short run, ethical thinking is essential to strategic planning. There is nothing unethical about making money, but money is not the currency of ethical thinking in business.

Part One

HOW TO MAKE A DECISION:
ELEVEN STEPS TO ETHICAL PROBLEM SOLVING

> *We're drowning in information while we're starving for knowledge.*
>> *Charles Steele (CEO and chairman,*
>> *Deloitte, Haskins & Sells)*

1. Define the problem.
2. Determine whether it is an ethical problem or "just a business decision."
3. Isolate the ethical dimension of the problem.
4. What are the ethical issues in the case? Ask yourself if it is a case of conflicting interests or a question of rights and fairness.
5. Who can help? Distinguish technical from ethical aspects.
6. Ask yourself whose problem it is. Is it a personal problem, a role-defined problem, a company problem, an industry problem, or a social problem?
7. Who is affected? The party with the ethical problem is very often *not* the party who may be the victim of the problem.
8. Reduce the number of alternatives to a manageable two or three; don't flounder all over the place.
9. Weigh the alternatives.
10. Given each alternative, ask yourself if there is a law against it. Is it a violation of a clear moral rule ("Don't cheat," "Don't steal")? Is it an offense to local customs or mores?
11. Ask yourself how it makes you look. Does it accurately reflect the kind of person/company you are or want to be? ("Can we get away with it?" is *not* a step in ethical reasoning.)

As an example, here is a scenario to which these steps can be applied:

You are head of personnel in a large department store that has been experiencing a damaging number of thefts by employees. You consider introducing polygraph ("lie detector") tests as a means of cutting down these losses.

1. What is the problem?

Will the use of polygraph tests in fact cut down theft losses without so infuriating the employees that the damage to morale and company loyalty will represent an even greater loss—even if more difficult to measure?

How dependable are the tests?

Is it fair to force an employee to take such a test?

Does an employee have the right to refuse to take such a test?

Is it fair to fire an employee for failing to take such a test?

Would the test have the desired effect if it were not mandatory?

2. Is it an ethical problem?

If the issues of "fairness" and "rights" arise, it is an ethical problem. This is quite independent of the severity of the losses or the question of whether it will "work."

3. Isolate the ethical dimension of the problem.

Are polygraph tests a violation of employee rights (even if "voluntary")?

4. What are the ethical issues in the case? Is this a case of conflicting interests or a question of rights and fairness?

It is not just a case of employee demands versus company interests (as in a wage dispute, for example). It is a question of rights—the right to privacy, the right not to be forced to incriminate oneself.

5. Who can help?

A polygraph expert can give advice on the accuracy of the tests, the possible foul-ups, the results in other companies where such tests have been administered. He or she is probably not the person to consult on the ethics of polygraph tests.

A few randomly chosen employees would provide a much more accurate ethical picture.

6. Whose problem is it?

A personal problem? Only if you have an ax to grind with the employees ("I'll show them!"), which is clearly not an ethical consideration.

A role-defined problem? It may be your responsibility to make the decision or the recommendation, but the policy will represent the company as a whole.

A company problem? Yes, so make sure that it is the company that makes and stands by the decision (or you might well turn out to be the scapegoat).

An industry problem? Probably not, although many department stores no doubt share the dilemma. Accordingly, it may be worth sharing information and concerns, but there is little point in adopting industrywide policies (as you would, for instance, in a standard pollution or product safety situation).

A social problem? No. It is a problem specific to retailing, not a problem caused by the nature of society. (For example, racism and unemployment are social problems, whose source and solutions by their very nature lie beyond the competence of any particular company or industry.) This is not to say, however, that the polygraph dilemma doesn't have broader social implications.

7. Who is affected?

The employees.

8. Alternatives?

Mandatory polygraph tests (anticipate employee resentment, and a few problem cases).

'Voluntary'' polygraph tests (anticipate confusion and low-grade resentment).

No polygraph tests, possibly combined with a well-worded talk to employees about the decision and alternative "get tough" measures.

9. Weigh the alternatives.

How well do the tests work in such situations? How dependable are they? How well should they work in *this* situation? The attitudes and anxiety of the employees should be the primary consideration, in terms of the ethics as well as of the technology.

How will you handle the problem cases? (Firing is emphatically not recommended.) Will resentment undermine employee morale, perhaps even *increase* the rate of theft? Are the employees justified in resenting this technological intrusion? Would *you* resent it (even assuming you had nothing to hide)?

Would voluntary tests do any good? Would they in fact be voluntary?

Would the *threat* of tests do any good?

Is there a way of getting employees to do their own policing, not under threat but by way of encouragement? (Or better, getting them to feel so involved with the store's success that they find it self-destructive to pilfer. (This is the optimal solution.)

10. Is there a law against the administering of such tests? Does it violate a clear moral rule? local customs or mores?

Let's assume that polygraph tests are legal in your state. (They are in most states.)

There is no moral prohibition as such. (Indeed, the moral prohibition would seem to be on the other side: "Don't lie!")

Polygraph tests do seem to be something of an established custom

(20 percent of the Fortune 500 companies use them), as opposed, for example, to all-night interrogation sessions for suspicious employees.

11. How does it make you look? What kind of person/company are you?

If you choose testing, you look like a company that doesn't trust its employees, a company that is tough, a company that is ready for desperate measures, but not a very good place to work.

If you choose not to test, and use proper publicity, you'll look like a company with a conscience and a real concern for the privacy of your employees.

There is no formula for ethical thinking; indeed it is the nature of most ethical dilemmas that they fall in the gray areas between prudence and propriety or consist of contradictions between equally valid claims (for example, the right of an employer to protect his stock and the right of an employee not to be subjected to humiliating tests). Nevertheless, the problem in many ethical dilemmas in business is the fact that ethical thinking is not employed at all. The alternative chosen after ethical deliberation may be the same one chosen on the basis of "strictly business" thinking, but ethical thinking increases the strength of that decision—and its justifiability—tenfold. (There is all the difference in the world between a company that does not *consider* its employees' rights and one that is ready with reasons that certain rights need to be overriden at times like these.)

Not infrequently, a minute of ethical thinking can avoid a disaster. The promise of an easy technological solution to a complex human problem is all too often tempting to resist.

THE BUCK STOPS SOMEWHERE: RESPONSIBILITY

Responsibility, n. A detachable burden easily shifted to the shoulders of God, Fate or Fortune, Luck or one's neighbor.

Ambrose Bierce

Thinking through an ethical problem doesn't mean much if you don't also take *responsibility* for the problem. Responsibility need not mean that you are the cause of the problem. It does mean, however, that you are in a position to do something about it and, just as important, that you *ought* to do something about it. A manager is responsible not only for his or her own actions but for those of subordinates—indeed, even if he or she has been unaware of what they have been doing. An executive is responsible not only for the actions of his or her subordinates but for those of the company as a whole. Responsibility is accountability, but it is also *do*-ability. Ethics begins (but does not end) with responsibility.

To participate in any practice is to have responsibilities. It is responsibility that distinguishes participants from mere spectators, and it is on the basis of responsibility that praise—as well as blame—is given. To be in business is to have responsibilities. To have a particular role in business is to have particular responsibilities. To be a manager, an executive, an assistant, or a personnel officer is to have those duties defined by the job. But responsibilities are not defined just in terms of participation and roles. One is always responsible *to* someone or some institution or community as well as *for* some action or state of affairs. Accordingly, a great deal of daily activity in the business world involves shifting, covering, or denying responsibility. Business ethics is very much concerned with pinning down responsibility, no easy task in the complex cobweb of loyalties and duties in the modern corporation. As any employee questioning company policy and some customers trying to get a refund will tell you, the buck doesn't seem to stop anywhere in most organizations but travels up and down the corporate hierarchy just one step ahead of those who pursue it.

Because responsibility is so important in business ethics, it is essential that we reject once and for all some of the most common excuses by which responsibility is so easily shifted from one person or one department to another. There can be no ethics without *taking* responsibility (which is not to say that you won't be *held* responsible when the fur begins to fly).

"IT'S NOT MY JOB." There are responsibilities defined by one's position, but there are also more general responsibilities determined simply by one's being part of a company. Protecting the company reputation is a responsibility of every employee, and protecting the reputation of business is the responsibility of every person in business.

"THE LAW DOESN'T SAY THAT WE HAVE TO." There are all sorts of responsibilities besides legal responsibilities. There are moral obligations that may not be part of the law, and there are obligations between people and between people and companies that may not be legally enforceable but are nevertheless very real.

"IT'S COMPANY POLICY." Policies are not the Ten Commandments. They are general, practical guidelines to facilitate decision making and give support to decisions made by the company employees. In most instances, that support is invaluable, such as when haggling with a supplier asking for "special favors." But such support is not absolute, and in cases where it is company policy itself that is being challenged, "It's company policy" will not do as an excuse. Policies back up ethics; they don't create ethics. Policies can be wrong, and in any case their application to any particular case is a matter of judgment.

"I'VE BEEN ORDERED TO DO IT." People are not computer parts, capable of doing only what they've been programmed to do. Employees are people and capable of making decisions, including the decision to quit. It may well be that one receives an order, but one also *accepts* that order and, in so doing, accepts responsibility.

"I HAVEN'T BEEN ORDERED TO DO IT." Did you have to be ordered to wash your face this morning?

"I CAN'T DO IT." Think again.

"MY OBLIGATION IS TO THE COMPANY I WORK FOR." But the company has obligations to customers, suppliers, and the community, and so does each and every employee. Company loyalty is half of business ethics, but social responsibility is the other half.

"I'M SORRY, BUT THAT'S JUST THE WAY IT IS." The way it is depends on what we do. The way it is can be changed.

"LIFE'S NOT FAIR." Perhaps not, but that doesn't mean that it isn't our responsibility to make it as fair as possible.

"RESPONSIBILITY INTERFERES WITH MY FREEDOM." Responsibility does not restrict one's freedom; it *defines* it. Freedom without responsibility is like weight without gravity in physics—a logical impossibility.

"WHY SHOULD I HAVE TO TAKE RESPONSIBILITY?" One of the older misunderstandings about responsibility is the idea that responsibility is a *burden* and that responsibility in business is largely a matter of liability for punishment. But responsibility is also a matter of pride and praise for a job well done. Responsibility is having a place in an organization and in a community as a full-fledged participant, and it is our responsibilities that also determine the perks and privileges of a position. There is nothing negative about responsibility—except when it is a responsibility unfulfilled or neglected.

FROM MICRO TO MACRO: SEVEN LEVELS OF BUSINESS ETHICS

It is often and rightly said that business ethics is no different from ethics in general; indeed, Peter Drucker, for one, has insisted that there is no such thing as "business ethics," that there is only ethics. But it is a mistake to think of ethics as a unique code of rules, and although there is in some sense a single set of rules for everyone—that is, morality—there are hundreds of other aspects of ethics that are specific to particular communities and practices, the practice of business among them. The language of business, some of which is concerned with the precision of finance but much of which is concerned rather with "code words" by which people in business recognize one another, is an expression of this special business ethos. And in that language, too, is an emphasis of the ethical importance of many matters—only some of them having to do with money—that define the special ethics of the business world: business ethics. This ethics is not different from the general ethics of society as a whole, but it nevertheless has its special features.

A person in business is only a business person part of the time, and even as a business person he or she has several levels of loyalty. But it is not as if there are walls between parts of the self, as if a person turns from ordinary human being to "Business Baron" at 8:30 A.M. and back again at 5:00 P.M., with possibly an interlude for lunch or shopping. A person belongs to several concentric communities at once; thus that person has several levels of ethical responsibilities. Most moments of the day, luckily, we can concentrate our energies on just one problem, with one aspect of ourselves, forgetting for the moment about the others. But the others are always there, and we live in a complex geology of ethical layers, some well known to us from childhood, others learned only with our careers, still others the highest and most difficult aspirations of the human spirit.

To begin with, we can distinguish three general strata of ethical thinking, three different ethical realms:

micro-ethics • the realm of the individual and relations among individuals
molar ethics • the realm of businesses, corporations, and industries
macro-ethics • the free-enterprise system, capitalism, and the world

These three strata meet and overlap, and where they meet we can discern discrete levels of ethical concern. Most business thinking occurs at the molar level, just as most personal decisions occur at the micro level. But it takes only a moment of reflection to realize that most business decisions made by individuals are both micro and molar, with macro implications. Accordingly, we can distinguish not just three but seven levels of ethics, each of them corresponding to a different ethos.

One can imagine these ethical systems as coexisting communities; for example, a businesswoman is a consultant in New York three days a week and a Hollywood mogul for the other two. For most people, most of the time, the different levels are more like concentric circles, smaller communities within larger communities, like neighborhoods within cities within states. The rules may be different—they tend to be more specific in the smaller circles and less specific in the larger—but they only rarely contradict one another. Moral rules, of course, are the same all the way through: "Thou shalt not kill" is just as much a matter of individual and neighborhood ethics as it is a rule for world order and a cardinal rule of every religion.

The seven levels of ethics are these:

1. individual human being
2. individual in the corporation
3. corporation (inside)
4. corporation in society
5. business world ("capitalism")
6. business in the world
7. spirituality and business (religion and the meaning of life)

1. At the level of the *individual human being*, the primary concern is, quite naturally, living well. But it is a bit misleading to talk as we do about the "individual," removed from all social context and treated as an isolated being. What we mean is an individual in a certain society, who has been brought up with certain community (not individual) values, with family loyalties and friends. In the strict sense, there is no "individual human being," only individuals in society. (Anthropologist Clifford Geertz says that a truly individual human being, devoid of culture and community, would not be a person but a pathetic monster, incapable of the most rudimentary human actions.) Accordingly, we also have to include at the individual level the whole network of immediate human relationships—family and friends, the neighborhood where one lives, the communal activities, from church to gossip and softball, that one enjoys in "private life." (It is worth noting how public much of our private life is.) This means morality as well, and though it makes no literal sense to talk about "individual morality" as most people do, it is important to distinguish ethics and morality on this individual, personal level from the larger framework of the corporation and the world. It is essential that ethics begins at home, but it is just as essential to remember that it doesn't stop there.

2. *The individual in the corporation* is a different person from the individual in his or her personal life. One dresses differently, talks differently, acts differently, thinks differently. At home, a person is mainly defined by personal characteristics—generosity, grumpiness, and so on. At work, a person is defined by his or her role and responsibilities, by contribution, by place in the organization. Loyalty to the company is of primary importance, not perhaps in the patriotic sense but at least in the sense that one works—for half of one's waking hours—for the good of the company and in its interests. The individual

in the corporation worries about status, respect from below, pressure from above. Obligations are in turn defined by status. (Thus friendships among workers, though one of the joys of working life, also raise some of the most difficult ethical dilemmas. Loyalty to the company and one's coworkers is quite different from the kind of loyalty one has to friends.) We might note here (there will be much more later) that it is at this level of life that ethics—business ethics—takes on many of the aspects of a game, defined by competition (within the company and with other companies) in which the sportsmanlike language of winning and losing makes considerable sense. The mistake is in thinking that this useful metaphor also applies to business life *outside* the corporation, in society as a whole (most of whose members, it is too easy to forget, are not in the game).

We should also note here that this distinction between individuals in their personal lives and individuals in the corporation is useful only in relatively large businesses (though many are officially called "small," with fewer than 500 employees). Truly small businesses—family grocers, seven folks working together—involve a sometimes enviably simple but sometimes disastrously confused synthesis of personal and organizational ethics. Our main concern here will be restricted to business life in organizations in which, simply defined, the ethics of intramural situations is not wholly settled by appeal to personal relationships. (In most businesses, organizational ethics kicks in as soon as there are six or seven people involved, and in odd cases it is evident even in firms of two.)

3. The ethics of the *corporation* is not the same as the ethics of the individual within the corporation, although, obviously, the one will have enormous influence on the other. The key to corporate ethics is the now much-abused concept of a "corporate culture." Too often, this term is unimaginatively restricted to the descriptive sociology of the organization, as one more ingredient in that potpourri called "management science." But a culture is essentially an ethos, and a corporate culture is defined, first of all, by its ethics. People in business know the ethics of corporations. Some corporations can be expected to act ethically under pressure; others cut corners as a matter of routine. And this is usually quite independent of the particular leadership at the time, since the corporate culture tends to determine the leaders rather than the other way around.

4. The *corporation in society* is, both in law and in ethics, a citizen, with the attendant privileges and obligations of citizenship. To begin with the obvious, corporations pay taxes and receive subsidies, enter

into contracts with the government and are expected to help out, even at some sacrifice, in times of emergency—in wartime, for example. But it would be a misunderstanding of corporate citizenship to think that it is limited—in both privileges and obligations—to financial matters. Of course, a corporation as such cannot enlist in the army, solicit for charities door to door, or sit in a box at the local opera house. But as a citizen, corporations have responsibilities to and an interest in national security, the well-being of the worst-off people, and the state of the arts. The key concept at this level of ethics is the "social responsibility of the corporation," a much-debated and much-misunderstood central concept of business ethics. In a less debatable sense, however, a corporation also has responsibilities of a more immediate kind, regarding its day-to-day workings. A corporation, like any individual citizen, has the obligation to consider its effects on the surrounding community ("impact"), to prevent unnecessary harm, and to correct what harm it causes.

5. The *business world* is no more of an abstraction than "the art world" or "the working class," and it is of considerable importance—especially in the sense of "class interest"—to keep in mind that there is a world of business and that it too defines privileges and responsibilities. For example, it is one of the privileges of the business world—and not of many others—that one not only profits from but is praised and honored for shrewd investment that may have taken little effort, skill, or time. Similar fortune in the art or intellectual world gets greeted with contempt, or worse. As for obligations, the business world itself has the obligation—its very reason for being—to improve the overall material well-being of the society. The individual in the business world also has an obligation to it—to protect its name and reputation and not make "business" a dirty word. This means something more than not indulging in sly dealings oneself; it also demands scrutiny and criticism of other people who would foul the world in which one prospers.

The business world is sometimes referred to as "capitalism," but this now archaic nineteenth-century word is really good only for starting arguments. The classic model of capitalism applies badly to the world of corporations (even small corporations) and makes the business world look too much like a giant, impersonal machine (the mechanism, or "magic" if you will, of the market), which it assuredly is not. One might note, however, that "capitalism" is not the only alternative to totalitarian communism and abject primitive poverty, and it is not a single economic system (cf. Japanese business, to take a prominent example).

6. *Business in the world* also suggests an ethical system, albeit an enormously confused one. Much of this is due to the enormous variations in culture—which make our world rich and interesting as well as dangerous and difficult. There is a dangerous sense among some business people that "global markets" will somehow change all of this and make everyone the same—namely, like us. But it is highly unlikely that this would happen in any but the most superficial sense (every society may soon have McDonald's hamburgers, color television, and electric guitars), and the resentment that comes with that superficial similarity may well be more dangerous than the cultural differences that preceded it. As ethics, the business view of the world must simultaneously juggle two uncomfortably antagonistic positions: respect for cross-cultural differences and compassion and concern for human interests everywhere. Neither alone will do. Respect for differences too easily degenerates into simpleminded relativism and indifference ("If they want to starve their babies to death, who are we to say anything?"). Trans-human compassion and respect too easily becomes bloated into moral imperialism—as if we, the "developed" countries, know what they, the "developing" countries, really want, whether they themselves do or not. The new world of business requires a new sensibility, not "us" and "them" but a shared world of differences— different needs, different talents, different cultures.

7. And then there are *spiritual questions*, for which answers may be intangible and most unbusinesslike but essential nevertheless. It is worth noting that this largest of all possible ethical frameworks circles back to the smallest—the personal life of the individual. The question

---

THE BOTTOM LINE OF THE FUTURE

It may prove difficult to give young people the education that would prepare them for ways of life in which community spirit and some measure of self-sufficiency are as important as is now the acquisition and accumulation of money. . . . In future societies, the most valuable people might be, not those with the greatest ability to produce material goods, but rather those who have the gift to spread good will and happiness through empathy and understanding.

René Dubos, *Celebration of Life*

of the meaning of life is the ultimate question for both the individual and (from our point of view) the universe itself. Our answer to this question in turn dictates those ultimate values that we supply in every other level of ethics, from our concept of individual success to our notion of corporate responsibility in both the community and the world. Too often, the modern intelligence declares with both arrogance and despair that life is meaningless, thus leaving both individual and corporate ethics without any foundation but greed (which is itself meaningless, of course). Or, God and Christianity are summoned at the end of the business week, as if to justify everything. But a blanket justification can be as empty as a trivial one, and the meaning of life is too important to be left to cynicism or to one morning a week. Life, after all, is what all of our business is about, and business is meaningful only insofar as it contributes to a meaningful life.

Part Two

MOTIVATION, MONEY, AND MORALS: MICRO-ETHICS

BEYOND THE PROFIT MOTIVE

> *The purpose of a business firm is not simply to make a profit, but is to be found in its very existence as a community of persons who in various ways are endeavoring to satisfy their basic needs, and who form a particular group at the service of the whole society. Profit is a regulator in the life of business, but not the only one.*
>
> *Pope John Paul II*

Discussions of business usually begin, understandably, with concepts of economics—products, profits, money, and the market. As economics, this is perfectly reasonable and unavoidable. Business is, one might say, applied economics; it is the practice of what economists theorize about.

Economic terms, however, are quite inappropriate as a basis for understanding business life and life in business. When the language of economics is used not just to explain "the mechanism of the market" but to describe the very human world of business, something bizarre happens: The concepts of economics become inhuman abstractions. Such pseudo-descriptions mistake the theoretical constructs of economics for the flesh-and-blood people who actually do business. These abstractions consequently invoke the peculiarly uninspiring myth of an absurdly inhuman and tedious creature—*Homo economicus*—whose motives are purely economic and who acts regularly on the basis of rational assessments of financial costs and benefits to itself. All other considerations—enjoying one's work, the feeling of accomplishment and the pride of expertise, admiring one's boss, the prestige of the next promotion, enjoying working with people or being good with numbers, having a beer with colleagues after work—are, at best, lumped together as "psychic income" or as the unknown variable x, if they are not left out of the equation altogether. Whatever else *it* may be, *Homo economicus* is none of us. (Does *Homo economicus* have sex, for instance?)

According to this classical economic view, a person's work or career becomes just another factor in the market. This is dubious economics,

"THE PROFIT MOTIVE"

Managers constantly complain about the hostility to profit. They rarely realize that their own rhetoric is one of the main reasons for this hostility. For indeed in the terms management uses when it talks to the public, there is no possible justification for profit, no explanation for its existence, no function it performs. There is only the profit motive, that is, the desire of some anonymous capitalists—and why that desire should be indulged in by society any more than bigamy, for instance, is never explained. But profitability is a crucial need of economy and society.

Managerial practice in most large American companies is perfectly rational. It is the rhetoric which obscures, and thereby threatens to damage both business and society. To be sure, few American companies work out profitability as a minimum requirement. As a result, most probably underestimate the profitability the company truly requires. But they, consciously or not, base their profit planning on the twin objectives of ensuring access to capital needed and minimizing the cost of capital. In the American context, if only because of the structure of the U.S. capital market, a high "price/earnings ratio" is indeed a key to the minimization of the cost of capital; and "optimization of profits" is therefore a perfectly rational strategy which tends to lower, in the long run, the actual cost of capital.

But this makes it even less justifiable to keep on using the rhetoric of the profit motive. It serves no purpose except to confuse and to embitter.

Peter Drucker, *Management*

but it is disastrous ethics. "Man does not live by bread alone" is a tired cliché, but it has never yet found its way into the economic view of business life. All values other than money that make a career worthwhile, all of the nonfinancial rewards of employment—and the hardships of unemployment—are forgotten by the wizards of econometrics. All of the excitement, expectations, challenges, and camaraderie of the business world get reduced to a single, purely imaginary stimulus—the "profit motive." It is the universal, irresistible force that theoretically drives not only the market but all of us. It is, according to the machismo economics of George Gilder, nothing less than our biological manhood at work, in a particularly modern—and male—environment.

What is this motive, to which everyone so readily refers, to which so many policy and political decisions have been appealed but which has been so little scrutinized? Who in fact is driven by this motive? Not the millions of people who staff the businesses of the world, who do a job and get a salary in order to live and buy the necessities and some of the good things in life. Not the hundreds of thousands of executives and managers who work for *other* people's profits; indeed they are defined by their "fiduciary responsibilities," which is to say that they are motivated by a set of sensibilities—ethical responsibilities—that are quite different from, though not opposed to, the personal profit motive. Of course, executives who do their jobs well are well rewarded, but to think of money as the motive rather than the yardstick of success is to misunderstand the motive as well as the measure of business.

Profits are not the motive. Money is a means by which to buy things and services as well as power, prestige, status, success, and other such intangibles. (Some say it will even buy salvation.) There is no profit motive. It has been fabricated by economists to explain the movements of their fictional, Frankensteinian monster, *Homo economicus,* which has been put together out of the dead parts of the social sciences and which desperately needs some spark of life to get moving. It is a fraudulent psychology created to support an extraordinarily uninspiring mythology. But business doesn't need a mythology, and it certainly doesn't need the profit motive.

THE ENTREPRENEUR: A HERO FOR OUR TIME?

The very term "profit motive" has become so familiar to us that we simply assume that it must apply to someone. Accordingly, the economic mythmakers have invented a hero, someone who actually has the temerity to act out the motive that most of us repress: the *entrepreneur*. In the mythic, heroic sense, this creature of ambition defies the fates and risks everything in pursuit of an elusive dream—

Fortune—obeying only one Supreme Law: the Law of Supply and Demand. In the classic model, he (it is usually "he") ignores friends and family, mortgages the house, or lives in squalor ("rags"), all in anticipation of future riches. He is rarely married, difficult to work with, and, in all likelihood, at least a little crazed.

There are such entrepreneurial maniacs, of course. Like rock stars and fashion models, they are essential symbols in our eccentricity-minded society. But the fact is that such entrepreneurial types are not the pillars of economic life in America today. They are rather rare (and not always enviable) exceptions. Most Americans do not mortgage the present for the future or see the risk of financial ruin as the test of their manhood. Most Americans prefer a secure and comfortable family life to fanatic ambition. They enjoy the camaraderie and stability of a job and are satisfied with a salary without insisting on the moon as well. Like George Gilder, most American males exercise their masculinity elsewhere. Indeed, if it is the all-or-nothing entrepreneur one is looking for, he can be found in considerable numbers today in the international cocaine trade.

The true entrepreneur is, according to recent research, probably married, more concerned with ideas than with wealth, and more in the mainstream than out of it. Entrepreneurs like to work for themselves—but mainly because of the conservativism of organizations, not because they are particularly difficult people. Contrary to the popular high-risk image, entrepreneurs dislike risk; the key is rather self-confidence. They are not organization people, but they are typically well organized. Most entrepreneurs are not heroes; they are simply independent people in business who have an idea and the drive to make it work. We will continue to celebrate the initiative, perseverance, and spectacular success of someone like Steven Jobs, of Apple Computers, but for every microchip millionaire there must be thousands of less inventive and less adventurous sorts who can run and maintain the house that Jobs built. A few entrepreneurs may be the heroes of the business world, but they are not, nevertheless, its substance.

It is the nature of the business world—if it is not human nature—to have heroes. In our freewheeling, individualistic, hardworking, innovative society, it stands to reason that one of our favorite public heroes—after cowboys, maverick cops, and pop singers—will be the entrepreneur, the person who has an idea and sticks with it, through thick and thin, on his or her own, with only a stockingful of savings to see it through. But the fact is that this bears little resemblance to the actual lives in business most people lead. Most people are not in

> I think if we want to understand the entrepreneur, we should look at the juvenile delinquent.
>
> Abraham Zaleznick
> (Konosuke Matsushita Professor of Leadership,
> Harvard Business School)

business by or for themselves. Most people do not have heroic aspirations or perseverance. Most people do a job, as part of a career, for someone else. They are paid out of the comptroller's office, not out of a stocking. Half of the businesses in the United States are family businesses, the other half is corporate America. Neither half is made up of entrepreneurs. The entrepreneur may be the seed that makes new businesses possible, but he or she does not tell us much about how businesses in America really run.

There is nothing wrong with heroes—and in particular heroes that suit our fantasies. But they've given up trying to be cowboys even in Texas, and it is high time we all stop trying to pretend that the American business world is the Horatio Alger fantasy of the lone entrepreneur. *Inc* magazine will continue to run its lead articles on "The Entrepreneur and How He/She is Changing Business Forever," but the fact is that 99 percent of the people in business have about as much resemblance to entrepreneurs as they do to cowboys. We can't continue to confuse the ethics of business with the eccentricities of entrepreneurship, no matter how much the former needs to encourage and celebrate the latter.

BUSINESS AND THE GOOD LIFE

> *When a friend asked him why he should dance*
> *around the subject of money all the time and never*
> *make any, [Paul] Volcker paused for a while, took*
> *a long pull on one of his cheap cigars and replied:*
> *"Couldn't you say the opposite? All of those fel-*
> *lows out there getting rich could be dancing around*
> *the real subject of life themselves."*
> John Brecher, Newsweek, *June 17, 1983*

Andrew H. was an ambitious young man with a good middle-management job in a branch office of a large national corporation. He knew
most of the people he worked with and had the respect of the people
in the community. He did his job well, made enough to live well, and
liked the friendliness and comfortable familiarity of the smallish town
in which he lived and worked. But Andrew had ambitions, and so he
was restless. Some of his friends from college were making more
money than he was. He received directives from the national office
written by people who had less ability and less seniority than he did.
He was happy, but he was also frustrated—when he thought about it.
He knew he could do "better," and so, when the promotion and
transfer to Metropolis came through, he readily accepted it.

It could have been much worse. Andrew's wife did not leave him;
his children did not get beaten up at school. The higher cost of living
in the city, while wiping out any actual gain in his standard of living
despite his much higher salary, did not impoverish him. He proved to
be as good as he thought he was at his new job and received a number
of promotions until—as the much-quoted "Peter Principle" would put
it—he reached his level of incompetence, and rose no higher. Andrew
no longer felt frustrated and restless. He did sometimes feel that he
was no longer so good at what he did, but he could never quite explain
why this would be so. He no longer felt on top of his work, and so he
no longer felt that same self-confidence and self-respect. Instead, he
felt only the pride of position, which too often felt to him hollow. He
missed the comfort and familiarity of his old town; he lost his interest
in some of the hobbies and the community matters that had formerly

Maybe I'm just getting old, but I'm worried about the investment-banking industry because I think the substance of many of the things we do is getting questionable. We do it. We do it well. It's very profitable. And we have to do it—we have to provide a service. If one company wants to buy another one or avoid a takeover, we have to be ready to do it, and do it as well as the next guy, using all the weapons that are available. But I guess I'm getting to be like a friend of mine, a very successful defense contractor, who says to me, "It's more and more difficult for me to run my business because I don't believe in the defense budget." Sometimes it's getting more and more difficult for me to do the things we do, because in the last analysis, I don't think that's what I want on my tombstone.

Felix Rohatyn, *New York Times*, August 5, 1984

preoccupied him. He would still say, when asked, that he was happy. But he knew that the sense of fulfillment that had once animated that answer was gone.

The Peter Principle has a corollary: that people who think only in terms of career success tend to create their own level of unhappiness. And, as with their incompetence, they may never know it. (They may even define it as "happiness.")

Why engage in business? For a few people (though much fewer than some business writers suppose) it may be the challenge and the fun of it, and for a few others—caught in the position that supplies writers in Hollywood with so many scripts—it may be the necessity of helping the family business, akin to the first-born's duty to take over the manor in feudal times. But for most people in business, the simple answer is "to make a living." A "living" is money and a place in society—the preconditions for *living well*. In fact, every question we ask in finance and economics—*Why* should one act rationally with an eye to costs and benefits? *Why* should a person want a profit?—ultimately ends not at the bottom line but here: *in order to live well*. It is an obvious point but easily lost sight of in the narrow focus of daily assignments and heated competition. It is also the key concept of business ethics. Business serves life, not the other way around.

The good life is the goal of business—not profits, not competition, not management or the work ethic. It is a matter of ethics, not of economics. Business and the market system exist and are justified insofar as they provide the good things in life, both for those people who are actually in business and for those who live in a world circumscribed by business. Business forms the core of our society because we believe that it promotes prosperity, freedom, and justice, and because we are a society that *wants* (demands) prosperity, freedom, and justice above all else.

Consider, for a moment, some of the alternatives:

- There is the view that the individual exists to serve the larger community or culture (a view that has been too closely identified with fascism and communism but in fact has hundreds of more amiable forms, in tribal societies and in small towns everywhere).
- There is the view that the individual serves history and the view that the very concept of the "individual" is a historical curiosity, limited to the last few hundred years of the second millennium.
- There is the view that the individual is nothing but a part of nature and serves only nature, a vision that can be as rapturous as Eastern mysticism or as gruesome as our "dust to dust" imagery of death.
- There is the view that the individual exists only to serve God, though it must be said that recent theology in the business world has quite conveniently found that God's divine purposes and the vicissitudes of the profit motive miraculously coincide.

We may have some qualms about the materialistic individualism of the business world, but we as a nation generally tend to prefer its abuses and excesses to the alternatives. Not everyone in the world would agree that living well is the ultimate end of life, and not everyone would agree with us about what counts as living well. But the premise of business ethics and the real bottom line of business is just this metaphysical view of life: that the individual and his or her happiness and well-being are the goal of being alive.

THE MEANING OF LIFE

Life is
_____ an adventure
_____ a game (make up the rules as you go)
_____ a puzzle (without knowing you have all the pieces)
_____ a maze (avoid the exit!)
_____ for my children
_____ a tragedy
_____ a learning experience

_____ a disease
_____ a matter of one's honor
_____ making it
_____ survival of the fittest
_____ a gift from God (to be paid for with gratitude)
_____ love
_____ meaningless
_____ a poker game
_____ a long hall of closing doors
_____ win or lose (most people lose)
_____ an investment
_____ art

SOURCES OF ETHICAL VALUES

FAMILY (parents, siblings, uncles, aunts and grandparents)
PEERS (playmates, schoolmates, friends)
INSTITUTIONS (church, school, clubs, armed services)
PREVIOUS EXPERIENCE (childhood trauma, success, status and disappointment, early work experience, attitudes and access to money)
MEDIA (television, radio, books, newspapers and magazines)
PROFESSIONAL ROLES AND MODELS (job expectations, leadership in the company, industry and company heroes)
COMPANY POLICIES
PERSONAL CODES OF ETHICS (developed after extensive experience with ethical conflict and pressures)

HAVING FUN—AND LOOKING OUT FOR NUMBER ONE

What is the good life? Let's begin by removing two of the most common false leads. It is often said—especially in fun-loving America—that the good life is the life of pleasure, a view that philosophers have long called "hedonism." Of course, there are many kinds of pleasure, from the pure physical ecstasy of a professional back rub to the job of cooking to the exhilaration of a conversation with one of the great minds of the time. But as soon as we recognize this broad variety of pleasures, we find ourselves perplexed. Some pleasures are more desirable than others; some, however intense, are not desirable at all. We would all—or most of us—relish the pleasure of receiving some great prize or title, whether it be the Nobel or Miss America. Few of us would tolerate the thought of a life consumed by alcohol or drugs—no matter how pleasurable intoxication may be. But what these examples show is that pleasure alone isn't the goal and doesn't make up the good life. Aristotle said it thousands of years ago: Pleasure is a key ingredient in the good life—one cannot imagine the good life without it—but that is because it almost always *accompanies* the good things in life. In other words, we enjoy doing things because they are good; they are not good just because we enjoy them.

Here is a small thought experiment: Imagine a small, tublike contraption—not unlike a flotation tank or a hot tub—that is wired in such a way that the occupant of the tub enjoys a continuous sense of total contentment, accompanied by frequent waves of pleasure. (Such experiments—with rats, at least—have been going on since 1955.) Entry and exit from the tank is wholly voluntary; a person can get up and leave anytime he or she wants to. However, in the years since these "happiness boxes" have been in operation, no one, having got into one, has ever had any desire to get out again. A built-in life-support system sustains vital functions indefinitely. Of course, after several months a person's body begins to look like a flesh-colored bean-bag chair, but no one has ever seemed to mind. Vanity, like ambition, dissolves in contentment. Life expectancy, needless to say, is far above average, with virtually no chance of accidental death. It is the life of perfect pleasure.

Would you like to step into the box?

Looking Beyond Number One

Another false lead is the popular American perversion summarized recently as "looking out for number one." Philosophers call it "egoism," but to most sober people it is just plain selfishness. The idea, simply stated, is that whatever people do they do because it serves their own interests. It has often been suggested that egoism thus provides the foundation for capitalism, and therefore the basis of business, too. It is worth noting—as a historical hint—that Adam Smith, the founding scholar of capitalism, would have no tolerance whatever for this idea. (It is often forgotten that before he wrote his earth-shattering *Wealth of Nations,* he became famous for a book on the "moral sentiments," in which he argued that the basis for much of our action is sympathy, not selfishness.) But, even more, if one thinks for half a second about the most oft-quoted reason for working—"I've got a family to support"—it becomes clear that egoism is a suspicious doctrine, at best. One might rely, "Yes, but it is *one's own* family"—thus stretching the concept of egoism to include everyone a person might care about—but even this fails to account for such everyday compassions in our supposedly selfish society as spontaneous sympathy and consideration for strangers, not to mention respect for the law (which is not the same as being afraid of getting caught) and that indiscriminate concern for others that the early Christians named *agape*, which today has the more secular name of "love of humanity." Whether or not such a divine passion is possible for most of us is not the point; we all (or almost all) feel needs and concerns that are not our own, whether a spontaneous impulse of generosity toward an employee, compassion for a widow in a wartorn nation filmed on the nightly news, or the vicarious anxiety felt with the hero or heroine in a movie. Our business society does not deny or ignore these passions; it encourages them (a virtue not easily described, however, in business language). Our own interests not only coincide with but also often *are* the interests of another, interests in which we have no personal stake. Egoism is a false psychological theory, but what is worse, it provides rationalization for selfishness by way of the excuse that "everyone else is selfish, too." What is worst is the fact that it is a view that virtually guarantees failure in the pursuit of the good life, for it sets the stage for antagonism (quite different from competition) and defensive isolation (very different from individualism) right from the start. For certain people at certain times, a little bit of "assertiveness training'' can be therapeutic and valuable. But as a vision of the good life, it is self-defeating.

Real Interests

Things I would do (if I could) full-time, for no salary:

_____

_____

_____

Things that I wish I could spend much more time doing:

_____

_____

_____

Subjects I would love to take courses or lessons in:

_____

_____

_____

If I had to give a public talk, it would be about:

_____

I would like to spend my next vacation:

_____

_____

The magazines I most *like* reading are:

_____

_____

_____

My hobbies are:

_____

_____

_____

My favorite part of the newspaper is:

_____

I'd like to see my son/daughter become a:

_____

EVERYTHING MONEY CAN BUY

> *Now that my ladder's gone,*
> *I must lie down where all the ladders start,*
> *in the foul rag-and-bone shop of the heart.*
> 　　*W. B. Yeats, "The Circus Animals' Desertion"*

It is inevitable, especially in the context of the business world, to talk about the good things in life, and, indeed, our first thoughts typically turn to material luxuries: a French-style château or a rambling ranch house, a Jaguar or a Town Car in the driveway, an expensive vacation and a table filled with food prepared by a clone of Julia Child. We too easily forget the presuppositions of our enjoyments—a secure society in which such possessions are possible, the good health to enjoy them, the public conveniences that make them useful (a Jaguar without roads would not be much of a luxury). We tend to imagine that the luxury and enjoyment of such things reside solely in the things themselves,

THE REWARDS OF WORK

No one regards it as remarkable that the advertising man, tycoon, poet or professor who suddenly finds his work unrewarding should seek the counsel of a psychiatrist. One insults the business executive or the scientist by suggesting that his principal motivation in life is the pay he receives. Pay is not unimportant. Among other things, it is a prime index of prestige. Prestige—the respect, regard and esteem of others—is in turn one of the more important sources of satisfaction associated with this kind of work. But, in general, those who do this kind of work expect to contribute their best regardless of compensation. They would be disturbed by any suggestion to the contrary.

John Kenneth Galbraith, *The Affluent Society*

rather than in the social context in which they have been earned. Much of what makes these things good is their agreed-upon value and status and the pride that comes with ownership—pride that must be spelled out in social, not material terms. The food we consider a luxury would be considered inedible in other societies; the things that we value—whether jewelry or garbage disposals—are valuable only because the society that we live in makes and deems them so. One might even go so far as to say that, except for basic nutrition and other biological necessities, there are no good things in life as such; it is only our agreed-upon evaluations and interpretations that make them so.

The clash of market and ethical values is most evident—and operates most to the deficit of business—in the area of human services. The facade of supply and demand disguises the complex network of social arrangements and expectations that precede every such question as "How much would you charge to do this?" To take the most obvious example, sexual intimacies are not ordinarily matters of supply and demand or haggling over price. Selling one's services when intangible values are at stake has a special name that both pervades and transcends the province of economics—*prostitution*. A female secretary who is asked to make coffee (which is not part of her job) may well feel not only offended but abused. An assistant who is forced to take verbal abuse may keep his silence in order to keep his job, but this is hardly what he is paid for. A person may be well paid for the job but nevertheless be bitterly resentful because he or she is making less than someone in a comparable position across the hall. Jobs have just as much to do with dignity and status as they do with material necessities;

every negotiation of jobs and salaries is an ethically charged inter-change, not just a matter of supply and demand.

It is one of the peculiarities of a market system that all values tend to be reduced to a single common denominator: money. Originally this was a matter of convenience; trying to barter a sheep for a set of roof shingles was a rather cumbersome business, to put it mildly. But one of the most persistent objections to business and business mentality is its tendency to assume that *all* values are market values, including art, religion, and human dignity. The convenience of cost/benefit analysis has been elevated to the status of rationality, as if any value that can't be quantified can't be rational but, at most, an "emotional" issue.

Ethical values can't usually be quantified. It is difficult enough for a court to settle the amount of damage in a straightforward financial suit, but how does one quantify the dollar amount of suffering, indignity, time lost, loss of pride, or physical disfigurement? Insurance policies of necessity put a dollar value on a life, but it would be perverse in the extreme to say that this is what a life is actually *worth*. The value of beauty can't be quantified either. A Rembrandt self-portrait is not valued primarily for its market value; nor is it literally "priceless," since it obviously can be bought and sold. But we are not impressed by the businessman who buys the painting solely for its investment value and is oblivious of its aesthetic virtues. Happiness cannot be quantified, and it is no surprise that the tragic figure in many American novels, plays, and movies is the man or woman who can count blessings in dollars but nevertheless is miserable—and can't under-stand why.

The good life consists not of things or services but of family, friendship, love, respect, admiration, a sense of personal dignity and self-esteem—intangibles, so called because economics cannot invent a measure for them. One might well, without blasphemy, call these "spiritual" values. That these values constitute the good life is one of the most ancient bits of wisdom. Business is not a matter of "making a buck," although that is (as in every profession) one of its essential aims. Business is first of all a relationship among human beings, in which money may be the medium but is not the only measure. Business life is not the market; it is a job, a position, a career, a life defined with and by other people, in terms of respect and status, in search of not only excellence but recognition, admiration, friendship.

If we want to find the motive behind the business world, we would do far better to look for such goals as being respected by one's friends and family and working with people one likes than to stalk the vulgar

A COST/BENEFIT ANALYSIS
(BY THE FORD MOTOR CO.)*

Benefits

Savings: 180 burn deaths, 180 serious burn injuries, 2,100 burned
                vehicles

Unit Cost: $200,000 per death, $67,000 per injury, $700 per vehicle

Total Benefit: 180 × ($200,000) + 180 × ($67,000) + 2,100 × ($700)
                = $49.5 million

Costs

Sales: 11 million cars, 1.5 million light trucks

Unit Cost: $11 per car, $11 per truck

Total Cost: 11,000,000 × ($11) + 1,500,000 × ($11) = $137 million

The social costs of a death:

Component	1971 Costs
Future Productivity Losses	
Direct	$132,000
Indirect	41,300
Medical Costs	
Hospital	700
Other	425
Property Damage	1,500
Insurance Administration	4,700
Legal and Court	3,000
Employer Losses	1,000
Victim's Pain and Suffering	10,000
Funeral	900
Assets (Lost Consumption)	5,000
Miscellaneous	200
Total per Fatality	$200,725

*"Fatalities Associated with Crash-Induced Fuel Leakage and Fires (in the Ford Pinto)" released by J. C. Echold, Div. of Auto Safety, Ford Motor Co. First published by Mark Dowie, *Mother Jones,* Sept./Oct. 1977.

and imaginary profit motive. People are in business because it offers them the good life, but to think that the business market determines all values and that the good life is just what money can buy is to misunderstand both business and life.

WHAT I LIKE ABOUT MYSELF

_____ ambition
_____ cheerful disposition
_____ courage
_____ helpfulness
_____ honesty
_____ creativity
_____ taste in clothes
_____ good looks
_____ in great physical shape
_____ independence
_____ dependence (loving)
_____ intelligence
_____ cleverness
_____ loyalty
_____ much loved
_____ obedience
_____ thrift
_____ courtesy
_____ restraint and self-control
_____ ability to express emotion
_____ dependability, responsibility

PLAYING GAMES: BUSINESS AND THE CASINO CULTURE

The news began to leak that General Mills was about to take on Post—
the war of the Wheaties and Grape Nuts flakes. It promised to be a
contest of epic proportions, corporate lives on the line for a few
percentage points of the market. About the same time, Coca-Cola,
after years of deliberation, introduced a new, diet Coke, to meet head-
on the perpetual challenge from Pepsi. According to the classical
pundits of the free-enterprise system, these would be examples of
entrepreneurial inspiration; business rushing to supply the needs of the
consuming public and to increase the wealth and well-being of the
nation. The truth of the matter, of course, is that the nation could
survive to eternity without a single new breakfast cereal, much less
another diet soft drink. But then how are we to understand the General
Mills–Post and Coke–Pepsi wars? Not in terms of supply and demand
and the "rigors of the market," which supply only the playing field.
And certainly not in the impersonal terms of business as an institution.
Forget about Adam Smith and the wealth of the nation. Forget about
the mechanism of the market. The metaphor for understanding much
of American business is not economics; it is rather the ethics of the
game.

Individuals as well as corporations engage in competition and thrive
on its challenge. Several years ago, business psychoanalyst Michael
Maccoby introduced the figure of the "gamesman" to characterize the
newly dominant image of recent business thinking. The gamesman—in
contrast to the craftsman, the company man, and the "jungle
fighter"—is in business mainly for the challenge, the chance to prove
himself (or herself). He is not the entrepreneur who works on his own
but a corporate employee for whom the large organization is the
essential playing field. Not everyone in business is a gamesman;
indeed, it would be hard to imagine an institution functioning without
mostly non-game-players. Nevertheless, the gamesman is the fellow
who gets his picture in *Forbes*, the fellow whose stories are spun into
contemporary legends. The ethics of business today is not just the
rules of right and wrong; it is also the ethics of good sportsmanship.

What makes business exciting—as well as rewarding—are its games.

There is game playing in every profession, of course, but it is mainly in business that this is considered a wholly desirable and acceptable attitude. Lawyers share the same sense of winning, but we do not think that the legal merit of a case is determined by winning. In business, on the other hand, merit is winning, pure and simple. Academics play games, for example, but this is generally considered one of the seedier aspects of academic life, not its essence.

Sometimes the business game is for small stakes—the acknowledgment of a supervisor or the personal satisfaction of a job well done. Sometimes business games involve gigantic stakes. Sometimes the game is routine—the normal competition between salesmen or the usual jockeying for promotion. Sometimes the game is in redefining the rules of the game itself, changing an industry or dramatically enlarging the market. Indeed, changing the rules of the game provides the most exciting of all games, and one can find no better example of business gamesmanship in all of its cleverness than in the historic battle for the heavyweight title: Cornelius Vanderbilt versus Jay Gould.

Vanderbilt owned the railroad from Buffalo to Chicago; Gould had just bought himself a competing railroad. To force Vanderbilt out of the market, Gould dropped the price to ship a carload of cattle by 17 percent, from $150 to $125. Vanderbilt retaliated by dropping the price on his railroad by an additional 20 percent, to $100, in return for which Gould dropped *his* price to $75. Vanderbilt lowered his price even more drastically, to $50, and Gould dropped his to $25.

By this time, the competition had become a test of wills rather than good business strategy. Profit was of secondary importance. This was rather a matter of winning. Vanderbilt triumphantly lowered his price to $1 a carload from Chicago to Buffalo, virtually a free ride. Gould waited a while, and then, apparently conceding defeat, raised his price back up to the original $150.

What Vanderbilt did not know, however, was that Gould had been buying up enormous numbers of cattle in Chicago and shipping them to Buffalo, on Vanderbilt's line, for $1 a carload, selling them at immense profit in Buffalo. Vanderbilt, though the "winner" of the railroad competition, swore once and for all that he would never compete with Gould again.

There are thousands of less dramatic tales, but the point is always the same: For many people in business, business is not just a way to make a living; it is a challenge, a sport, a source of excitement ("better than sex" once said one famous CEO). We live in a sports-loving society where not only business but politics, sex, conversation, war, neurosis, and even life itself are discussed as games, in terms of playing well or poorly, winning or losing, having fun or being a bad sport. This gives our lives a little levity and challenge. (Compare the life-is-a-burden philosophy of some cultures.) But it also provides us with an apt model for understanding business. Games, for example, are paradigmatic *practices,* with rules and well-defined roles. Business, which is too often defined as a free-for-all, is much better understood as a game, as a practice with distinctive rules, roles, and goals. But it is also the game metaphor that gives rise to some of the most serious misunderstandings about business and ethics.

The first problem is that most of us are taught to think of one kind of game only, the head-on competitive game in which beating the competition is the goal. It is what game theorists call a "noncooperative zero-sum game," and it is aptly illustrated by the General Mills–Post and Coke–Pepsi games. The market is more or less established; every bowl of Wheaties eaten is, presumably, one bowlful of Grape Nuts flakes still in the box. Every can of Coke consumed is one more can of Pepsi still cooling in the vending machine. But most games are not zero-sum games, and even zero-sum games are not as noncooperative as they may seem. Airline companies, for example, may engage in desperate competition in terms of fares, schedules, and fringe services, but between them there is a much more basic interest in protecting the market as a whole. A basic rule: Praise as you will your on-time record or pampering by your flight attendants, but never—*never*—criticize the safety record of *any* airline, for that would threaten the market as a whole. Many nervous consumers would rather take the bus.

The second misunderstanding comes from the fact that games, no matter how seriously played or followed, are in general not very serious. Business, on the other hand, is serious. It may not be the life-and-death Darwinian struggle, but neither is it just fun and games. In a game of football, everyone plays hard for two hours and then goes home to "real life." But business is *in* "real life," and what happens in business is not an isolated entertainment, "just for fun." (The day after Superbowl Sunday is, after all, just another Monday.) Indeed, when a company or the market is threatened, the game mentality tends to come to an abrupt halt, not infrequently coupled with a desperate request for a change in the rules (that is, government intervention).

Business is not just a game. The metaphor has considerable value, but it also has its limitations.

1. Within the corporation, games take the form of competition for position and promotion. But such games are more the exception than the rule, and most business "players" view such competition with anxiety and distaste rather than sportsmanship. And such games are always limited by the well-being of the corporation and the people in it. Some corporations accept as a matter of policy the belief that intramural competition spurs performance. (Citibank of New York, for example, has a reputation for engendering fierce competition among its young bankers by keeping only a modest fraction of those it hires.) But it is important to note that it is performance, not competition, that is the standard. Winning isn't the *only* thing (Vince Lombardi to the contrary).

2. Competition between corporations is the most familiar form of competition in business—Quaker vs. Kellogg, Ford vs. GM, McDonald's vs. Burger King. But, again, such competition is almost always limited by shared interests in the market and careful cooperation. It may be true that competition succeeds in improving quality and lowering prices for the consumer and in improving efficiency and performance within the company, but it is *healthy* competition that makes this difference, and that means taking into account the health of the firms and the people in them as well as the well-being of society. The goal of the game is prosperity, but prosperity is not just the goal of the game.

3. Competition among businesses is one thing—looking at businesses as isolated players. But businesses are also in the world, and in this sense business is not a game at all. The public may well be entertained by megamerger shenanigans and will be delighted by oil-company price wars. But when the game begins to show the least threat of increased prices or uncontrolled power, the public is fast to show another face. Watching football may be entertaining, but *being* the football is not.

Game playing may be ineliminable from business, and indeed, as a metaphor it has its virtues. It suggests fun as opposed to toil, challenge and vigor as opposed to begrudging duty. But in the past decade, we have seen what happens when the games take on a life of their own, when speculation and what we might call "the casino culture" takes over the business world. The very idea of "production" gets short-circuited, and the pursuit of profits becomes an end in itself. Forget about customers. Forget about employees. Forget about products. Ultimately, they only get in the way. In his bestselling book, *Liar's Poker*, Michael Lewis brutally details life on the trading floor, and it is not an inspiring sight. With the deregulation of the savings and loan industry in the 1980s, one of the most conservative and respected industries (if often suspect as well) turned into a giant casino system—and the house, of course, always won. With federally insured deposits, there could be no losses, except on paper. With the ceiling on interest rates removed, high premiums ensured a constant flow of money, which could then be safely speculated on newly respectable "junk bonds," buying property (with hefty depreciation write-offs), playing stock market futures on 6 percent margins, taking or threatening to take over giant corporations (*who cares what they produce or contribute to society?*), and so on. The whole depressing story is old news by now, but the guilty metaphor has not wholly been uprooted. Business is not a game, and the point is not just to "win." The point and purpose of business is to ensure prosperity and create value, not just pocket the profits.

THE ETHICS OF GAME THEORY

> . . . *a fair field and no favor and the right will prosper.*
>
> *Thomas Carlyle*

Marvin Schell is an oil producer in an unstable oil market. He has only one serious competitor in the area, but the idea of reaching a mutually satisfactory agreement is out of the question. Marvin can cut prices, or he can make some risky and expensive capital expenditures to build up the business. He cannot afford to do both (nor can his competitor). If he decides to make the expenditures and his competitor cuts prices, the results will be ruinous. If he plays it safe and cuts prices, then at least he cannot lose badly, and if his competitor exhausts his resources with expenditures, he can capture the market. The best possible outcome, however, would be if both of them developed their businesses further and carried out exploration and research for the long term, but neither will tell the other what he plans to do. What should Marvin do?

Looking at Marvin's situation as a game allows us to apply the precise mathematical method called "game theory." Game theory was developed by the American mathematician John von Neumann earlier in this century. The idea is that as long as it is only Marvin's profits or "payoff" that is in question, the various factors of risk and probability can be calculated to determine the best or most rational strategy. Naturally, Marvin wants to come out of the competition with the greatest possible profit. But this is not the whole story.

Winning isn't everything, and it certainly isn't the only thing. The key to playing a game is *playing by the rules*. The rules are essential because games serve purposes: to entertain, to exercise, to train, or, in the case of business games, to spur productivity and increase availability of products to consumers by motivating business people according to their own self-interest. But this means that every game must be viewed in a larger context—in terms not only of its internal rules and goals but also of its external purposes and restrictions. Game theory, in other words, is properly a part of ethics.

The purpose of the oil game is to encourage exploration, maintain supplies, and make essential energy products available at the lowest feasible cost to the consumer while earning the supplier the highest rate of return. The oil game, like every game in business, has at least three payoffs, and three ethical dimensions as well.

- to the player (Marvin);
- to all of the players (or the industry as a whole);
- to everyone else (the consumer, but also those in the community who don't consume but are, nevertheless, indirectly affected).

Marvin's game strategy is aimed, first of all, at his own profits. But it is possible for him to profit illegitimately, and if he does, he may win the game but lose something more valuable. He also knows that how he plays the game determines the fortunes of the other players as well. One decision could be ruinous to his competitor; another might benefit his competitor as well as himself. Some decisions can put a whole industry down the tubes, and Marvin also knows that there are decisions that might be good for everyone in the industry but nevertheless disastrous for everyone else—thus the restriction on collusion, which may benefit all players but endangers the whole point of a free market.

Marvin's situation is an example of a classic game, sometimes called the "prisoner's dilemma." (Suppose a prosecutor separates two partners in crime, Mr. A and Mr. B, and offers to make a deal with each of them. If one confesses and the other does not, the confessor will get a light sentence; the other will get the maximum. If both confess, they will both receive stiff sentences. If neither confesses, both will receive shorter sentences since the evidence will be weak and plea-bargaining more likely. If you were one of the prisoners, would you confess?) In this sort of game, there is a particularly delicate tension between your own profits and the profits of your competitor (and perhaps of everyone in the industry). There is also the strong temptation to change the game through collusion (impossible for the prisoners but an ethical dilemma for Marvin and his competitors). The ethics of business games is something more than good sportsmanship. Ethics keeps the game in perspective, and at the same time protects the game itself by preventing changes in the rules.

According to game theory alone, Marvin's most rational response is to play it safe, to cut prices and not take the risk of exploration and development. Indeed, game theorists would point out that if both players were to adopt what would turn out to be the best outcome, a good game theorist would have to suspect collusion, for the decision would be too irrational otherwise. (Why would both parties choose an option that would most likely be to their disadvantage?) But if every oil producer followed the optimum individual strategy and did not agree with competitors to take shared risks, where would the oil come from? In other words, the rational strategy for each individual might turn out to be disastrous for everyone.

THE PRISONER'S DILEMMA

	First Prisoner's Strategy	
	Confess	**Don't confess**
Confess	Both get eight years	First gets ten years Second gets one year
Don't Confess	First gets one year Second gets ten years	Both get two years

(left label:) **Second Prisoner's Strategy**

THE STATION'S DILEMMA

	First Station's Strategy	
	Price at 25.9	**Price at 23.9**
Price at 25.9	Both get fairly high revenue	First gets high revenue Second gets low revenue
Price at 23.9	First gets low revenue Second gets high revenue	Both get fairly low revenue

(left label: **Second Station's Strategy**)

The prisoner's dilemma is one of the keys to business ethics. It has as its corollary a larger problem that we might call the "collective dilemma." Suppose that you are considering driving to work, as opposed to taking the bus. It would be absurd to suggest that your decision presents you with an ethical dilemma; it is simply a matter of personal taste and convenience. But suppose that one million other commuters are at the same time considering whether or not they should drive to work. If they do, traffic will be hopelessly snarled and everyone will be worse off than if no one—or only a few people—drove to work. (A Bentley in a traffic jam is no less frustrating than a small Chevy.)

In business, the collective dilemma is the mathematical antidote to an overly exuberant conception of free enterprise. There are times when the most innocuous activities have the most disastrous results collectively, and then the overall perspective and purpose of the business game takes precedence over the individual goals—as a way, ironically, of making those goals once again possible.

Game theory is a valuable tool in strategic analysis, but its precision too easily hides its inherent limitations. Harvard Business School students play a "business game" in which the assumption is pure competition, with no room for negotiation, no understanding about what is really at stake, and certainly no ability to appreciate the larger social factors that in fact limit every game. Indeed, the worst feature of game theory is the assumption that business is inherently competitive, rather than a cooperative venture between businesses and society.

The most familiar kind of game is the zero-sum game—the game in which there is a fixed total market, in which the total of all profits and losses for all parties is zero. It is this game image of business that gives rise to the view that business is "dog eat dog" and a desperate competition in which winning is all. The fact is that business situations almost never consist of zero-sum games. Even the most inelastic market allows for innovation and expansion. Imagination is never far from good business, and one of the functions of imagination in business is to see the numerous ways beyond zero-sum thinking. Most markets can be expanded; most companies can find new markets, if they need to. But the classical image of ever-expanding capitalism is itself in part the product of zero-sum thinking, the idea that one company's gain is necessarily another's loss. The fact of daily life, however, is that the vast majority of companies in America lead a comfortable existence with their own more or less dependable markets (which is not to say that they can take them for granted). As in so many other aspects of American life, we pay so much attention to dramatic changes that we tend to miss the comfortable regularities that define most of business life. Doing business is not, for the most part, zero-sum competitition; it is doing one's job and continuing to earn one's share of the market. Business life is more like a cooperative game of "catch" than a winner-take-all game of poker.

The prisoner's dilemma, like a zero-sum game, is a noncooperative game; that is, a competitive game in which one person's gain tends to be another's loss. But again, because of our emphasis on the importance of competition in business, we tend to ignore the fact that most business games are cooperative rather than (or as well as) competitive, that one company's gain may well signal an opportunity for others as well. The fast-growing computer field, for example, is not a case of one company crowding out the rest so much as it is a case of various companies making discoveries that enrich not only themselves but dozens of other companies, which quickly attach themselves to the innovative coattails of the first. The fact that eventually the field becomes crowded and some inevitably fail should not blind us to the happy fact that such competitive failure comes only after a very significant period of mutual enrichment. Most industries *share* in good times (and bad).

This happy fact is not limited to fast-growing, innovative fields. It is also true of many stodgy, static industries. Indeed, stodginess can be a great virtue in business. It breeds familarity and a sense of comfort. It discourages new competition because there is so little challenge. But challenge is only one aspect of business—the key to the most dramatic business games, to be sure, but only one aspect nonetheless. Banking is an industry that is greatly disturbed by even the smallest change—in federal banking laws, for example. What benefits one bank generally benefits the industry, and although there may be the facade of competition for ordinary checking accounts, the fact of banking life is that it is not a scramble for a limited resource, not a hotbed of intrigue and strategy, so much as it is business as usual. As it should be.

Finally, it is essential to remind ourselves that the greatest games in business, the games with the greatest challenge, are not zero-sum or competitive games at all but rather games of cooperative exploration, games in which the payoff is not just profits but a place in history. The companies (AT&T, ABC, CBS, NBC, Hughes, MCI, Western Union, Lockheed) that pooled their resources to develop, build, and launch the first communications satellite—a feat far beyond the resources of any one of them—faced a challenge far more invigorating than any marketing campaign, and far more valuable to everyone. The best business games are not the poker games enjoyed by the gamesman. They are games in which an enlightened business world sees itself as a single cooperative game, whose goal is the enrichment of everyone.

BUSINESS AND POKER: A DANGEROUS ANALOGY

Several years ago, business writer Alfred Carr raised a ruckus by arguing that business was immune to the usual rules of ethics.

It would not be an argument worth discussing, if it were not already so prevalent—if less articulate—in so many people's minds. We have already agreed that business might well be understood as a game, and like all games it does have special rules, its own goals and codes of conduct. The rules and customs of poker are not the rules and customs of chess. But the argument that business is like poker in its divorce from the prevailing morality of our society misapprehends both business and poker.

1. Bluffing isn't lying. Poker has rules for deception and a keen (sometimes violent) reaction to cheating. Bluffing is a strategy of increasing uncertainty, but it is very different from lying, which is just as forbidden in playing poker as it is in business negotiations. Most of business is transacted in conversation, where truth and mutual trust are essential.

2. Poker, like business, is a practice, and the integrity of the game is essential to its very existence. Deception has its limits, and just as Carr interprets bluffing as lying, he confuses strategy with unfairness. It is the uncertainty and the psychological skill of poker that make the game worth playing. It is the uncertainty of business ventures that not only makes them a challenge but, more important, promotes the competition that motivates quality and lowers production. The rules of the game serve the ends of the game: entertainment in poker, productivity in business.

3. Business is not so insulated as poker. A poker game involves only its players; business is essential to the well-being of the entire society. The rules of poker protect the game and the players; the rules of business protect everyone else too.

4. There is nothing productive about a poker game; it merely redistributes the income of a small group of people. Business is not primarily concerned with redistributing income but rather with production. It is a cynical and pointless view of business that perceives it as an activity divorced from productivity and consumer satisfaction. It encourages the casino culture, and encourages not an alternative ethics but, so far as the public good is concerned, no ethics at all.

5. Carr's view exaggerates the gap between business values and the morality of the larger society. Indeed, there is no gap at all but rather two concentric circles, the one securely within the other. The goals of business are, not surprisingly, the same as the goals of the larger society—material well-being, the optimal production and distribution of goods, and the most efficient and effective services to promote the good life for every individual and the wealth of the nation as a whole. A game may have its own goals and rules that define it, but these should not be confused with the overall purpose and place of the game itself.

6. Carr's suggestion ignores that core of ethics that does not vary

---

BUSINESS AS A POKER GAME

We can learn a good deal about the nature of business by comparing it with poker. While both have a large element of chance, in the long run the winner is the man who plays with steady skill. In both games ultimate victory requires intimate knowledge of the rules, insight into the psychology of the other players, a bold front, a considerable amount of self-discipline, and the ability to respond swiftly and effectively to opportunities provided by chance.

No one expects poker to be played on the ethical principles preached in churches. In poker it is right and proper to bluff a friend out of the rewards of being dealt a good hand. A player feels no more than a slight twinge of sympathy, if that, when—with nothing better than a single ace in his hand—he strips a heavy loser, who holds a pair, of the rest of his chips. It was up to the other fellow to protect himself. In the words of an excellent poker player, former President Harry Truman, "If you can't stand the heat, stay out of the kitchen." If one shows mercy to a loser in poker, it is a personal gesture, divorced from the rules of the game.

Poker's own brand of ethics is different from the ethical ideals of civilized human relationships. The game calls for distrust of the other fellow. It ignores the claim of friendship. Cunning deception and concealment of one's strength and intentions, not kindness and openheartedness, are vital in poker. No one thinks any the worse of poker on that account. And no one should think any the worse of the game of business because its standards of right and wrong differ from the prevailing traditions of morality in our society. . . .

Alfred Carr, "Is Business Bluffing Ethical?"
Harvard Business Review, January/February 1968

---

from community to community—which we call "morality." Morality consists of those basic rules, which are not merely a matter of a single game or practice but provide the preconditions for every game, every practice. Carr may be trivially correct when he says that the rules of poker are different from the rules of other games and practices, but he is quite wrong when he suggests that this constitutes a divergence from morality.

IS IT EVER RIGHT TO LIE? (ON TRUTH IN ADVERTISING)

Is it ever right to lie?
  No.

Now, let's get down to business.
  It may never be right to tell a lie, but nevertheless it is often prudent, preferable, and—if the way people behave is any indication at all of morals—popular as well.
  Consider the familiar dilemma of HGT sales representative John G., who is asked whether his product is in fact as good as a Xerox. One curious fact is that John G. owns a Xerox himself, but another not insignificant fact is that he is employed by the HGT company to sell their line of products, not to express his personal preferences or conduct a neutral survey of product quality. What does he do? What can he do? Of course, he says, "Yes—and better besides." Is he lying? Or just doing his job? He is doing both, of course, but should we say that he is thereby doing wrong?
  "Truth" and "falsehood" are evasive qualities even in an academic seminar or a scientist's laboratory; they are even more so in the real world. Is a lover lying to himself when he says that his love is the "most wonderful woman in the world"? Is a salesman lying to a customer when he praises an imperfect product? To be sure, there is such a thing as outright deception—the standard case in which a used-car salesman insists that an old convertible is in excellent mechanical condition, knowing full well that the unhappy new owner will be lucky to get the heap off the lot. But one can also argue that shopping at certain used-car lots (the kind advertised by a hand-painted sign that says "Honest Harry Has the Bargains") carries with it the knowledge of risk on the part of the buyer, risking a trade-off for the bargain. What counts as "honest" is already put into question. Of course, there are outright lies—falsification of the odometer reading or the false claim that the engine was overhauled 3,000 miles ago, but there is a certain latitude in lying that depends on the context, the customer, and the costs. Not only lying but giving misleading information is intolerable in the health-care industry—for example, not mentioning the side

effects of a new drug. Showing hyperdramatic demonstrations of "action" toys to children or giving technical information to people who cannot possibly understand it may involve neither false nor misleading information but nevertheless may be morally dubious (given the huge proportion of the adult population that can be swayed by mere adjectives such as "scientific" or "natural"). Cost counts, too. Exaggerated claims for the cleaning powers of an inexpensive soap product or the convenience of a household gadget advertised on TV for (inevitably) $19.95 are more easily forgiven than even mildly bloated praise for the value of a new house or bulldozer. On the other hand, it is clear that it is not only self-defeating but cruel to tell a customer *everything* horrible that might befall him with his product. (Imagine the warnings that would have to accompany even such a simple household appliance as a food processor.)

Lying may always be wrong, but some lies are much more wrong than others. Truth may always be desirable, but the "whole truth and nothing but the truth" is just as likely to be a nightmare.

To say that it is never right to lie is not the same as to say that one should never lie. It is rather to say that a lie is always a later resort, a strategy that is not a first choice. If the salesman could sell his wares by saying nothing but the truth, he could, should, and would do so. But one must always excuse a lie, by showing that some greater evil would result from telling the truth or, most often, simply by showing that there is minimal harm done by lying and that, in this context, the

---

WALL STREET LIES

There are lies and damned lies. Then there are Wall Street lies.

What distinguishes Wall Street lying is that it is pervasive and routine, an accepted part of doing business in a fiercely competitive marketplace, according to industry executives and traders. . . . Wall Street's willingness to use deceit as a business practice and to cut corners in the interest of profit is being blamed for promoting a culture that tolerates borderline behavior, and thus increases the likelihood that laws will be broken.

"There's a competitive pressure to do it more than the next guy, and then if you do it more then they do it more, and it gets out of hand," says J. Gregory Dees, a professor who teaches ethics and entrepreneurial management at Harvard Business School.

—*The Washington Post* (weekly edition)
October 14–20, 1991

lie was not wholly inappropriate. The one thing that a person cannot do is to think that telling a lie—*any* lie—is just as good or right as telling the truth, and so needs no special justification for doing so.

Lying has almost always been considered a sin or an immoral act. In a best-selling book, Sissela Bok has argued that lying is always wrong because, in a variety of ways, it always has bad consequences—worse, that is, than if the lie had not been told. Common experience indicates otherwise, perhaps, for the general attitude both in business and in society is that lies have a perfectly proper social place. Indeed there are clearly contexts in which it would be wrong *not* to lie. Lies can prevent family fights and quarrels among couples. They can prevent bad feelings and help avoid misunderstandings. And, often, they can help an employee keep his or her job. ("I was caught in traffic" is a transparent lie but sometimes an acceptable excuse for being late; "I hated the idea of coming to work so much that I forgot to set the alarm" is, though true, utterly unacceptable.)

We can all agree, looking only at short-term and immediate benefits, that the harm done by some lies is considerably less than the harm that would be done by telling the "unvarnished truth." An employer forced to fire a mediocre worker is certainly not to be blamed for saying that "financial exigencies" have forced him to lay off several low-seniority personnel, instead of telling the truth, which is that the fellow borders on incompetence and doesn't have either the charm or the imagination of a pocket calculator. An advertiser would be judged an idiot, not honest, if he baldly stated that this pain remedy is no more nor less effective than any other on the market, though its packaging is prettier. Nevertheless, there are reasons for saying that lying is always wrong.

The first reason has to do with the enormous amount of effort involved in telling a lie—any lie. The truth—even the incomplete truth—is an enormously complex network of interlocking facts. Anyone who has found himself caught in the nervous web of fabrications involved in even such a simple lie as "We don't know a thing about what our competitors are doing" ("Then how do you know that . . . ?") knows how many seemingly disparate facts can come crashing in when a lie has torn just a small piece out of the truth. As recent national politics has so prominently displayed, the cost of a cover-up is often many times more than the damage done by the lie itself, even if the cover-up is successful.

The second reason looks beyond the short-term benefits of lying to the longer-term damage, which may be harder to see. Every lie diminishes trust. A lie discovered is guaranteed to undermine faith in the liar, but, more subtly, *telling* a lie diminishes one's trust in others. ("If I'm lying to them, they are probably lying to me as well.") Most Americans now look at television advertising as if it were nothing but a tissue of lies—ironically making the more successful ads just those that ignore substantial content and concentrate on memorable associations and effects. A businessman may make many a profit through deception—for a while—but unless one wants to keep on the road for the rest of one's life (sounds good at twenty, not so good at forty), deception almost always catches up and destroys just the business it used to ensure. As long-term investments, lies are usually a bad risk.

The third and strongest reason for thinking that it is never right to lie was suggested by Kant. He asked himself the question, "What would happen if lying were generally accepted? For example, what would happen if it were an everyday and unexceptional feature of the business world that one person would borrow money from another with no intention whatever of repaying the loan?" His answer was that telling the truth and, in the example, borrowing money would both become impossible, so that if I were to approach you and ask for a $10,000 loan, which I would promise to repay on the first of the year, you would simply laugh in my face, since everyone by then would know that such promises were not to be taken seriously. Lying, in other words, must always be wrong, since to treat lying as acceptable undermines just that trust that makes telling the truth meaningful.

Does this mean that one should never lie? Well, no. But it does mean that it is never right to tell a lie; that telling a lie always requires extra thought and some very good reasons to show that this cardinal violation of the truth should be tolerated.

This said, perhaps we should clear up a few common misconceptions about the place of lying in business. It is sometimes suggested that advertising is always a lie, since it tells only one side of the story and that side, needless to say, in the best possible light. But now it is important to distinguish—in facing any such accusation—among the following:

1. telling less than the whole truth;
2. telling a biased truth, with one's own interests in mind;
3. idealizing one's products or services;
4. giving misleading information; that is, true statements that are intended to be misunderstood or misinterpreted;
5. stating obvious falsehoods;
6. stating vicious falsehoods.

HOW NOT TO TEACH BUSINESS VALUES

By the age of twelve, many children find it easier to decide that all commercials lie than to try to determine which are telling the truth. . . . They become ready to believe that, like advertising, business and other institutions are riddled with hypocrisy.

Thomas Bever (professor, Columbia University)

An obvious falsehood, for example, is the displayed claim of some toothpaste manufacturers—that use of a certain gel will overnight convert Shy Sam or Plain Jane to Fabulous Fred or Super Sally, the heartthrob of the high-school prom. One might object to other aspects of such advertising, but "It isn't true" seems too silly to say.

Vicious falsehoods, on the other hand, are those that are not at all obvious and are a deliberate and possibly dangerous form of deception. Saying that a product will do such and such when it will not is vicious deception, as is intentionally withholding information—for example, the flammability of children's pajamas or the side effects of a popular over-the-counter drug. Misleading information can be as vicious as false information—indeed it is only a matter of logical nuance that allows us to distinguish between the two.

It is impossible to tell the "whole story," especially in the limited time of a fifteen-second radio or TV slot or in the small space available on a paper package. But advertising isn't supposed to be a scientific study, even if it utilizes some (more or less) scientific evidence on the product's behalf. Of course advertising expresses a bias on the behalf of the product. Of course it idealizes the product in its presentation. But neither bias nor idealization is lying, and it is surely foolish to insist that advertising, unlike almost every other aspect of social life, be restricted to the simple, boring truth—that is, that this product is not much different from its competitors and that people have lived for hundreds of thousands of years without any of them.

It is often challenged—these days with Orwellian overtones—that advertising in general and TV advertising in particular have turned the American consumer into something of a supermarket zombie, without a will of his or her own, without judgment, buying hundreds of innocuous but sometimes tasteless products that no one really needs. But the zombie image contradicts precisely what lies beneath the whole discussion of truth—namely, the confidence that we are, more

---

MEDALS FOR HONESTY?

What is universal about these examples [of lying in business] is that these managers, each functioning on a different corporate level, are concerned with one thing—*getting the job done*. Most companies give numerous awards for achievement and accomplishment, for sales, for growth, for longevity and loyalty; but there are no medals in the business world for honesty, compassion, or truthfulness.

Richard O. Lundquist (Equitable Life Assurance Society)

---

or less, capable of making value judgments on our own, and that if we buy or even need to buy products that are of no particular cosmic importance, this does not signal either the end of civilization or the disintegration of the human mind. Encouraging someone to buy a product that is only a fad or a mark of status is not deception, and to call it that tends to undermine the ethical distinction that is of enormous importance—between vicious falsehoods and any number of other "varnishings" of the truth. These may be vulgar. They may encourage us to compete for some pretty silly achievements—the shiniest (and most slippery) floor, a car that can win the grand prix (to be driven in bumper-to-bumper traffic up and down the freeway), a soap that makes one speak in a phony Irish brogue. But to condemn all advertising is to make it impossible to attack vicious advertising and thus to bring about the logical conclusion imagined by Kant—an entire world in which no one believes anything, in which advertising serves at most as a source of amusement and seduction of the feeble-minded.

Let's end our discussion of lying by commenting once again on Alfred Carr's suggestion that business is like poker, that it has its own rules, which are different from ordinary ethics. One of these rules, supposedly, is the permissibility of lying. But business (like poker) forbids lying. Contrary to Carr, a generally accepted practice of lying would undermine the business world faster than any external threat that has ever faced it. Promises and contracts, if not good faith, are the presuppositions of all business. The exact nature of truth in advertising may be controversial, but advertising in general must be not only based on fact but believable and trustworthy. If it were not, the commercial world in America would be about as effective as the provocations of Hari Krishnas in America's airports—an annoyance to be ignored as we all go on with the rest of our lives.

Honesty isn't just the best policy in business; it is, in general, the only possible policy.

MORALITY: THE BASIC RULES

> *I don't like violence. I'm a businessman. Blood is a big expense.*
>
> *Mario Puzo,* The Godfather

Ethics is a matter of *ethos*, participation in a community, a practice, a way of life. Business ethics is a function of the business ethos. Within itself, the mentality of business may be a game mentality, but not all of business ethics is defined by this gamelike business *ethos* or by the business community. The nature of business is circumscribed by society, which tends to encourage or discourage particular aspects of business on the basis of its own ideals and well-being. But there is also a more general set of basic rules that are not part of or partial to any particular society, community, or practice. These rules apply everywhere and determine the legitimacy of every practice. These are the rules of *morality*.

Morality is not the same as moralizing, and being moral does not mean being righteous. It means only *doing right*. Most of the time, being moral is no big deal. One doesn't praise an accountant for not cheating on the corporation's tax return, and one doesn't praise an employee for not stealing from the company. Morality is most noticeable in its absence, except, perhaps, when a person succeeds in remaining moral under enormous pressure to be otherwise. But morality in general is not heroism; it is simply not doing what no one should

---

A MATTER OF PRINCIPLE?

Abe Lincoln once threw a man out of his office, angrily turning down a substantial bribe. "Every man has his price," Lincoln explained, "and he was getting close to mine."

From the lunchtime collection of Tom Stewart

---

think of doing in the first place. In practical business contexts, morality is rarely an issue, not because the possibility of immoral but lucrative behavior does not exist at every turn but because it is assumed—it *must* be assumed—that no amount of gain will justify a breach of morality. Morality and business are mentioned together when a business venture is *immoral,* and there is never a question of which— business or morality—will win that competition. Moral rules are the trump cards of every business transaction.

Given the importance of moral rules, one might like a list of them, but such an exercise is probably a waste of time. Anyone who doesn't know them already isn't going to learn anything. (It's not like learning a new computer language.) But, for starters, how about

Thou shalt not kill
Thou shalt not steal
Thou shalt not commit adultery
Thou shalt not bear false witness
Thou shalt not cheat on thy taxes
Thou shalt not knowingly do harm
Don't be cruel
Etc.

We could go on. There are moral rules that are in dispute, such as the morality of premarital sex and the morality of children's advertising. There are moral rules that conflict—especially in times of extreme stress, in wartime or the corporate equivalent thereof. But of morality itself there is surprisingly little to say (until we get to a highly theoretical level, which is not appropriate here). Moral laws are unambiguous and not open to debate. They simply say,

DON'T DO IT!

Against breaches of morality there are no good arguments, whatever a person's status, however powerful the company, however great the profits. In fact, considerable damage may be done by a company spokesman trying to argue against a moral rule, perhaps more damage than the original transgression itself. In this context, we should recall once again the Lockheed spokesman's heedless complaint, defending himself against a morally ambiguous charge: "When a company wants its products to be bought at all costs, [can it] realistically decline the request [for payoffs] on the grounds that it is not a good thing from the ethical point of view?"

The answer to that question is, simply, "Yes."

The practical problem with moral rules is never whether or not to accept them; it is rather how to apply them. Granted that one must accept the principle "Thou shalt not kill," does that include the lives of animals? Does it prohibit any risky industrial activity like mining coal, in which some employees will lose their lives? Does it prohibit the manufacture of any product, like guns or knives, that *might,* if abused, cause fatal injuries? Granted that one accepts the principle that one should not steal—that is, take someone else's property without paying a fair and agreed-upon price for it—does that mean that one should not take advantage of a company in trouble by buying up inventory or perhaps the company itself? Should a business person take advantage of the stupidity or negligence of a supplier or a customer—for example, if the first forgets to send a bill or the second overpays one? Granted that one should tell the truth and ought not to cheat on taxes, does that preclude such common business practices as tax deferrals and shelters?

What is morality, given that it occupies such an unchallengeable place in our (and every) society? Simply stated, morality consists of those rules that circumscribe legitimate activity for every citizen (or visitor). Such rules are the boundaries of a tolerable social life and guarantee the security of those things a society values most—individual life and well-being, obviously, but, in our society at least, extraordinary freedom, private property, personal and social relationships, freedom from terror, and the "pursuit of happiness." But beyond this essential function, the nature of morality is a matter of violent dispute. There are those who insist that morality is inextricably tied to religion—or to a particular religion—and impossible without. There are those who insist on a strict interpretation of an exact set of moral rules, with no room for other interpretations and no exceptions based on current social facts and needs. And there are those who believe that morality is nothing but a set of local social restrictions that (with some risk) can be flouted or bypassed at will. (One sometimes finds people in business who defend the ultrastrict view of morality in their personal lives but are virtually amoral in professional life, thus provoking the most vehement critics of business.) But whatever else it may be, morality is at least the following:

1. MORALITY IS A LIVING PHENOMENON, no matter how ancient its codes and principles. Our primary moral precept is the autonomy of each individual and every generation to rethink and decide for themselves what is right and what is wrong.
2. MORALITY IS WHAT ONE DOES, not what one says or how loudly and publicly one regrets doing wrong afterward—a recent fashion. Apologizing on the national news after being convicted of a crime is not necessarily a mark of morality.
3. MORALITY IS A SHARED SENSE OF VALUES. It is possible that only one person in the company is right and everyone else is wrong, but how do we recognize when that lone voice is indeed correct? Only because that lone voice finds a much larger audience outside the company, and agreement on the moral principles with which the company itself will be condemned.
4. MORALITY ISN'T ACCIDENTAL. It is not what one does that counts but what one does *knowingly*. Promoting the right person by mistake isn't being moral. Giving money to a charity by mistake isn't charity.
5. MORALITY REQUIRES COMPASSION. Cold-blooded obedience of the rules isn't enough.
6. MORALITY IS A WAY OF LIFE, a state of character. It's not a matter of forcing oneself to comply. The self-satisfaction of being a "good person" is motive enough.
7. MORALITY IS NOT A SUBSTITUTE FOR LIFE. We are a "crypto-moral" society that delights in clever criminals and charming con men, and not only in the movies. We are a law-abiding society, but we are also attracted to people who break the rules. No one who knows our society should ever expect a morally perfect business world. But such characters and their stories provide the spice of business life, not its substance. To be moral is an unquestioned good. To be a moralizing bore, a dogmatic stick-in-the-mud in the name of morality, is not good. In the words of Tom Peters, "the line between ethical purity and arrogant ego-centrism is a fine one."

THE MOTIVATION OF MORALITY

Check the six items below that you find most important in motivating you to remain aware of ethical issues for you and your company.

_____ 1. Fear for your job.
_____ 2. Explicit, clear, and applicable company policies.
_____ 3. Knowing that the company expects it of you.
_____ 4. Knowing that your family expects it of you.
_____ 5. The sense that your role in the company is important.
_____ 6. Living up to the responsibilities that you know are yours.
_____ 7. The knowledge that you'll be rewarded.
_____ 8. Your concern for the company's reputation.
_____ 9. Knowing your company is already fair, and wanting to keep it that way.
_____ 10. Strong pressure to "toe the line."
_____ 11. Knowing you'll get caught.
_____ 12. High personal standards of ethics.
_____ 13. High corporate standards of ethics.
_____ 14. You really respect your manager and wouldn't want to get him or her in trouble.
_____ 15. The dictates of your religion.
_____ 16. You always hear your mother's/father's voice in the back of your mind.
_____ 17. You'd hate to be on television for such a reason.
_____ 18. You welcome the opportunity to show what a good person you are.
_____ 19. You're being paid to uphold company standards.
_____ 20. Ethics helps motivate everybody; unethical behavior turns people into cynics.

ETHICAL STYLES

One of the most important but least often addressed aspects of ethics is the difference among ethical styles. It is a problem that surfaces in almost every discussion of actual cases, whether in business school or in the boardroom, whether the topic is South Africa or advertising for children on television. Different people have different premises, different ways of arguing, different ways of doing the right thing. There are ethical styles just as there are social styles and styles of management and marketing. A clash of ethical styles can be far more disruptive and destructive to business tranquillity than differences of opinion or clashes of personality. In a conflict of ethical styles, each party typically thinks the other "immoral"—or worse. Negotiation breaks down, not because there is no common point of interest but because there is not even agreement on the kinds of interests that are relevant to the case.

The most familiar clash of ethical styles—one that emerges in almost every management context—is the sort of seemingly irresolvable conflict that we find between Manny K., who feels absolutely constrained by the letter of the law, and John Stuart, who is more concerned with the practical specifics of the case at hand. For Manny K., it does not matter that the rule in question is outdated or impractical. It does not matter that it became a matter of law or policy under another administration, which is now out of office. It does not matter that the rule will no doubt be changed someday. Manny K. believes that one should obey rules, whatever their origins and whatever the consequences. Any other way of thinking, from his standpoint, is amoral.

John Stuart, on the other hand, is a self-consciously practical person. Rules serve a purpose, a function, and they are to be obeyed just because—but only because—they serve that purpose or function. A rule that proves to be impractical no longer deserves our respect or obedience. A rule that was formulated under very different circumstances or was legislated by a different administration should be carefully scrutinized and not given too much weight. John Stuart makes his decisions on the sole ground that a certain course of action has the best consequences for everyone involved. If that fits the rules (as it usually does), then so much the better. If it does not, then so

much the worse for the rules—and so much too for that stubborn
Manny K., who for some unfathomable reason refuses to see the point.

Manny K. considers John Stuart to be nothing but an amoral
opportunist, a man who does not respect authority and the rules. John
Stuart considers Manny K. to be utterly unreasonable and impractical,
if not "impossible." When general utility conflicts with an established
rule, John and Manny are certain to misunderstand each other. There
can be no compromise, because each of them considers his own
position to be beyond question and cannot understand the other,
except, perhaps, as pathology.

Why has so familiar a scenario found so minimal a role in studies of
organizational behavior and business ethics? Ethical styles have been
ignored by business writers because we tend to assume that ethical
principles, unlike personalities and public policies, are universal and
nonnegotiable. One executive interrupted at the beginning of one of
our seminars and, crossing his arms in defiance, challenged the very
purpose of our discussion, saying, "There is right, and there is wrong.
There is nothing more to discuss, in business or anywhere else." We
responded, of course, with a case designed to bring out the conflict of
established rules with practical necessities, and the John Stuarts in the
group soon rose to the occasion, making our point for us. One of the
more destructive legacies of our Judeo-Christian tradition in ethics is
that it tends to encourage dogmatic and intolerant thinking precisely
where understanding and tolerance are most necessary.

There are a number of ethical styles, of which Manny K. and John
Stuart exemplify but two. There are styles that emphasize painful
wrestling with problems and styles that rely on sheer intuition. There
are styles that emphasize pity and compassion, and there are styles
that stress the importance of being detached and objective. Not every
attitude in ethics is an ethical style, of course. Being immoral is not an
ethical style. Selfishness, despite its occasional vogue as an "enlightened" ethics, is not an ethical style. There are, however, many styles
of ethics in business. Here are eight of them:

1. RULE-BOUND. Thinking and acting on the basis of rules and
   principles, paying only secondary regard to circumstances or
   exceptions. (Manny K.)
2. UTILITARIAN. Weighing probable consequences, both to the company and to the public well-being. Principles are important only
   as rules of thumb. "The greatest good for the greatest number of
   people" is the ultimate test for any action or decision. (John
   Stuart.)

3. LOYALIST. Evaluating all decisions first in terms of benefit to the company and its reputation. The concern with reputation (motivated by one's own pride in the company) also ensures general conformity to laws and principles and concern with the company's role in the larger social picture. (Also called the "company man.")

4. PRUDENT. Weighing probable consequences to oneself and one's own concerns but always including long-range considerations of company reputation, public trust, customer and supplier relations, ability to obtain loans, etc. Prudence is not the same as selfishness or crude self-interest (though it is sometimes called "enlightened self-interest") since it has built into it the mutual dependence of one's own interests and company interests. The primary difference between the prudent strategist, the loyalist, and the utilitarian is that the first is concerned primarily with himself and only secondarily with the rest of the world; the second is concerned primarily with the well-being of the company without special regard for him- or herself. The utilitarian takes the broader social view and, though naturally concerned with one's own and one's company's success, thinks in terms of the overall good. The prudent strategist lives on the border between ethics and self-interest and unlike the loyalist and the utilitarian is not unlikely to give up his tentative ethical stance under pressure or conflict. A special case is the person Maccoby calls the "gamesman," whose ethical commitment might be said to be limited to the "rules of the business game," within which the primary motivations are to be challenged and to win, without respect for the rules he has to obey (in order to play) and without regard for the actual consequences of his actions.

5. VIRTUOUS. Every action is measured in terms of its reflection of one's character or the company reputation, without immediate regard to consequences and often without paying much attention to general principles. The virtuous style can vary in both scope and method; it can be identical in its concerns to the company concerns of the loyalist, or it can encompass the social world—as in the actions of some of the great business philanthropists. It can pride itself on obedience to the rules, or it can pride itself for its unerring intuitions, but it is one's own virtue that is the source of pride rather than the autonomous motive to obey the rules, for example.

6. INTUITIVE. Making decisions on the basis of "conscience" and without deliberation, argument, or reasons, the intelligence of

which may not be immediately apparent. Intuitive thinkers tend to be extremely impatient with more deliberative, rule-bound, and utilitarian types. It is a style that usually flourishes only at the top of the decision-making hierarchy, and continued success (by moral, utilitarian, and prudential standards) is essential, since errors in intuition, unlike errors in deliberation and strategy, cannot be readily explained or rationalized.

7. EMPATHETIC. Following one's feelings, in particular feelings of sympathy and compassion. "Putting oneself in the other's place" is the modus operandi of the sentimental style, whether the "other" be a competitor ("How would we like it if he . . .") or a customer ("Suppose you found yourself stuck with . . .").

8. DARWINIAN. Whoever survives must be right. In some versions, this is clearly not an ethical position (e.g., "If we win, we're right, but if they win, we were wronged"). But a consistent Darwinian fully accepts the possibility and even the desirability of his or her own failure to a superior competitor, without complaint.

Ethics is thinking in terms of the "larger picture," not ignoring or neglecting one's own interests and well-being (a faulty view of ethics) but not overemphasizing one's own interests either. When, as is usual, one's own interests coincide with company interests, the distinction does not even arise (which is why the prudential strategist can be tentatively included in the list of ethical styles). And when, which is also usual, the (long-term) well-being of the company coincides with its positive contributions to society, there need be no distinction made between company loyalty and the more general good (which is why the loyalist has an ethical style rather than just a sociological attachment). In fact, in such amiable circumstances, ethical styles overlap or remain hidden from view; "business as usual" usually takes ethical considerations for granted (which is not to be confused, as it so often is, with the supposed irrelevance of ethical considerations in business). It is in times of conflict or crisis that differences in ethical styles become prominent, and it is in those times that such differences must be understood and negotiated instead of—as happens so often—being allowed to make a bad situation that much more explosive.

We said that each of these styles has it characteristic advantages and disadvantages; for example, the lack of practical flexibility in rule-bound moral thinking, the sometimes impossible complexity of utilitarian calculations, and the untrustworthy (because only tentative) ethical

---

ETHICAL STYLES

1. Rule-bound	obedience to law, rule, principle
2. Utilitarian	consequences for everybody
3. Loyalist	the company first
4. Prudent	our long-term advantage
5. Virtuous	character, reputation are all-important
6. Intuitive	spontaneous judgments
7. Empathetic	"how must he feel?"
8. Darwinian	whoever survives is right

---

dependability of the prudential strategist. But this is not the place to explore these in detail; rather we wish to stress the variety of ethical styles, each of which defines its own criteria for right thinking (e.g., in the rule-bound style, thinking about applying the right rules; in the intuitive style, minimal thinking) and right action (good for the company, good for society, good for others). Understanding the differences and resolving conflicts among ethical styles can sometimes be as important and as difficult as resolving the ethical problems themselves.

AN ETHICAL STYLES QUESTIONNAIRE

(Personal)

1. You are driving across the country. On a long stretch of Interstate Highway 10 between Phoenix and the California border, the six newly paved, nearly perfect lanes are virtually empty. There is nothing but soft brush for miles on either side of the highway, it's late afternoon, and you're driving a brand-new, Hertz-rented Thunderbird (turbo). The posted speed limit is 75 mph. How fast are you driving? Why?

2. There is a drought in your area, and the city council mandates water rationing. You have a beautiful lawn and flower bed in your backyard, which are dying. Dutiful compliance with rationing has brought water usage down to safe levels. No one will see you. Should you save your garden?

3. Your regular golf partner doesn't show up on Saturday morning as scheduled. You call his house but get no answer. You end up wasting the entire morning waiting for him. You are rightly frustrated, upset, and angry. That evening he calls and tells you that he and his wife had an enormous fight that morning; he was first angry and then depressed and in the emotional turmoil simply "forgot" to call you. What is your reaction to this excuse?

4. Your softball team is one run behind when it starts to rain. In fact, it is pouring, and it doesn't seem likely to stop. It's getting cold too, but by the rules of the league if the game gets "called" the other team wins. Your best batters are about to come up, and the team really needs this win. You are cold and miserable too. Everyone is shivering and the children are crying. But, as captain of the losing team, it is your decision whether or not to stop the game. What do you do?

5. You are invited to a private club that does not admit blacks, Jews, or orientals. Nothing has been said about this policy, but a recent "incident" has made it quite clear. Many of your best friends and most important business associates are members of the club. What do you do?

6. Leaving the theater parking lot, you nick the fender of the Porsche parked next to you. It is virtually invisible, but you know how Porsche owners are. No one is around. Do you leave a note?

(Managerial)

7. Company policy dictates that "an employee shall accept no gift, from any actual or potential customer or supplier, with a value in excess of $50." A long-time client who has since become something of a friend offers you two football tickets (to a game you really would like to see) worth $27 each. Do you accept them?

8. One of your employees, it turns out, lied about his military experience on his resume. On probing, he confesses to you that he had an extremely humiliating experience in the army and has tried to repress

all memories of that period of his life. Do you understand why he did it? Do you forgive it? Do you make public his humiliation?

9. A good client about to close a deal asks you, casually, whether your fees are the best in town. You know, for a fact, that your fees are 10 percent higher than one of your competitors, for essentially the same service. Do you tell him this? Do you simply laugh good-naturedly? Do you admit that your fees are higher but exaggerate the differences between the services rendered?

10. Your assistant is offered a similar job, but at better pay, by one of your competitors. You can't afford to match the offer, but you have spent so much time training this person and given so much personal attention to her development and progress in the company and she has become such an integral member of the "team" that you can't imagine how you will undo the loss. Do you feel "betrayed"? Or does this seem to you to be a perfectly predictable part of the free-enterprise system?

11. You discover that a small but nevertheless significant error in your bookkeeping has resulted in an extra $1.40 service charge for each of your checking account customers. It will cost you almost $3.00 per customer to refund and explain the mistake. What do you do?

12. You are offering a contract to redo your offices and, after considerable deliberation, you decide to go with company X. Having made this decision, a representative of company Z asks to fly you to Miami Beach for a few days to discuss the same contract. You are virtually certain that you will go with company X, but it's early February, you've been overworking, and company Z has a well-earned reputation for putting out an elaborate "welcome mat." Do you accept the invitation?

13. One of your more enterprising managers drops by your office at lunchtime and places on your desk in front of you a slightly blurred photograph of a confidential offer to one of your clients from one of your competitors. What do you do with this information?

14. You have been seriously thinking about making a lateral career move and getting out of administration and more into the operations side of the business. A position opens up at exactly the right level, and you are sure that you would have a good shot at it. Then your assistant, whom you have been grooming for a promotion, walks into your office

and asks you to recommend him for the same position. Your letter could probably land him the job. What do you do?

Ascertaining Your Ethical Style
(A = agree, D = disagree)

_____ 1. "It really bothers me when someone ignores or breaks one of the company rules. It's the same kind of feeling I get when I see someone run a red light, even if no one else is on the road."

_____ 2. "I get so irritated when one of the bureaucrats at the office insists on following the rules when there just isn't any point to it. I mean, rules are made to be broken, right? At least as long as no one gets hurt. The important thing is productivity, not kowtowing to bureaucrats."

_____ 3. "My feeling is that anyone who can't stand behind company policy—100 percent—just shouldn't be here. If they think that the company is doing something wrong, they should quietly leave. Otherwise, they ought to support it."

_____ 4. "You've always got to ask 'How will this benefit us in the long run?' I don't believe in short-term solutions. But I do believe that if we can make our company prosper over the long haul, it will be best for everyone—and especially for us. I'm not saying we should be selfish, but no one is going to prosper if we sacrifice ourselves."

_____ 5. "I always ask 'Will I be able to look at myself in the mirror in the morning and say, "I'm proud of you."?' It's the same with the company. I'd hate to have to explain to my friends that, sure, the project has given us a black eye in the press, but we stand to make nearly a quarter-billion on it. You want to make an impressive profit to bolster your reputation—with the board and the stockholders, with your friends and family. If you sacrifice your reputation, what's the point of making money?"

_____ 6. "I just know when something's wrong. It's as if I can *smell* it. Don't ask me how I know, but I'm hardly ever wrong."

_____ 7. "I always put myself in the other guy's shoes. It's not that I'll always give in if he's hurt, but I have to know how he feels. If it's a customer who's bought a bum product, I think of how I'd feel cheated if it were me. If it's a competitor who's lost a fair fight, I still ask 'How does he feel?' but at least I know he doesn't (or shouldn't) feel cheated.''

_____ 8. "Rockefeller, Frick, Mellon, Carnegie, Vanderbilt—I mean, you're not talking about nice guys who fought a clean fight. They did whatever they had to, and they won. History says that they're right, and it's the same with all of us now. No one ever made the history books by being right in business and going broke.''

STRATEGIC PLANNING—FOR THE GOOD LIFE

Young business people are often encouraged these days to make out a "plan" for themselves—where they would like to be in a year, in five years, perhaps more. An entire course at Harvard Business School is devoted to career planning—what sort of position to seek first, when to move, etc. But what is tragically lacking is analogous *life* planning, with an eye not only to such obvious life stages as marriage, children, and retirement and one or two hobbies for one's "spare time" (a revealing phrase) but also to other interests and aspects of one's personality. Not surprisingly, an informal survey of 1983 MBAs six months out of Harvard showed that nearly half were already frustrated with their jobs and their lives, though they had been equipped to understand and analyze only the former.

There is a sense, of course, in which the good life cannot be planned. Emergencies and tragedies are usually not predictable, and in business the details of the job market, politics, and the business cycle—even if explicable to future historians—provide the wild cards in the game of life. Planning when to get married—when one does not already have a specific person in mind—strikes us as not only unromantic but also foolish. Risks are a part of life—and sometimes desirable. But risks can be foolish as well as invigorating, and they can be planned for.

Chance may be as essential to life as the search for security, but chance—paradoxically—does not "just happen." Chance too can be planned and evaluated, and there is a world of difference between being ready to welcome unexpected opportunity and being shocked and unprepared for it. Much of our unhappiness, in fact, is not the result of misfortune or bad luck. It is bad planning, or no planning, no sorting out of priorities *before* we find ourselves neck-deep in responsibilities and obligations or over our heads in a life we never really wanted in the first place.

Life in today's fast-moving world is not so unpredictable as the future shockers would tell us. Modes of communication and transportation—not to mention warfare—may be evolving at a terrifying speed, but the essentials of the good life remain remarkably constant: friendship, family life and time to enjoy it, a sense of fulfillment, the respect of one's neighbors and self-respect besides, the basic comforts of life, good health and the "good things" that money will buy (whatever those happen to be this year or decade). Is there really so much difference between wanting to own an expensive car in this century and desiring a fine carriage in the last one? Were the food and wine better in the Middle Ages, or was friendship any more enjoyable in ancient Rome? As we become ever more efficient and productive, how is it that we seem to have less time rather than more, and have fewer ideas about what to do?

A plan for the good life means something more than listing one's career ambitions and possibilities and something more than listing the things that one enjoys. A plan for the good life means, first of all, knowing your needs, your ideals and aspirations as a human being. One joins a firm with business and management objectives in mind; it is not unreasonable to keep in mind also a set of life management goals. If one can set one's sights on a promotion by the end of the first year, why not set a goal of friendship for that period, too? One might argue that in life, "management by objective" is compulsive and neurotic—if indeed it is pursued in too businesslike a manner. But when business life is so carefully planned and orchestrated, the rest of life is too easily forced into the odd or spare moments, or neglected altogether. Strangely enough, the risks and shocks we think of as the challenge of business are reserved for our personal lives, where they are usually much less welcome. Ethics and the good life get sacrificed not because of immorality or stupidity but simply because they are not part of the only plan in town.

What kinds of questions go into a plan for the good life? First of all, questions about yourself, what you want, expect, enjoy and need:

STRATEGIC PLANNING—FOR THE *NEXT* LIFE

From *How Rich Will You Be?*, a brochure distributed by the Reanimation Foundation, an investment fund based in Liechtenstein. The foundation offers investment accounts for individuals who plan to have their bodies frozen at death in the hope that they can be brought back to life in the future.

Q: How long will it take for me to be reanimated?

A: Experts predict that in 50 to 150 years medical science will develop the technology to bring suspended patients back to life. How long it will take for you to be reanimated will depend on how well you're suspended and on your physical condition at the time you're suspended.

Q: If it takes one hundred years until I'm reanimated, how much money will I receive?

A: If you assume a conservative annual rate of return of 8 percent on your investment, the amount of money you will receive in a hundred years is as follows: If you invest $100,000, you will receive $219,976,130. If you invest 10,000,000, you will receive $21,997,613,000.

Q: Who will be investing my money?

A: A major Swiss bank with an excellent reputation for safe and prudent investments.

—*Harper's*, December 1990

---

security, freedom, companionship, privacy, power, friendship, great wealth, or just to be recognized as a success.

1. What do you consider the most important things in life? Success, family, companionship, romantic love, money, status and position, respect, friendship. Which could you live without, or have only in small doses? Which could you not live without, or have only in substantial doses?

2. What do you most enjoy doing? Imagine yourself left entirely to choose on your own, without financial pressures, without expecting rewards or compensations beyond the activity itself. What would (or do) you choose to do? Listen to music? Play tennis? Build things? Have a quiet dinner with an intimate friend? Be alone, doing nothing? Work?

3. What kind of people do you like to spend your time with? Work with? Are they the kind of people you are spending time with now? Are you the kind of person they would want to spend time with? Do you enjoy people who inspire you? What are your primary expectations in a friend? In a colleague? In a boss?

(Most of us conscientiously choose our subordinates; it is much more important to be careful in choosing a boss.)

4. How do you see yourself, ideally? How would you describe yourself in a paragraph, say, for a future *Who's Who*, emphasizing not positions and awards but character and accomplishments? How well are you working toward that now?

5. How important is so-called spare time to you? How much do you need? What do you (or would you) do with it? Is spare time to you just time to relax and get ready for more work? (Living to work used to be a virtue, until psychiatrists gave it a pathological name: "workaholism." But the fact remains that loving one's work is one of the few dependable roads to happiness.) Is your spare time more important than your work? (Then why are you working so hard?)

6. Where would you draw the line in your job? What would you not do, even at the risk of being fired? Work seventeen-hour days, and weekends? Have to fire a good friend? Make false reports? Lie to your boss? Get ahead at the expense of someone who deserves it more? Be responsible—even indirectly—for some innocent person's death? (Better to be clear about these things *before* the topic comes up unexpectedly, under pressure.)

7. What is your ethical style? What kinds of arguments do you use to support your ideas? What kind of person do you find immoral? Do you resent people who obey the letter of the law? Do you find people who don't give arguments to be frustrating?

8. Whom do you want to please? ("Yourself" is the fashionable but usually false answer. "My mother" and "my father" are a bit overworked, thanks to Freud. Try again.)

9. How much money do you need? How much do you want? Why? Suppose you suddenly inherit $400,000. What would you do with it? Is that so important?

10. What do you want to be doing next year, this time, in your job and out of it?

11. What do you want to be doing five years from now—what kind of job, what kind of life? Does the idea of doing just what you are doing now (plus a little status and some cost-of-living increases) horrify you? Or does it give you a sense of pleasant comfort?

12. Looking back over your life and career from your rocking chair, what would you like to remember—and how would you like to be remembered?

Part Three

IN, OUT, AND UP THE ORGANIZATION: MOLAR ETHICS

WHAT DO YOU DO?

It is a very American question: "What do you do?" Europeans joke about it. Asian visitors are confused by it. But for us it is a very natural and seemingly inescapable opening question: the first line after "hello" in a casual conversation; the first serious question in an interview; the sometimes fatal question when one's job is on the line.

We identify ourselves through the work that we do. For most of the business world, that means identifying the role one plays in a company: "I do financial analysis at Prudential-Bache" or "I'm an accountant with Kinsey-Ross." One's identity turns on the identity of the company and its reputation, both in general and in that particular field. "Oh, then you must be very good," or, "Well, uh, I hear you've been having some difficulties lately." We may think of ourselves as individualists, riding on our own merits, but the fact is that our ethics are tied up with our company identities—our sense of worth, our sense of righteousness, our sense of belonging. It is worth noting how quickly and willingly we accept the corporate pronoun "you" in the sentence "I hear *you*'ve been having trouble." It would be a poor (and probably temporary) employee who would fend off the question with "Not me, *THEM*" or "I refuse to accept any responsibility for their stupidity."

We are what we do, and what we do is, for the most part, what the company says that we do. We identify with the company, and, to a large extent, its interests are our interests. One's position is a source of pride, the core of our responsibilities, the heart of most people's public identities. Our ethics are entangled with our jobs. No matter how hard one tries to remain "clean" in a dirty world, the ethics of one's company color one's sense of self. And, more positively, it is very hard indeed to be dirty in a world that is visibly and self-consciously clean. Unethical behavior in business is supported if not

135

encouraged by the ethics of the business, and ethical behavior is, too. Nothing ensures ethics in business as much as an ethical job in an ethical firm in an ethical industry.

WHY I LIKE (DISLIKE) MY JOB (OR WHAT I'D LIKE IN THE NEXT ONE)
(L = Like, D = Dislike)

_____ the people I work with
_____ location
_____ opportunities for promotion
_____ my status in the company
_____ my relation with my boss
_____ the people who work for me
_____ my sense of power
_____ what I actually do on the job
_____ the meetings
_____ the challenge
_____ the salary
_____ opportunities for professional growth
_____ the pressure
_____ the sense of accomplishment
_____ time for family and personal life
_____ opportunity to improve my skills
_____ the contacts I make
_____ being left alone
_____ the potential for making more money in the future
_____ the reputation of the company
_____ the reputation of the industry
_____ the *kind* of people I work with

CORPORATE CULTURES

> *Most of our guys are having fun. They are the kind*
> *of people who would rather be in the Marines than*
> *in the Army.*
>> *Personnel spokesman, Pepsico, Inc.*

Jake and Art have the "same job" but at different companies.

Jake Hackworth dreads the office the way the Little Rascals dreaded school. If he can be sick, he's sick; if he has an excuse to leave at 3:30, he's out of the building before the boss can change his mind. The boss, by the way, is Simon ("Legree") Timmons, the founder of the company and the "miss not a trick" overseer of its 340 employees. Although the company prides itself on its efficiency and its incentive system, the fact is that the main motivation is fear of mortification. Indeed, the best-known employees are those who have been most often chewed out for lack of efficiency, always publicly and personally, by the boss. Jake has never suffered this humiliation, because he obeys the rules and does his job, if only the way a freeway driver obeys the speed limit with a cop on his tail. He is known by very few of his fellow workers, which is just as well. He couldn't imagine anything worse than having to face any one of them in his precious hours and days away from work.

Art deVotee, on the other hand, can't wait to get to the office in the morning. He works for a huge office-systems corporation, but he feels as if he knows almost everyone in the company. This is absurd, of course, since the company has branches in thirty-one countries and even his home office has 5,100 employees. But he feels such camaraderie with his fellow employees that he and his friends have often joked about making up company T-shirts (and other items of clothing) to express their undeniable team spirit. Art often sees his coworkers on the weekends, which is not difficult, since many of them live no more than a few blocks away. His children play with their children. His wife works with some of their wives. He has been with the company for only three years, but he "can't imagine working anywhere else."

Every corporation is a culture. What is a culture? Anthropologists define a culture as a way of living, a way of talking, dressing, thinking,

---

LIFE AT "BIG BLUE"

The IBM man was not a visible part of the roaring twenties and the dissolute life that distinguished them. First of all because he was a serious fellow, intent on making something of himself, but also because Mr. Watson would fire him in a minute if word of excessive frivolity, and drinking whatsoever, or unacceptable incidents of boisterous or embarrassing conduct got back to the leader. . . .

There were no specific rules about decorum, grooming, and apparel, but a certain style was expected because Mr. Watson approved of it.

William Rogers, *Think*

---

defining time, eating lunch. But, first of all, a culture is a set of values, a way of relating to one another. In economic and scientific management theory, and in too much political rhetoric as well, the corporation is an impersonal and sometimes socially irresponsible institution whose sole purpose on earth is to make a profit for its owners or shareholders. In law, on the other hand, the corporation is a fictitious "person" whose existence is virtually limited to pieces of paper and whose responsibility is, to put it politely, problematic. Whatever virtues either of these conceptions of the corporation may have, however, neither has much to do with business life and very little to do with the true nature of corporations. From the inside, corporations are neither impersonal nor irresponsible, and they are certainly not fictitious. They are living communities in which a great many Americans make a home for themselves. Corporations are cultures within which much of our ethics and many of our ways of thinking about ourselves and each other are created and enforced. The ethics of the individual in business will be, sooner or later, for better or for worse, the ethics of the company he or she works for.

As a culture, the corporation encompasses almost every aspect of an individual's waking life, or at least that half of one's waking life that we call "work." Jake Hackworth's corporate culture embitters his entire life; indeed he does not so much "relax" in his own time as hide from his work, and his whole image of himself is bound up in the fact that he hates his job and, like everyone else, fears his boss. Not surprisingly, he often talks about business as a matter of sheer survival and sneers at the very idea of business ethics. Art, by way of contrast, sees his corporation as a gift to the world; "progress" and "service"

SNAPSHOT OF WORKPLACE 2000

Employees of the future will have to be quick-change artists to keep pace with the evolving workplace. These are some of the turnabouts to expect.

• Short-lived assignments. Expect to work on a contract basis or spend time on several project teams.

• Workers will have at least three careers in their lifetime.

• Thirty-hour workweeks.

• Nonprofits: the next career frontier. Corporations and government are going to play an ever-reduced role in terms of jobs.

• Flexible schedules, telecommuting and virtual offices. . . . Companies save money in reduced office space.

• Working at a desk from 9 to 5 will be history for some workers as offices become as close as a computer and modem.

—*Black Enterprise* "Career Issue," February 1996

---

are familiar words in his vocabulary, and, not surprisingly, he looks with pity and disdain at men like Jake, who simply do not understand the importance of what they are doing or are failing to do anything of any importance. What may be surprising is that, on paper, Jake and Art have exactly the same job, but in two very different corporate cultures.

As a culture, the corporation defines not only jobs and roles and rules for proper behavior; it also sets goals and establishes what counts as success. It circumscribes one's most probable circle of friends, both directly, by setting up peer relationships and arranging daily face-to-face introductions, and indirectly, by cultivating characteristic ambitions, aspirations, and expectations as well as the overall sense of competition and cooperation that defines so much of business life and ethics. Although Jake started his career with a naive optimism, he now believes that business is nothing but ruthless competition in which he may be a survivor but never a winner. Art was never naive, but he did know that nothing is accomplished without cooperation. "Winning" is an attitude that he always shares.

Corporations are communities. No matter how much we distinguish our business associates from our friends, it is not coincidental how many of our friends turn out to be in business and in similar businesses, at comparable levels of advancement and with similar goals and values. (It is worth noting that most of Jake's friends are also disgruntled

---

BESIDE THE POINT?

We will not get very far if we try to evaluate corporations morally in terms of the personal character or motivation of the persons who participate in corporate activity, e.g., as managers or employees. I do not subscribe to a conspiracy theory of moral evil and I am quite ready to admit that corporate officers are moral people or at least that they are as likely (or unlikely) to be honest, hardworking, kind, unselfish and patriotic as the rest of us. But whether they are or not is beside the point.

John Ladd (professor and chairman,
Biomedical Ethics Program, Brown University)

---

employees of other tyrannical bosses. They spend a lot of time complaining about the work they are so anxious to forget.)

In a seminar with executives of one well-known corporate culture this year, a significant number of "company men" insisted right from the start—so that there would be no misunderstanding—that they clearly separated their business and personal lives, and therefore also their business acquaintances and their friends. But after the briefest discussion, it became apparent that they all lived in the "corporate ghetto," as they called it, and spent almost all of their time at company-sponsored functions or with other employees of the company. They did not all spend time with the same people they saw at the office during the day, but they saw almost exclusively people at similar stations and with similar responsibilities in parallel sections of the company. Most of their friends "from the outside"—apart from an occasional old college or army drinking buddy—turned out to be in similar corporations and at a similar rank. One would be foolish to generalize from such examples, but corporate cultures set up the network of people and positions with whom we feel comfortable, and given the enormous power of peer pressure in ethics, one should not be surprised that the culture of the corporation—rather than "individual values"—is the primary determinant of business ethics.

CORPORATE ETHICS

> *The corporation must be considered a full-fledged*
> *member of the moral community and a proper*
> *subject of moral blame and credit.*
> Peter French (professor, Trinity University)

Corporations differ widely as cultures, however much the stereotypical portrait of corporations as profit-making institutions makes them seem all the same. The simple difference between the products two companies manufacture and market may already characterize the most enormous differences in corporate cultures and corporate ethical viewpoints. (See, e.g., Terrence Deal and Allan Kennedy, *Corporate Cultures,* 1982.) One company makes detergent and toothpaste and consequently orients almost all of its thinking toward advertising in the domestic market and convincing large proportions of an essentially homogeneous and anonymous public that its products are more desirable than others from which they are indistinguishable. Another company is in the fast-changing computer and electronic-communications business; its orientation, accordingly, is toward innovation and experimentation. It is a culture of change rather than a culture of spreading the word. It is easy to infer how different life in two such cultures will be, including the average age of most members of the cultures and the basis for their security and status within the organizations. It is easy to imagine the differences in the ways employees and managers will treat each other. Different businesses provide different cultures, and different cultures define different values, different ethics, different lives.

It is no secret that morals are watched more closely and so tend to be more orthodox in a small town than in a huge, fast-moving city. So too with corporations. The kind of life that is possible in a small, private corporation of a hundred or fewer employees is utterly impossible in a national or international corporation with tens of thousands of employees. The size of one's circle of friends in the two cases may be comparable, but the range of acquaintances could not be more different. In a small corporation, as in a small village, it is not only not difficult but expected that every person will have some idea of what

CORPORATE CHILD CARE

The Best:

Acuson	Levi Strauss
Apple Computer	Lockheed
AT&T	McKesson
Bank of America	Mervyn's
Chevron	Morrison and Foerster
Citibank	Pacific Gas and Electric
Clorox	Raychem
Hewlett-Packard	Syntax
Kaiser Permanente	Wells Fargo

—*Coleman Advocates for Children and Youth*

THE CULTURE OF CREATIVITY

Akio Morita, chairman of the Sony Corporation, delivered the commencement address at the Wharton Business School. An excerpt follows:

I am not a believer in the idea of a "post-industrial" society. For me the very essence of business, in fact the very foundation of a nation's economy, is manufacturing. Why? Because manufacturing creates. It takes resources and material and by applying knowledge to them creates products. By knowledge I am referring to technology and creativity.

The knowledge and value-added results of manufacturing are products which can provide utility, convenience, and enjoyment to all people— and thus enrich their lives. This is the mission of the manufacturing business. And in this case, my business is Sony.

We strive to succeed at this mission by establishing a supportive corporate culture. An environment where creativity is encouraged, where group dynamics are fostered, and where individuals can find meaning and satisfaction in seeing their efforts blossom into tangible results. This is not unique to Sony, but in many ways, it may be unique to the world of manufacturing.

I know the glamour of Wall Street may be enticing, but I have personally found that the creative, future-oriented, and tangible essence of the manufacturing industry offers substantial opportunities for discovering meaning and purpose. And it offers the chance to reach and enrich the lives of thousands of people you will never know, through the products you create.

WHERE WOULD YOU RATHER WORK?

Compare the following two items, which appeared in *The Wall Street Journal* on the same September day:

Merck

Merck & Co. is marking its centennial with an unusual one-time gift to each of its 37,000 employees: options to buy 100 shares of Merck stock at potentially hefty profits.

How hefty—and how much employees will profit—depends on how much Merck's stock rises in value over the next five to ten years.

Employees, while liable for taxes on gains, could profit handsomely. Assuming a 5 percent annual compound growth in Merck's stock through 1996—yielding a price of $162 a share—an employee who bought and immediately sold 100 shares would then realize a $3,475 profit. At a 20 percent growth rate, or $317 per-share price, the gain after five years would be $18,975. After ten years—with a $788 per-share price, the most optimistic scenario outlined by the company—the profit would be $66,075.

"We need to find ways to get everyone on board in terms of our goals and objectives," said Steven Darien, vice president, human resources.

Food Lion

The United Food and Commercial Workers charged that Food Lion Inc., a supermarket chain operating in the southeast and mid-Atlantic regions, earns a hefty chunk of its profits by illegally paying employees for fewer hours than they actually work.

The UFCW told the Labor Department that it has found violations of federal wage-and-hours law involving 141 Food Lion stores in eighty-eight cities in seven states. It said a conservative estimate is that the company derives $64.6 million in illegal annual savings from "off-the-clock" work. Food Lion had a pretax profit of $284 million in 1990, and its net income was $172 million on sales of $5.6 billion, the UFCW said.

The company, in a prepared statement, called the complaint "simply one more example of the union's attempt to harass and coerce Food Lion management into recognizing the union without regard to the sentiments of our employees."

LAYOFFS AND TRADE-OFFS (PRODUCTIVITY VS. PEOPLE)

	Percent change 1990 to 1995	
	in employees	*in productivity*
Digital Equipment	− 50.2%	+ 82.0%
McDonnell Douglas	− 47.5	+ 43.2
General Electric	− 25.5	+ 38.0
KMart	− 32.4	+ 37.1
GTE	− 31.2	+ 35.3
IBM	− 32.5	+ 32.5
General Motors	− 6.9	+ 23.4
General Dynamics	− 71.7	+ 5.7
Boeing	− 35.1	− 6.6
Sears	− 40.2	− 9.8
10-company total	− 29.1	+ 27.9

—*Business Week*, February 24, 1997

The net gain of 2.1 million jobs from October 1994 to 1995 was substantially less than the almost 3.4 million jobs created during the same period the year before.

—*Black Enterprise*, February 1996

the others are doing. At the same time, there can be a high tolerance for eccentricity—"Oh, that's just the way Joe does things these days." In a larger corporation, as in an urban society, one hears about other segments of the organization—even those that directly impinge on one's own work and are essential to one's very survival—only indirectly, through reports and gossip or memos or, sometimes, through a rather extraordinary effort to "familiarize oneself" with a very different segment of the company. Consequently, outward signs of conformity are considerably more important even if there is also much more room (outside of work) for individual idiosyncrasies. In a small company, ethics is just a matter of living together. In the larger corporation, ethics becomes mainly a function of management. This is *not* to say that small businesses are always more ethical. It is to say that matters of ethics in a small business are much like personal ethics—matters of personality. (A small business tends to be nasty or nice in much the same way that individuals are nasty or nice, and one deals with them in much the same ways.) A large corporation, on the other hand, may be populated entirely with morally upstanding personnel and yet have an ethics problem. In impersonality there is always the danger that

---

FIVE KEYS TO CORPORATE ETHICS

to employees	fairness
to consumers	quality
to suppliers	dependability
to superiors	trustworthiness
to the community	responsibility

---

ethics will degenerate into a set of abstract rules rather than remain a living community of interpersonal relations, and abstract rules can too easily be compromised (or reinterpreted) under the pressures of the corporate hierarchy.

But size isn't everything. The same differences appear between relatively large corporations. An international giant like ITT (368,000 employees worldwide) not surprisingly places an enormous amount of emphasis on the importance of hierarchies of power and responsibility, whereas the somewhat smaller 3M Corporation (87,000) is much more concerned with internal coherence and corporate loyalty. Thomas Watson, Sr., ran giant IBM on the model of a family, and it is not unusual to find a "small" business of only a few dozen employees run as impersonally and as hierarchically as one of the giant corporations. An enormous corporation may be broken up into small units that give it the corporate culture of a small village, perhaps even a sense of intimacy, like those global Japanese companies that divide up their staff in "quality circles," each of them assigned its own project and within which the relationships are completely personal.

In his book *Corporation Man* Anthony Jay suggests the tantalizing "sociobiological" thesis that the ideal group size for any human organization—built right into our genes—is about twenty-five to thirty, the same size as a small primitive tribe or hunting group. This makes possible maximum group solidarity and flexibility at the same time. Of course, very few businesses could afford to operate on this small a scale, but Jay's hypothesis does suggest that within any business there will be a "natural" size of organization into which (if evolution has time to work within corporations) groups of employees will tend to cluster for maximum effectiveness and, we can add, maximum ethical awareness. But this means that, first of all, there may be many corporate cultures within a single corporation and, second, that a corporate culture and its ethics may depend upon whether the organi-

CULTURAL HEROES

America's boardrooms need heroes more than Hollywood's box offices need them. Heroism is a leadership component that is all but forgotten by modern management. Since the 1920s, the corporate world has been powered by managers who are rationalists, who do strategic planning, write memos and devise flow charts. But we are not talking about good "scientific" managers here. Managers run institutions; heroes create them. . . .

Companies with strong cultures are quite adept at recognizing and creating situational heroes. Many place their potential candidates in bellwether jobs—certain critical positions that epitomize what the core of the culture is all about.

When people know what the hero-making jobs are, they're energized. They know what's expected of them; they're free to be innovative. And over a period of time, the company becomes more innovative.

Employees don't have to be leaders or young Turks to win the rewards of heroism. Strong-culture companies create heroes throughout the corporation. The following line from IBM's house organ, "Think," is a case in point: "All those happy faces, you'd think he was the Prince carrying the glass slipper to Cinderella, when in fact he's dropping off a Selectric that the customer recently ordered." Yet this line anoints salesman Joe McClosky a hero for being a 30-year member of the company's highly honored Hundred Percent Club. The trick? IBM deliberately sets their sales quotas so that roughly 80 percent of the force makes the club.

Terrence E. Deal and Allan A. Kennedy,
Corporate Cultures

zation of the corporation makes possible or impossible groups approaching this ideal size. When an employee has a sense of belonging to a small community, even a giant corporation has an effective medium for instilling and enforcing its values. When an employee feels isolated and anonymous, even in a small company, he or she can too easily adopt the Darwinian "survivor" mentality and poison the entire ethical atmosphere.

CORPORATE CULTURE AND ETHICS CHECKLIST

	Yes	No
Is your company		
friendly	—	—
proud of its products or services	—	—
comfortable and personal (whatever the size)	—	—
anonymous and impersonal (whatever the size)	—	—
proud of its reputation	—	—
concerned with only an elite clientele	—	—
concerned with the mass market	—	—
fearful	—	—
fair in promotions, salaries, firing	—	—

	Yes	No
Does your company		
trust its employees	—	—
have a company hero (who?)	—	—
have a corporate hierarchy (how formal and rigid?)	—	—
encourage aggressiveness	—	—

	Yes	*No*
condone "cutthroat" competition	——	——
condone "cutting corners"	——	——

	Yes	*No*
Do you (or fellow employees)		
feel as though you're being watched all the time	——	——
trust the company	——	——
trust the competence of those at the top	——	——
trust the decisions made from the top	——	——
trust the decisions made below you	——	——
feel equal in dignity to those above you	——	——
feel equal in dignity to those below you	——	——
feel that ethics is an explicit concern of those around you	——	——
feel that ethics is an explicit concern of those above you	——	——
feel there is unethical behavior that "goes on all the time" around you	——	——

ENDS, MEANS, AND METHODS: THE RATIONALITY OF BUSINESS

> *Productivity should be the servant of humanity and not its master.*
> William Gomberg (emeritus professor of management, The Wharton School)

Fred M. knew that his division had fallen short of its stated goals by almost half a million dollars. He could not stand the thought of a reprimand and the probable loss of a small promotion he had been expecting. By a bit of creative accounting, he presented a report that, on paper, gave the division a small profit. His career would have been saved, perhaps would even have prospered, if it hadn't been for those damned auditors. But what was most infuriating was the attitude of his superior, who told him after the hearing that the company would certainly have forgiven a yearly loss but could not possibly forgive his unethical behavior.

Sally K., on the other hand, was recognized by everyone she worked with as a conscientious, unerringly ethical worker. Indeed Sally was a perfectionist, and whatever task she tackled would assuredly receive more attention than any other task or project in the department. The problem was that Sally's tasks were always so thoroughly perfected that the projects themselves were almost always late and often over budget. The department did poorly, despite the fact that everyone recognized its internal excellence. And Sally, we might note, was never very satisfied with her job, herself, or the people around her.

Business life is a hierarchy of objectives, goals, and strategies. A company seeks to make a profit for its owners, to build a new parking lot, to cut back on paperwork and improve its accounting department, to make sure that this year's Christmas party is not like the last one. An individual working for the company takes on the goals of the company, but he or she also has a large number of personal goals, objectives, and strategies: to keep one's job, to get promoted, to get to lunch before the noon rush, to come back with an equally cutting comment to the wise guy across the hall, to get along better with the secretary, to please one's superiors, to be respected by one's subordinates, to enjoy one's work, and, last but by no means least, to live well and not have one's life wholly absorbed by the demands of one's job. Not all of these objectives and goals are of the same magnitude of importance.

Most of human action consists of *means, ends,* and *methods.* Goals and objectives are *ends,* the intended and desired results of an action. Within any practice, there are also specified means to achieve those ends. One scores a point in soccer by kicking the ball; one scores a hit in baseball by hitting the ball with a stick. Many ends will be means to further ends—getting a hit in order to bring in a run in order to win the game in order to win the pennant. In addition to the particular actions that are the means to an end, there are also systematic *methods* that tie these means together—strategies, tactics, techniques, and general patterns of behavior, including habits, rituals, and emotional attachments. Ends, means, and methods do not exist in a vacuum, however; they are rather precisely specified as part of an ethical practice. Fred M. was one of those business casualties who saw only the immediate end and lost sight of both his own and the company's larger goals and standards. Sally K. displayed a more subtle form or bad business strategy: She focused so intently on the means that she lost sight of the ultimate ends of her projects.

Ethics, we can say, is the adoption of the right methods and means toward the right ends.

There are correct and incorrect means. Gaining a market with higher-quality and lower-cost products is the exemplary means of getting ahead in business. Gaining a market through extortion and trickery is not. There are right and wrong methods in business. Being smarter, working harder, and being one step ahead of everyone else is ideal. Stealing ideas, putting off one's creditors, deceiving consumers, and using underpaid immigrant labor is not.

There are also correct and incorrect ends. Trying to make a profit to expand the plant and to make production more efficient, to pay the stockholders who have waited patiently for a dividend, and to give the local community employment and prosperity is to work for indisputably right ends. Trying to capture the market to put one's brother-in-law out of business is not.

Just as a miser comes to confuse the means of wealth (money) as the end, it is all too easy for a business to confuse the means to further investment (profits) with the end (prosperity, the well-being of everyone in the company, further development and improvement). A very common mistake is the elevation of stockholder satisfaction to ultimate end, when in fact it is a means for most companies. "Perfectionism" is often a problem of excessive attention to means, losing sight of the end. Maccoby's "gamesman" threatens a company with a parallel error: getting so caught up in the methods of doing business that the ultimate goals of the company are sacrificed.

The distinction among ends, means, and methods allows us to make three other distinctions that are equally important to business ethics:

1. OBJECTIVES, GOALS, ULTIMATE GOALS. Not all ends are of equal importance. An immediate end is an *objective;* it is limited, a means to further ends. The *goal* is the larger end. The immediate objective of a play in football is to reach the forty-yard line; the goal, of course, is to score a touchdown. The *ultimate goal* is to win the game. "Management by objectives" works only if the objectives are coordinated toward the goal in question. Profit, we might add once again, is virtually never the ultimate goal but rather one of several essential intermediate goals in business.

2. TASK, JOB, CAREER. The critical function of ethics in business is keeping the larger perspective in view. Most of one's day—at every level of the corporate hierarchy—is spent doing particular *tasks,* from returning a phone call to negotiating a contract with an important client. A task is a specific result to be achieved through a narrow range of means. Several (usually many) tasks together make up one's *job*. A job is defined by the larger set of goals and objectives that give the specific tasks meaning. Jobs, however, are also limited and rather specific. Good jobs are part of a *career*. A "dead-end job" is one that doesn't lead to a career. A "meaningless" or "irrelevant" task is one that has little to do with one's job.

3. POINT, PURPOSE, AND POSSIBILITIES. Every practice has its point and every profession its purpose. The *point* and *purpose* of business is making a profit through productivity. But the rules of every practice allow room for many activities that, though they do not serve (and many even encounter) the point of the practice, nevertheless are permitted. Hostile takeovers and "unfriendly acquisitions," still in the news these days, are (for now) permitted when antitrust considerations are not involved. Men who make millions from these dramatic corporate battles describe themselves as champions of free enterprise. But there is an essential distinction between the *point* of free enterprise and what freedom

of enterprise *allows*. Freedom of speech allows the *possibility* of pornography, but that is hardly the point or the purpose of that freedom.

Good business requires a perspective of means and ends. A good example of the loss of that perspective is in the movie *Bridge on the River Kwai:* The ultimate goal of the British officer (played by Alec Guinness) is to do his part in winning the war against the Japanese. His immediate objective, while a prisoner of war, is to keep his men as healthy as possible, and his means for doing that is to keep them busy building a bridge for the Japanese. But the goal of building the bridge becomes so important to him that when the Allies come to bomb the bridge, he loses all perspective and tries (unsuccessfully) to stop them. So, too, an unfortunate number of businessmen, who truly love their jobs, make the mistake of getting so caught up in tasks and objectives that they lose sight of the goal, and of their careers.

Getting Straight: Ends and Means
(5 = ultimate end, 1 = mere means, 0 = not relevant)

_____ wealth
_____ power
_____ respect and friendship
_____ independence and freedom to do what I want
_____ a happy family
_____ my own happiness
_____ pleasure
_____ an exciting life; adventure
_____ inner peace
_____ a comfortable life
_____ eternal salvation
_____ self-esteem
_____ admiration
_____ wisdom
_____ love
_____ a sense of accomplishment
_____ doing something for my community
_____ doing something for my country
_____ improving chances for world peace and prosperity

Rank the following goals for your company:
_____ please the stockholders (high profits)
_____ make the employees happy
_____ have a good reputation
_____ keep management jobs secure (well paid)
_____ quality products/services

ETHICS, EFFICIENCY, AND EFFECTIVENESS

Success is a matter of means and ends. But in any chain of ends and means of any significant length or complexity, it is possible to fail to meet one's goal even though—even because—one succeeds in the smaller tasks and objectives that are aimed at that goal.

The managerial name for clarity about ends and means is *effectiveness*. Effectiveness is getting done what one wants to get done. It is to be distinguished from *efficiency*, which is often confused with effectiveness. Efficiency is the elimination of waste, but as such it is the limited achievement of subordinate ends. An administrator may be extremely efficient in terms of getting the paperwork through his office, but such efficiency is not commendable if nothing else gets accomplished as a result. A manager may be extremely efficient through the use of threats and force with his subordinates, but resentment and timidity may well make the department wholly ineffective. What makes efficiency dangerous is that it so often looks impressive, since it has to do with relatively short-term and limited goals that are easy to measure. But success depends on effectiveness, and effectiveness may be long-term and harder to measure by the moment.

Effectiveness is what the business world is all about. Efficiency, we might add, is an overvalued and often much misunderstood virtue, for what improves efficiency may often—and subtly—undermine the effectiveness of an organization. One neglected example is the popular

In Japan, we tend to think of a business as something that really should go on regardless of short-term performance—not as something to be thrown away or shut down because of temporary difficulties. . . . We learned a great deal about systematic long-range planning from American business, and yet we often feel that in the management of businesses the Japanese have a longer-term orientation than Americans have.

Yotaro Kobayashi (*Fuji Xerox*, Japan)

complaint about *meetings*, almost always number one on the list of activities that are a "waste of time." It is true that meetings are almost always—by their very nature—inefficient and filled with seemingly aimless chattering that interferes with the nagging tasks waiting for everyone back in his or her own office. In terms of office efficiency, meetings are indeed a waste of time. But what meetings do—however hard it is to appreciate this in the midst of one—is to force familiarity and contact, or confrontation, among people who are working together. Meetings reinforce a sense of teamwork and camaraderie. Meetings air suppressed tensions and disagreements—in style as well as substance. Meetings humanize the workplace and remind us that humans are not in fact defined by their efficiency.

Meetings, in other words, make an organization more effective but with an intentional sacrifice in efficiency. Meetings are a necessary communal activity that breaks down isolation in a company and gives social significance to work relationships. This is why "efficiently run" meetings, however welcome at the moment, may be a long-term liability, and it is why, whatever the charm and efficiency of the "One-Minute Manager," that little parable remains a parable—and nothing more. A one-minute reprimand may make an unpleasant managerial task more palatable, but there is no substitute for "quality" time spent with your employees.

Large corporations are not generally known for their efficiency; nor should they be. Milton Friedman has often attacked government inefficiency. But John Kenneth Galbraith, comparing his own work in government with his time at *Time* magazine, comments that there is no question in his mind that *Time* was the less efficient organization. Inefficient organizations are not necessarily ineffective, however, and the larger the organization, the more room for inefficiency may be necessary for maximum effectivness. This is no small point in under-

THE BASIC PHILOSOPHY

Things have certainly changed since that first convenience store opened in 1927, but our philosophy, the foundation on which the industry was built, has not changed. It's all built around service—giving the customers what they want, when and where they want it.

Jodie Thompson (senior executive vice president,
Dallas, Southland Corporation, "7-Eleven")

Computers spew out production reports and sales figures hourly. And managers eat them up.

Investors hunger for bigger dividends and faster earnings growth.

No matter what the economy, much of American business continues to feast on short-term results. Expecting profits to be served up like fast-food burgers. And economic solutions dished out like instant pudding.

Right now we believe all of us must work to correct a fundamental flaw in the way American business is operating. Short-term results cannot be allowed to become our only criterion for success. Investors must be willing to relax some of the pressure on managers to produce immediate results. Managers must be given more security to make long-term investment decisions.

In turn, those in management must be prepared to make long-term commitments to invest in innovation—in new products and new technologies. And at the same time, to make long-range plans to restore our older industries to full strength.

From an advertisement for W. R. Grace Co.

---

standing corporate ethics. A company that demands maximum efficiency may be inviting unethical behavior, by isolating component departments and goals, by sacrificing the inefficient "socializing" that creates team spirit and cooperation. On the other hand, a company that emphasizes only effectiveness without any attention to efficiency may well lose the coordination and the organization that holds its parts together.

Overcoming the myth of efficiency is perhaps one of the most important demands of business ethics. A manager who bullies his or her subordinates and takes pride in "discipline" may make an impressive show of departmental efficiency, but long-term effectiveness will virtually always suffer. Worse, it is in such "efficient" environments that business ethics is often sacrificed to the more immediate fears of a firing or a reprimand. Effectiveness, on the other hand, typically involves considerable understanding and slack—room for an employee to have a bad day, to fail, to complain, just to talk and gossip and to feel that he or she is working *with* and *for* the company rather than (in his or her own mind) *against* it.

Efficiency is a means; effectiveness is the end. Every efficiency measure should face the following test:

How efficiently does this have to be done to achieve our overall goals and objectives? Does efficiency (for example, no "wasted" meetings, no long lunches, no hanging out at the water cooler) actually interfere with the morale of the company and, consequently, its long-term effectiveness?

AS EASY AS X, Y, Z: THE MEANING OF MANAGEMENT

> *[The Manager] is like a symphony orchestra conductor, endeavoring to maintain a melodious performance in which the contributions of the various instruments are coordinated and sequenced, patterned and paced, while the orchestra members are having various personal difficulties, stage hands are moving music stands, alternating excessive heat and cold are creating audience and instrument problems, and the sponsor of the concert is insisting on irrational changes in the program.*
> Leonard R. Sayles (professor of management, Columbia University)

The current emphasis on management "science"—in one minute or more—has tended to obscure the basic fact that management is a relationship among people. For the manager, management is getting

MINTZBERG'S LIST OF MANAGERIAL ROLES

Figurehead (representing the department or the company)

Leader (hiring, training, motivating, approving and disapproving, rewarding and punishing, setting the standard)

Liaison (making contacts above and below, keeping the chain of command intact)

Monitor (collecting information, editing gossip and speculation)

Disseminator (passing on information)

Spokesman (giving information outside, "making a case" for the company, advising stockholders and government)

Entrepreneur (improving and changing the company)

Disturbance handler (confronting disgruntled employees, averting strikes, handling irate customers and suppliers)

Resource allocation (deciding who will get what)

Negotiator (working out deals with customers, suppliers, unions, etc.)

others to do what you want them to do and what the company expects them to do. As such, management is an intrinsically ethical enterprise. The question is not only *what* to get people to do but *how* to get them to do it. And answering this latter question goes deep into questions about ethics and attitudes as well as into questions of motivational psychology and the nature of "human nature."

Henry Mintzberg has studied managerial roles, with an eye to dispelling the heroic image of the manager as orchestra leader. He has delineated at least ten different roles, few of them as glamorous as the manager-as-hero image promoted by Peter Drucker and others (in the neoheroic "managerial revolution"). But what is also evident in Mintzberg's study is that the manager is also the ethical nerve center of an organization. Policy may come from the top, but day-to-day questions of fairness and mutual consideration within the company lie within the province of middle management.

Note that virtually all of these involve distinctively ethical decisions and concerns. The ethical stature, image, and policies of the head of a department or company set the tone for the activities and the pressures on everyone else. A leader who insists on results "no matter what" inevitably encourages corner cutting below, whereas a leader who insists on integrity gives ample opening for any manager or employee who is disturbed by questionable conduct within the company. Handling information is not just a matter-of-fact role; it is also deciding

---

THE MEANING OF WORK

Work is still the complicated and crucial core of most lives, the occupation melded inseparably to the identity; Freud said that the successful psyche is one capable of love and of work. Work is the most thorough and profound organizing principle in American life. If mobility has weakened old blood ties, our coworkers often form our new family, our tribe, our social world; we become almost citizens of our companies, living under the protection of salaries, pensions, and health insurance. Sociologist Robert Schrank believes that people like jobs mainly because they need other people; they need to gossip with them, hang out with them, to schmooze. Says Schrank: "The workplace performs the function of community."

Lance Morrow, *Time*

---

who should know what, and who should not. Handling disturbances, allocating resources, and negotiating are explicitly ethical roles that are rules by the question of fairness.

One cannot be a manager at all without being concerned every day with ethics. If a person wants to avoid making value judgments, he or she has no role in management. Management is setting and enforcing the ethical policies of a company.

Theories of management tend to emphasize motivation, but every theory of management is also a theory of ethics. In other words, adopting an approach to one's employees is not only working on a certain model of what makes people work (or not); it is endorsing and to a certain extent *creating* a situation in which everyone has expectations, demands, and, when it goes wrong, disappointment or resentment.

Consider the now well-established and cleverly named theories of work called "X," "Y," and "Z." Theory X asserts that people are basically lazy and will not work unless tempted by rewards and threatened with punishments—including, of course, the loss of the job. Theory Y counters that people want to work and want to assume responsibilities. Theory Z, formulated by William Ouchi as a way of characterizing the much-touted success of Japanese industry, does not stress individual rewards or punishments or some innate desire to work. Instead, it emphasizes membership in the group, and working hard becomes more a matter of team spirit than of individual motivation.

THE ETHICS OF PRODUCTIVITY

The real cause of the commitment gap lies not with the new cultural value or with an erosion of the work ethic, but with a striking failure of managers to support and reinforce the work ethic. This means that practical solutions are possible.
                    Daniel Yankelovich and John Immerwahr,
                    Putting the Work Ethic to Work

1. Reduce disincentives. Put justice to work. *Reward* extra effort. Seventy-three percent of the work force say that the quality and effort they put into their job has very little to do with what they are paid (72 percent say they want to do the best job possible, regardless of pay).

2. Distinguish between factors that enhance job effectiveness and those that increase job satisfaction. Some factors may make a job more agreeable but not make people want to work harder or better. But also emphasize the "soft" factors of productivity—dedication, commitment, creativity, responsibility, quality, entrepreneurship. They can't be measured, but the company or the manager that ignores them will in fact have less to measure.

3. Enforce high standards of quality. Nothing corrodes the work ethic more than the perception that employers and managers are indifferent to quality.

4. Flatten the hierarchy! This is the most important, most radical, and most difficult part of the solution. Traditional organizations give the strong impression that individual job holders are less central to the success of the enterprise than are the managers. Indeed, the recent "managerial revolution" often underscores this impression, that the corporate culture is ultimately a managerial culture. So why are workers not committed? The less the distance between workers and management, the more that workers will share in the goals of management. The more isolated the middle manager, the more likely he or she is to subvert productivity instead of enhancing it.

Adapted from *Putting the Work Ethic to Work*

But the following should be evident even in this crude characterization of these three theories:

1. They are not just theories about the "way we are" but approaches to management that *create the conditions that they describe.* A company that offers large rewards and threatens firing as a punishment will set up an atmosphere of individual ambition and

---

FAMILY MANAGEMENT

HDL Publishing Company of Los Angeles has released *Mafia Management*, a book "for executives in legitimate businesses who might improve the way they manage their organizations by studying the Mafia." It costs $59.95.

—*The Progressive*, March 1990

---

fear, inevitably causing competition and resentment and inspiring workers to do no more than they have to in order to get a desired and plausible reward and avoid getting fired. A company that treats work and responsibility as in themselves desirable will attract people who feel that way (and lose the others). A company that runs on team spirit will attract team-minded employees, but it will also tend to build just that form of community in which everyone reinforces everyone else and personal accomplishment becomes one with group achievement.

2. They are not just theories about the way people are but theories about the way they *ought* to be. In other words, to adopt a theory of management is to embrace an ethics. We aren't talking about "science"; we are talking about the kinds of people we want to work with and the kind of place we want to work in. Management theories reinforce the attitudes we like and dislike—and establish the basic ethical foundation from which the rest of our decisions and policies must follow.

PRESSURES AND PYRAMIDS: AUTHORITY AND AUTONOMY

No one in business is unethical without a reason. One finds occasional spite and perversity in business, as anywhere, and every once in a while a monster appears who is truly malevolent. But even greed is a relatively rare motive for unethical behavior, not because people aren't greedy but rather because, perhaps fortunately, most of us rarely have the opportunity to be truly greedy. Unethical behavior is typically a response to pressure—the pressure of unreasonable demands, the pressure of overwhelming competition, the pressure of a demanding boss or board of directors, the pressure of an impending investigation or bankruptcy. The primary way to prevent unethical behavior, therefore, is to understand and if possible reduce such pressures, but in any case to make sure that the most likely response to pressure is not to throw ethics to the winds.

The likeliest victim of corporate pressure is the man or woman in the middle, pressed from above for results, sufficiently anonymous to believe that no one will pay attention to the means, sufficiently powerful to pull it off, sufficiently frustrated and perhaps embittered to be heedless. Middle managers are rarely the authors of their own projects or ethical policies. It is an unusual manager who can effectively challenge imposed expectations as unreasonable or who can take the initiative in imposing his or her own set of ethical standards on a department. Indeed it is an exceptional manager who is able or willing to resist unethical demands or ethical indifference from above and insist on his or her own moral standards. ("When you accepted this position, you should have known that you might have to. . . .")

The most visible behavior is, quite naturally, where the power is— which is why ethics is always an issue at the top of the organization. The most common unethical behavior is therefore in the middle, where it is virtually invisible outside the company and where its effects are— usually—modest, easily contained and hard to pin down. But we can understand why this is so if we look at the two key factors in ethical responsibility: *authority* and *autonomy*.

Authority is established and accepted power, power legitimized by the company. It is the person in authority who can get things done, who is responsible, and who deserves (and often even receives) the praise or blame due for projects well or improperly completed. Where authority is not clear (because power is not clearly legitimate, or because it is not clear who has it), responsibility is in question. Where responsibility is in question, ethics is endangered. The worst case, accordingly, is where a manager or an executive has a responsibility without the authority to get it done. This rarely happens at the top (or it wouldn't be the top), but it often happens in the middle, where lines of authority and responsibility are not always coordinated, where a person can feel pressure impersonally applied without having the

---

STRESS AND ETHICS

What makes an ethical executive tick? Nobody knows for sure, but
London House thinks they may be happier, less tense, and more responsible than people who are more willing to tolerate unethical behavior.

The consulting company tested 111 executives, middle managers, and
professionals attending seminars the past two summers at the University
of Chicago. The most striking finding: The more emotionally healthy the
executives, as measured on a battery of tests, the more likely they were
to score high on the ethics test. High-ethics executives were also less
likely to feel hostility, anxiety, and fear. The matter needs further study,
says London House researcher Alan Nerad.

—*The Wall Street Journal*, April 11, 1991

---

power to do what must be done. Responsibility without authority is a
sure-lose situation for a manager. Authority without responsibility, on
the other hand, is a surefire recipe for department tyranny and ineffectiveness.

Autonomy, on the other hand, means independence, regardless of a
person's role in the corporate hierarchy. In a strict moral sense, the
lowliest employee is just as autonomous as the chief executive officer,
because either of them can say "No!" if necessary, though at considerably different personal cost. But in a practical sense, autonomy
varies enormously in every organization, and in ethics as in budgets
most people are severely restricted in their ability to make decisions.
A middle manager suffers not only from considerable uncertainty
concerning autonomy. Ambiguous authority makes it more likely that
a middle manager will feel forced to use what power he or she has
unethically, in desperation. Uncertain autonomy makes it less likely
that a middle manager will feel capable or willing to challenge unreasonable or unethical pressures.

In any position with status and responsibility, pressure is the stuff
of the job—as long as it is *reasonable* pressure. Authority is necessary
to get the job done, but it must be *real* authority, not just its appearance. Autonomy is essential not only to prevent stifling rigidity in the
organization but also to allow for independent decision making when
it may be most necessary: in the midst of a middle-management crisis.
An ethical problem may emerge in a single act or set of acts in the
middle of the organization, but the real problem is probably in the
structure of the company as a whole. There is not enough authority

Relations with superiors are the primary category of ethical conflict. Respondents frequently complained of superior's pressure to support incorrect views, sign false documents, overlook superiors' wrongdoing, and do business with superiors' friends.

Brenner and Molander, *Harvard Business Review*

where there is responsibility, or there is not enough autonomy where there is authority. Pressures in business distort both means and motives. And though these pressures may manifest themselves in the middle, the responsibility—and the ultimate authority and autonomy—are always at the top.

What can be done about excessive pressures that lead to unethical behavior? One can hire employees and managers on the basis of their ability to stand up to pressure without bending the rules, but this is only part of the story. It is part of the executive's job to see that pressure is not unreasonable, or he or she may be to blame for the inevitable excuse. ("If I was going to make the quota, I had no choice but to. . . .") Chief executives may also be responsible for insufficient moral guidance, which can be as relatively innocent as preoccupation with other matters or failure to provide an explicit policy or code of ethics (see the next chapter) or as incriminating as the explicit announcement "I don't want to know and I don't care how it gets done, so long as it gets done." Then there is the undeniable responsibility that is sometimes so embarrassingly evident at the top (for example, once a newspaper story breaks), whether it consists of setting a bad example or explicitly (or implicitly, but unmistakably) ordering unethical behavior. Then, of course, there is no doubt whom to blame.

Responding to Pressure

1. Can you envision a possible or probable situation in your present position where you would be forced to compromise your ethical values? (Are you in one now?)
2. How could such a situation be corrected to your satisfaction?
3. What could you do?
4. What is the point at which you would threaten to quit?
5. Would you at any point turn against the company (go to the media, to the government, to a competitor)?

LOST IN THE CORPORATION: MORAL MAZES

> *What is right in the corporation is not what is right in a man's home or in his church. What is right in the corporation is what the guy above you wants from you. That's what morality is in the corporation.*
>
> —*Robert Jackall,* Moral Mazes

Every member of the corporate community—especially the CEO—knows about pressure and the compromises and sacrifices it engenders, but usually, in all but the worst corporations, our view of the moral horizon is not entirely blocked. We still know the difference between right and wrong, and we can still see our way between ethics and corporate duties. There are some reasonable people, if not just above us then somewhere above them. There is still some flexibility in the company, and there are those people to talk to. There seems to be some way of maintaining our integrity and doing what we have to do. (If none of the above is true, then by all means *start looking for another job!*) Nevertheless, even in some of the best corporations the pressures can be such and the road to success can be so convoluted that we encounter the familiar phenomenon documented in detail by Robert Jackall in his book *Moral Mazes* (New York: Oxford University Press, 1988). Our view of the moral horizon is indeed blocked. Our access to our own integrity is restricted. Jackall writes (quoting an unnamed vice president), "What is right in the corporation is what the guy above you wants from you." One loses one's moral compass. Jackall goes on, "Bureaucracy breaks apart the ownership of property from its control, social independence from occupation, substance from appearances, action from responsibility, obligation from guilt, language from meaning, and notions of truth from reality." In place of morality and merit, "bureaucracy makes its own internal rules and social context the principle moral gauges for action."

No one can deny the familiarity of this sense of frustration and humiliation. Luckily, relatively few corporations put such pressures on their employees and managers much of the time; those that do are usually condemned to failure. (We must always allow exceptions for a few "business scum." As long as there are unemployment lines there will always be unethical and exploitative companies that take advantage of them.) But in the big picture, Jackall ultimately makes too much of this clash between morality and corporate politics. To be sure, clashes and conflicts are inevitable in any company of any size, but only once in a while will or can these clashes be so bold an affront to morals as such. More often, they demand compromise, negotiation, and sometimes some threats or pleading. Jackall concludes, "In such a world, notions of fairness or equity that managers might privately hold, as measures gauging the worth of their own work, become merely quaint," and it [the corporation] is "a society where morality becomes indistinguishable from the quest for one's own survival and advantage."

It should be obvious by now that I reject this gloomy portrait of the corporation, but without denying the pressures and the sometimes unreasonable behavior that bring about such perceptions. Jackall fails to appreciate both the multitude of ethical styles and the importance of compromise and negotiation rather than purity in ethics. As Tom Peters has said, "a 'pure' ethical stance in the face of most firms' political behavior will lead you out the door in short order. . . . The line between ethical purity and arrogant eccentricity is a fine one." To be sure, there may be no easy deciding between integrity and the duties of one's job or position, but the truth is that the conflict is mapped in shades of gray (or overlapping colors) rather than black and white. This may be a painful realization, but the search for a perfect world is futile—and not only in the corporation. One does the best with what one has, but maintaining ethical ideals in the face of pressure is nonetheless essential. Not only institutions but people are naturally flawed. What, after all, were all of those Greek tragedies about? But it is simply not true, except in exceptionally unfortunate cases, that there are "no intrinsic connections between the good of a particular corporation, the good of an individual manager, and the common weal."

There is no reason to retreat in desperation, pretend a false and ultimately self-defeating sense of integrity or, worse, encourage total absorption in one's company or community role so as to be incapable of seeing beyond it and its failings. The twin answers to the problem of "moral mazes" are judgment and integrity, which mean, among other things, keeping the big picture in mind and having the courage, when need be, to speak up for what one believes. For the corporation itself, the answer is an open line of communication, a clear set of values, and the behavior to exemplify them (often summarized today in the cute phrase "walk the talk.") But, going from the other direction, exemplary behavior on the part of upper management is not enough unless everyone else in the pyramid knows what is going on. Accordingly, one way to break up the moral mazes and keep the ethical hallways obvious and accessible is to have a corporate code of ethics.[1]

CORPORATE CODES OF ETHICS

Regarding corporate policy manuals, former Avis chairman and popular iconoclast Robert Townsend suggests, "Don't bother. If they're general, they're useless. If they're specific, they're how-to manuals—expensive to prepare and revise." The exception, however, seems to be in the area of ethics. Townsend concludes: "If you have to have a policy manual, publish the Ten Commandments."

The Ten Commandments may be the ultimate corporate code, if only because their authority—unlike the temporal decree of some senior VP—is undeniable. Corporate codes are important to business ethics because they provide visible guidelines and a court of appeal. An employee or a manager squeezed from above has a place to look for guidance and, if necessary, an indisputable reason (*within* the company) for rejecting an unethical request: "I'm sorry, but it's against company policy." Of course, the act might well be unethical quite aside from the company guidelines, but it is not always easy or possible for a subordinate to turn to his superior and enforce his own sense of morals. "It's company policy" solves that problem without awkwardness or danger to the subordinate and without unnecessary embarrassment to his superior.

Corporate codes of ethics are not just decoration, and they are not

1. Material in this section has been adapted from my essay, "Corporate Roles, Personal Virtues, Moral Mazes," in *Business Ethics and the Law,* C. Coady, ed., Federation Press, Australia, and from *Above the Bottom Line,* 2nd edition.

IN THE MUTUAL FUNDS INDUSTRY

It's illegal, but profitable, for a mutual funds manager to trade with advance knowledge of a fund's buying or selling plans. Personal integrity—plus, perhaps, fear of the Securities and Exchange Commission (SEC) and jail sentences—serves a generally reliable preventative. But a fund's best fraud fighter is its code of ethics. The code of ethics is no mere set of grandiose principles that mutual fund managers tack up on their walls. It's a legal document written by each fund company that spells out the rules for portfolio managers' personal trades. It's the heart of a mutual fund's self-policing system.

So far, the funds' ethics codes have worked well. Relatively few front-running cases have been uncovered. But ultimately, a fund group's honesty depends on the people it hires. Even the strictest code of ethics can't regulate unbridled larceny, nor can the SEC.

—*Kiplinger's Personal Finance Magazine,* April 1994

---

just directives for the lowliest employees, lessons in business etiquette for shipping clerks and secretaries. Even the CEO can turn to the board of directors and say, "That would violate our code of ethics." A clerk or secretary can thereby be empowered by the company as a whole to resist an unethical offer from even the most powerful customer or supplier, and the middle manager caught in a squeeze can find in the code not only an excuse but an opportunity to make a show of his or her autonomy and sense of responsibility even without the necessary authority. A code of ethics also provides an unchallengeable basis for firing an unethical employee, even when his or her action is not, strictly speaking, against either the law or the specific terms of the job.

Codes of ethics provide an important kind of stability to an organization. They protect middle managers and executives alike from the pressures of the market, which—however valuable in inspiring a sense of competition—tend to incite desperation and unethical behavior. A code of ethics can make gray areas clear, for example, by simply specifying that no employee may accept from a client gifts worth more than $50. The amount may seem arbitrary (one might still ponder the acceptibility of two $27 football tickets), but it eliminates a range of dilemmas to which there might otherwise be no clear answer.

What goes into a code of ethics? The Ten Commandments (or at least most of them) might be a good beginning, but obviously a code

INTERVIEW WITH DAVID R. CLARE, PRESIDENT, JOHNSON & JOHNSON (in *The Corporate Conscience*, 1985)

CC: Since you brought up Tylenol and that's sort of the most eventful, most famous development in the recent history of J&J, I'd like to ask a little bit about some of the ethical challenges that you faced there, the choices you could have made within the limits of the law, the choices that you chose to make out of a sense of public responsibility. Could you characterize, first, the climate of the time?

CLARE: The reporter called from Chicago saying, "What's going on?" The climate was one of sheer unbelieving that this had happened: shock, absolute unhappiness associated with the obvious fact that people were dying, that they were dying potentially through the use of one of our products and we just didn't know what had happened. We did not know how extensive it was, what the cause was, what the problem was in any dimension. It appeared to be localized, but we weren't sure. So one of the immediate dilemmas—if you may remember the first instance—we started recalling batches of product. . . . But then we found that the products, the packages implicated, were produced at two different plants in two different states, so that the batch recall was an inappropriate response. So the key decision, the first decision, was how far do we go? And we were in an ethical dilemma from the standpoint that at least there were those who were arguing that you should not withdraw, because all you're going to do is demonstrate to some sick individual that they can have a major nationwide impact on a major product through their individual action at some locality. So there was the argument: "We should not withdraw. You're going to enhance the copycats. You're going to enhance the process of adulterating a product for the copycats." And that was discussed for a period of about forty-eight to seventy-two hours as we argued out: "What was the right thing to do?" And [we] finally came down on the side [that] there was no choice from our standpoint. We had to act to protect the public, whether it was more widespread than it appeared to be or whether it was a condition that could be repeated by other copycats using our product. So the first and foremost, we had to protect the public.

CC: The cynical listener might wonder if there wasn't really some hidden ulterior PR motive behind the recall? How do you respond to such a person?

CLARE: If there were a hidden PR motive, it didn't come up during the intensive seventy-two hours that we were struggling with the issue. It didn't surface in the discussion. We were reacting to a set of circumstances, and we were reacting against those circumstances with a set of principles, the first principle of which is you have to act in every way to protect the consumer and . . . to do it promptly in the Tylenol example was, [in our judgment,] the only way we could do it. Now, we think ultimately it also turned out to be good for business, not only for J&J and the business of Tylenol or for J&J and the image of it as responsible business citizens, but also we had inherited a very strong reputation with the consumer. Let me turn it around if I may. As a consumer, how would you feel about J&J if we hadn't done that? If you were an employee, how would you feel about J&J if we had not acted according to our published standards of performance? If you were a part of the community at large, not even a consumer of analgesics, how would you have perceived us as a company if we hadn't acted as we did? Our belief is that our perception [by the public] would have been very negative, in retrospect, that we would have come out of this with an entirely different image than the one we had inherited of a very responsible company. And we're going to maintain that position.

CC: You mentioned employee attitudes. How did the decision to recall one hundred million dollars worth of Tylenol affect employee morale here?

CLARE: I've been with the company almost thirty-eight years now, and I've been involved in all sort of activities, from managing plants to managing sales forces and so forth. Never in my career have I seen a single incident bond together the employees as closely, as quickly, and as effectively as that single decision did.

needs to be more specific than that. It must also be something more than the law—law is at best the minimum standard allowing a business to operate at all. A useful code should be adaptable to the particular business—a manufacturing firm will need a very different code of ethics from an advertising agency. A useful code should supply precision where precision helps rather than hinders (for example, in the limitation on gifts to employees), and it should be unambiguous. Of course, every general principle has its ambiguities in interpretation, but a code that says only "We treat our customers right!" hardly gives anyone a clue about how to handle an irate and irresponsible customer who feels cheated because he dropped the merchandise when taking it out of the box. But even the most amorphous codes, such as "Be fair" and "Use good taste" make an important point and succeed in reminding every employee to look beyond the bottom line alone and in providing a touchstone for appeals through the hierarchy.

Codes of ethics are important because they provide a point of focus for everyone in the organization. It is easy to understand how an employee or manager inside a large organization can get so caught up with internal pressures and problems that he or she forgets the purpose of the business; a code of ethics acts as a beacon, even if only dimly perceived, keeping those overall goals and standards in view. College professors sometimes get so caught up in publishing and trying to get tenure that they forget that their ultimate job is to teach; thus college presidents feel compelled to make a certain number of speeches emphasizing teaching of undergraduates. Managers can get so caught up disciplining difficult subordinates and trying to please demanding superiors that they tend to forget that the business of business is the well-being of the company, earned by best serving the public; thus it is no small part of the executive role to keep that in view, and corporate codes are a simple, effective, and excellent way of doing that.

It is sometimes argued that corporate codes—which must of necessity consist of short aphorisms rather than of treatises on ethics—are vague and hard to apply. But a code is not just an abstract set of principles on paper; it exists as a living part of the organization. Abstract rules are spelled out *in practice*, through daily examples and company tradition. A code that is not applied or applicable isn't a code. "Thou shalt not steal" is vague, too; it does not give us a clue about what can or cannot be taken or under what circumstances. But in our daily practice, we know full well what counts as stealing and what does not; the commandment has meaning because we apply it every day.

One last point: There is no reason to have a code if its principles are not enforced. A manager who fails to meet a deadline is penalized; he or she must be just as sure of a penalty for ethical wrongdoing. It serves no purpose—except hypocrisy—to have a set of standards that is sacrificed when need be in the face of financial exigency. Ethics need not contradict the bottom line but must be, at least, above the bottom line.

THE ETHICAL ADVOCATE: THE BOARD OF DIRECTORS

Ethics is often a matter of perspective. Being ethical is remembering and reminding ourselves of the larger picture, of other people's interests and views. It is easy to get caught up in an argument about whether to do X or Y and never even think of Z. It is like one of those tricky geometrical proofs where the solution lies in looking outside of the drawn figure, or a riddle in which one is led to look for the answer in the wrong place. One can try for hours and fail to see the solution, but as soon as it is pointed out, it is obvious. So too with ethics. The coach of a junior-league baseball team becomes so caught up in the game and the competition that he forgets to pay attention to the well-being of the kids. The vice president of marketing becomes so caught up in the campaign to sell a new product that he neglects to pay attention to the abuse of the product caused by the heavy promotion. Ethics is important enough that it deserves its own authority, and not just as the offshoot of the legal compliance department.

Former Bush cabinet secretary Louis Sullivan was once a director of General Motors. Under his direction, the number of black executives, promotions, and suppliers increased enormously. He also helped investigate such issues as pollution, community problems, and energy consumption, and he reports that he found that, in general, the executives of General Motors were concerned and more than willing to help him. What they lacked was not the interest but the focus that Sullivan as ethical advocate provided.

Ethics becomes a problem in most companies not because of ethical indifference or ignorance but rather because it is just not part of the conversation. The research department describes the new discovery. The engineer explains the production process. The marketing executive examines the distribution and outlines an optimal marketing strategy. A strategic planner plots a new course for the company while the financial analysts calculate probable costs and earnings. The discussion is enthusiastic, optimistic, intense. All bases are covered, it seems, from the initial design to the advertising campaign. But what about the impact of the product? What about compliance with moral and local norms as well as with the law? What possible contributions might be ignored? What possible harmful consequences? In other words, what about ethics?

There is nothing unethical about most business discussions, but too many business decisions do not include ethical input when it is needed. Ethics requires attention and research just as much as product design or marketing do, but it is too rarely the case that there is an "expert" in ethics to provide that input. That is the role of the ethical advocate.

The ethical advocate is someone whose job it is to think of and raise the right ethical questions. He or she should not have absolute power, of course, but should not be just a kibbitzer either. The ethical advocate need not be a special addition; he or she might well be someone already in the organization, perhaps even the chairman or an assistant. Theodore Purcell has suggested adding an "angel's advocate" to the board of directors, with the understanding that such an advocate has the full support of the company.

An ethical advocate can help set up a code of ethics for a company, but his or her ethical role in the company should be much more than that. The importance of an advocate is that he or she can participate in the actual planning and decisions of the company, making concrete suggestions and specific proposals, organizing particular research projects where they are needed to ascertain the impact of a product, the cost of alterations, the moral implications, the unseen possibilities.

The ethical advocate cannot simply "solve" ethical problems; that takes the concerted effort of the entire company (and sometimes of an entire industry). But the ethical advocate can be a valuable force in focusing attention on possible problems of compliance and overlooked possibilities for contributions as well as unwanted consequences that can be avoided.

The real power in the corporation, at least in theory, lies in the hands of the board of directors. They are in charge of the company, and although they do not run the company on a day-to-day basis they are responsible for hiring and overseeing those who do. Until recently, however, the board served not so much as overseers much less as rulers but rather as a congenial club of Olympian-like advisors who were brought in (wined and dined) with little to do in the company. Many boards of directors are composed of other corporate officers who are friends of the company CEO, public celebrities, ex-politicians, university presidents, and other people who may be in no position to understand, much less supervise, the workings of the company in question. Their briefings of the policies and problems of the corporation are indeed brief, and their contact with the company may be

---

FIVE ETHICAL GUIDELINES

- Look for the ethical way. Don't wait for problems to arise (when it is almost always too late).
- Don't pass the buck. Responsibility isn't a burden; it should be a source of pride.
- Look for solutions, not excuses.
- Never give up an ethical issue. (They don't just go away.)
- View ethics as an opportunity, not as an unwanted complication or obstacle.

---

limited to a single board meeting every month or so. Their approval often amounts to a "rubber stamping" of executive decisions, and, when something goes wrong, the "directors" may be among the first to express shock and surprise, denying any knowledge or responsibility for wrongdoing. Sometimes the relationship between top management and the board may be anything but supervisory. In recent scandals about the extravagant paychecks chief executives were getting, it became quite clear in a number of corporations that these excesses were granted by the board in exchange for proportionally extravagant salaries for their own minimal contributions. Again, one should view such behavior as the exception rather than the rule, but the number of merely perfunctory boards of directors forces us to think again about who really runs the corporation and, more to the point, where the moral conscience of the corporation is and ought to be found. Sullivan's presence on the board of GM is an important indication of where the future is leading us in this regard. At now-defunct E. F. Hutton, by contrast, eighteen out of twenty-three company directors were insiders, providing little correction for the now-infamous ethical abuses that drove that firm into bankruptcy.

The board of directors is an institution that has lately come under increased scrutiny. Members of the boards have been subjected to lawsuits for the doings of their company, and with this their awareness of their responsibilities—and their role as ethical leaders—has started to change the institution. One immediate reaction, of course, was to head for cover. Civic leaders started to turn down lucrative directorships because the shadow of a ruinous lawsuit threatened. Some of them started demanding, and corporations started offering, liability insurance for the directors. But the healthier and more promising reaction is to take these responsibilities more seriously, and this is already changing the role of the board and making board members into ethical advocates, not just visiting gourmets.

CORPORATE LOYALTY

We're not a captive employer, but after training someone, we expect a little service in return.
                                        Coca-Cola executive

Corporate loyalty used to be taken for granted, not least because good jobs were hard to come by and most important promotions came from the inside. But in the days of "fast-tracking" MBAs and the dramatic increases of salary and status that became possible only through job hopping, corporate loyalty became a problem. *Why* should an employee stay with a company if all the advantages seemed to lie elsewhere? According to Sterling Robert in *Fortune* magazine (February 9, 1981), the turnover of younger managers *quintupled* in twenty years, and most corporations assumed that they would lose more than half of their younger recruits in five years or less. Yet if business were to hold together as a practice and corporate competition were to be more than a free-for-all in which no one could trust anyone, company loyalty would have to continue to be an essential ingredient of business life. One couldn't very well play a game of football if the players kept deciding to switch teams in the middle of play.

Today, the business world has changed. Corporate mobility has radically diminished. Executives are often thankful to have jobs. Accordingly, the question of loyalty has returned, as a matter of prudence as well as of ethics. Corporate loyalty is the ultimate responsibility of every employee within the organization. (There are further responsibilities beyond the company, of course.) Whatever the responsibilities of any particular job or position, it is ultimately the company one works for to which one owes loyalty. Loyalty carries with it obligations. For example, an employee is expected to act when necessary for the good of the company, quite apart from the question whether an act is part of the job or not. ("Why should I tell them that their marketing campaign is offensive? That's not my job.") An employee is expected to speak well of the company and not to spread rumors (true or not) about its weaknesses and failures. An employee is expected to have some sense of product loyalty. (One does not expect to see Lee Iacocca driving around in a Toyota.)

Some aspects of corporate loyalty are virtually a matter of legal obligation. An employee in a sensitive position must be trusted not to share corporate secrets with the competition. This is so even where this is not, strictly speaking, illegal or a matter of contractual obligation. Information is just as much the private property of a corporation as its furniture or equipment, even if physical possession is more difficult to define. Some companies demand that employees sign an agreement that they will not divulge company secrets during or after their employment, but almost all companies expect that their employees will respect company secrets as they should any other property rights.

We can all agree that it is unethical to sell or trade secrets to the competition when one has signed an agreement not to. Indeed, we would probably all agree that selling or trading secrets to a competitor is unethical even if there is no such explicit agreement. But the privacy of information is of little force if there is not a more general sense of corporate loyalty. Suppose an employee rejects a bribe from the company's competitor, who is trying to buy the formula for a process, but soon after accepts an offer of employment from that same competitor, taking the formula with him? Is this a breach of trust and loyalty? Clearly that depends on the good faith of his own company. Loyalty is not an abstract principle but rather a question of mutual obligations. What a company can expect from its employees—including ex-employees—depends on what employees expect, and have got, from the company.

It is every employee's right to switch jobs when and as he wishes, but this right—like all rights—has to be balanced with obligations. The free market exists for executives just as much as it does for skilled laborers and inventors. But, as the Coke executive said, after training someone, the company expects a little service in return. Every employee has some obligation to the company, if only for having the job in the first place. One can be expected to move for a much better job, but moving "just for a change" (after a few months of service) is suspect at least. What counts as a reasonable amount of time in a job depends, of course, on what one has already given back to the company and what one has received in return—especially nonreturnables, like training and settling-in expenses. To a certain extent, the question of company loyalty is a question of fair exchange—like so many ethical issues in business.

Some older discussions of corporate loyalty tended to focus just on the obligations of the employee and his or her obligations to the company. This is no longer acceptable. Loyalty is a two-way affair, and it is the responsibility of the company to inspire and to deserve loyalty. What has changed is not just the mobility of executives. There is also an increased awareness of employees' rights and a sense that a company is expected to nourish its employees, improve their skills, maximize their responsibilities, and not let them get bored, restless, dissatisfied, or frustrated (for the company's sake as well as the employees'). A few politicians, executives, and social critics might lament the passing of the (imaginary) old days of blind company loyalty and hard work without such incentives, but the fact is that today's employees and executives alike are asking not only what they can do for their company but what the company can do for them.

Corporate loyalty is a matter of the market as well as of morality, and a company has to attract and produce loyal employees; it cannot take them for granted. A company that consistently hires from the outside instead of promoting on the inside, offering little hope for its own best employees, has no claim to long-term loyalty. A company that fires its employees en masse without regard to individual merit cannot expect loyalty. A company that abuses its employees sends out an unmistakable message: "This company is not to be trusted, only used" (Simeon Tourestsky, "Changing Attitudes: A Question of Loyalty," *Personal Administrator*, April 1979).

Concepts of corporate loyalty have also changed because the nature of corporate work has changed. In simpler times and simpler companies, most employees were trained on the job, and their skills were more often than not specific to the needs and circumstances of that particular company. Today, many executives and virtually all other professionals are trained in schools before they ever see their first job. Their skills are applicable to any number of companies, and their loyalties by virtue of training are minimal. Many of today's corporate personnel have professional rather than corporate identities (as ac-

---

FOUR STEPS TO INSPIRING LOYALTY

Step 1: Set high standards, model them through one's own behavior, and demand them of others.

Step 2: Be fair and consistent in the administration of these standards. Loyalty flies out the window when people perceive their leaders as unfair and inconsistent in their management practices.

Step 3: Clarify expectations and supply feedback. People need to know what is expected of them in clear, specific terms. People also need to know when they have done well, and when they have failed to meet expectations.

Step 4: Involve the whole person. People need to have their total being involved—mind, heart, and soul. This sort of total involvement becomes the basis of innovation, creativity, and quality, which in turn contribute to the building of even greater loyalty.

—Alexander B. Horniman, *Executive Excellence*

---

countants, as strategic analysts, as specialists in this and that). They are more like inside consultants than like corporate members.

Loyalty is not just a matter of incentives in the obvious sense. High salaries and promotion opportunities may encourage people to stay but might not inspire loyalty. You can't buy loyalty any more than you can buy love. (At most you can buy its expression.) W. E. Burdick, of IBM, insists, "You have to win loyalty." The kind of loyalty that you can trust requires a sense of personal attachment and gratitude, which comes not just from being treated well but from a genuine feeling of "belonging" and being "at home."

The advantages of corporate loyalty to the corporation are obvious—and well worth the expense. What are not so immediately obvious are the advantages of loyalty to the employee, given the number of opportunities that will always appear to be "out there." But what this means is that although the ethics of employee loyalty may be undeniable, the need to motivate corporate loyalty is indispensable to most corporations. Robert Townsend, emphasizing the importance of promoting from within, notes, "How to do it wrong: go outside and get some expensive guy . . . and a year later . . . you'll still be teaching him the business" (*Up the Organization*). If, that is, he isn't "just passing through," and if he pays any attention at all to his performance in addition to his dossier. Corporate loyalty may be the best investment a company can make. It is also the best guarantee of internal ethical dependability—having employees to think of the company as they do of themselves.

A GOOD DAY'S WORK: THE ECLIPSE OF MERIT

One of the critical problems in corporate life, and in the free-market system in general, is the increasing failure of meritocracy, along with the increasing suspicion that hard work is not rewarded and good ideas are more likely to be ignored or stolen than compensated. The obvious result: strategies for "survival" start to replace devotion to tasks, and research and development are replaced by the search for short-term results and demonstrable increase in the bottom line. To be sure, the skills involved in good management are not like the tangible results of a trade or profession, such as carpentry, computer programming, or accounting. Management skills are "people skills," matters of facilitation and, at their best, inspiration rather than production as such. Thus an excellent manager knows that excellence in management is often evident in what does not happen or what seemingly happens with little effort rather than in any dramatic or breathtaking performance. The insecurity that inevitably results from this should not be taken to mean that "excellence" has no place in managerial life, however, or that management circles are by their very nature doomed (as some seem to be) to an insistent mediocrity, a "don't rock the boat" mentality. To the contrary, one of the key themes of the new world of global competitive business is to encourage and insist on excellence and to defend the ideal of a meritocracy, a system in which excellence is rewarded and mediocrity ("not rocking the boat") is not. In managerial circles, "excellence in management" is too often such a mask for mediocrity. In *Moral Mazes,* Robert Jackall frets, "What if men and women in the corporation no longer see success as necessarily connected to hard work? What becomes of the social morality of the corporation—the everyday rules-in-use that people play by—when there is thought to be no fixed or, one might say, objective standard of excellence to explain how and why winners are separated from also-rans, how and why some people succeed and others fail? What rules do people fashion to interact with one another when they feel that, instead of ability, talent, and dedicated service to an organization, politics, adroit talk, luck, connections, and self-promotion are the real sorters of people into sheep and goats?''

Merit is the idea that everyone gets and gives and is seen to get and to give what he or she *deserves.* In some societies, this may depend on such accidents as birth and social status. In our society, to be sure, it also depends to a much larger extent than we usually want to admit on good luck and mere celebrity, but nevertheless we like to think that good fortune has at least something to do with what one *does* or *has done.* The free-market system is often celebrated and defended for rewarding hard work and good ideas, but the simple fact is that this isn't quite accurate. Friedrich von Hayek argued years ago that the virtue of the free market was to be found in its freedom, not in fairness. To the victor go the profits, but that is no proof that victor is virtuous. Ingenious inventors find themselves without a stake in the realization of their ideas. Founders find themselves undermined, bought out, taken over, not because they failed but because they succeeded, and the market undercuts them. (The old-time successful manufacturer, played by Gregory Peck in the movie version of *Other People's Money,* was a poignant illustration of this point.)

But in business, the market is not everything. In fact, *within* the corporation, the market plays a relatively minor role. Personal politics, as everyone knows, plays a more sizable role in determining one's success and status within the company. Much depends on how well one "fits in," whether or not one is or seems to be a cooperative "team" member, how one influences and inspires others. But because success in the corporation does not wholly depend on the sometimes brutal vicissitudes of the market, it is also possible to insist, as a matter of corporate policy, on the seeking out and rewarding of merit. Such a policy does not escape from the politics of the organization, of course, but it becomes part of that politics, and the net result is a concerted effort—even if it is in the name of individual advancement—toward quality products and a cooperative if not harmonious work environment. A company that encourages buttering up and schmoozing instead of productive work and accomplishment, on the other hand, or a company that is quick to blame and therefore requires the skills involved in evasion of responsibility and "C.Y.A." rather than the skills of productivity and effectiveness, is not just a lousy company to work for; it is also a company that will be, sooner or later, on its way out of the market.

Part of the problem in any corporation of significant size is "the measurement problem." Any given result is almost always the product of dozens or hundreds, even thousands, of individual and collective actions and decisions. It is hard to know how to reward individuals for their particular contribution. But if the goals and purposes of their collective actions are in fact the well-being of the company and its various stakeholders, the precise distribution of merit is not of any particular importance. "Quality" refers not just (or even primarily) to individual merit, but rather to the overall quality of the results. As in a sports team, credit ultimately goes to the entire team, and overt displays of individual excellence may indeed jeopardize rather than improve the quality of play. Quality, in other words, is not primarily an individual virtue. It is the virtue of the individual in being a devoted part of the group.

The idea that individuality has to be submerged into larger collective projects and purposes too readily gives way to some erroneous objections to corporate life as such, the image of "the man in the grey

ANNUAL VACATION TIME (IN WEEKS)

	By law	By bargaining
Austria	4	4–5
France	5	5–6
Germany	3	4–6
Greece	4	—
Italy	—	4–6
The Netherlands	3	4–5
Spain	5	5
Sweden	5	5–8
Switzerland	4	4–5
United States	—	2–4
United Kingdom	—	4–6

Source: *Utne Reader*

flannel suit'' and the anonymous corporate drone. But to be part of a group in which one's own contributions cannot be measured except by reference to the overall effort and success of the group is not to say that the individual is not thereby responsible for his or her own efforts as well as the overall success of the group, nor does it undermine the idea of merit just because individual merit is as such hard to measure. In most team sports, the idea of measuring the contribution of any given individuals, whether in the indisputable terms of ''goals scored'' or ''runs batted in'' or the more difficult measures of the efficacy of a lineman or a guard, is pretty much beside the point. The important thing is that the team did well and that merit shines on all of its members, more or less equally. So, too, in business, we should not confuse group effort with the loss of individual merit and accomplishment, and to insist overly on the unique importance of the latter may well undermine the former—and make any accomplishment impossible.

CORPORATE POISON

> *The executive suites of thousands of corporations in the United States are filled by men who have become professional eunuchs. The drive and potency they once possessed has been spent . . . they spend their days doing things that often seem meaningless.*
> *O. William Battaglia and John J. Tarrant,*
> The Corporate Eunuch

Corporations that breed a sense of futility or injustice poison themselves. The poison is *resentment,* that seething, vicious sense of impotence rendered infuriating by the continuous sense of victimiza-

ANTIDOTES TO CORPORATE POISON

DO tie remuneration directly to performance that enhances the efficiency and effectiveness of the enterprise.

DO give public and tangible recognition to people who keep standards of quality and effort that exceed average satisfactory job performance.

DO accept wholeheartedly the principle that employees should share directly and significantly in overall productivity gains (however defined).

DO encourage jobholders to participate with management in defining recognizable goals and standards against which individual performance can be judged.

DO give special attention to the difficulties that middle managers face in supporting and enforcing programs to restructure the workplace.

DO NOT permit situations to develop where the interests of employees run counter to the well-being of the firm—e.g., by introducing new technology in a way that threatens employees' job security or overtime.

DO NOT attempt to improve standards of quality unless you are prepared to accept its full costs—e.g., discarding substandard products, paying more for better components, or transferring or dismissing people who cannot do quality work.

DO NOT permit a significant gap to develop between management rhetoric and the actual reward system—nothing feeds employee cynicism as much as management blindness or insincerity about the forms of behavior that really "pay off."

DO NOT pretend that programs designed to increase productivity are really intended to enhance job satisfaction and the dignity of work.

DO NOT support special privileges for managers that serve to enhance the status of managers by widening the gap between them and those who do the work—e.g., giving bonuses to managers at the same time that employees are being laid off.

Daniel Yankelovich and John Immerwahr,
Putting the Work Ethic to Work

tion. "I can't afford to leave this company, but I can't get anywhere either, and I can't even get what's coming to me." At best, such an attitude breeds indifference and apathy. An employee goes through the motions without taking the initiative and without ever doing more than the minimum. At worst, the resentful employee becomes a liability who can poison the attitudes of everyone else, or a real danger—a corporate saboteur who will disrupt the work process or sell out the company. But resentment is not just a function of an employee's personality; it is a product of inattention on the part of the company. Resentment is caused. Resentment can be avoided.

The first sign of resentment is a sense of separation between "me" or "us" on one side and "it" or "them" (the company) on the other. Such a separation is usually initiated by the more powerful partner— the company. Repeatedly passing over a deserving employee for promotion is a sure way to create resentment. Allowing good work to go unpraised while consistently criticizing small errors and lapses is another. Anything that makes an employee feel impotent without at the same time affirming his or her place in the company tends to produce resentment. It is natural and necessary for a corporation occasionally to put individuals in positions where they feel overwhelmed, but that is where explicit support and guarantees of authority and autonomy are of the utmost importance. Nothing breeds resentment like responsibility devoid of authority, except, perhaps, too few or too demeaning responsibilities. (The vice president who spends his or her time ordering the office furniture is a good candidate for resentment. So is the smart secretary with an administration background who spends his or her day typing memos.)

Resentment is a reaction to impotence and injustice, real or imagined. Real injustices should be sought out and corrected. (You can't expect an already resentful employee to mention them; he may feel the matter is beyond hope.) Imagined injustices can be corrected through conscientious explanations: "No distinctions without stated differences" is a good rule of thumb. Of course, no amount of effort can dissolve the resentment of a paranoid employee, but so long as the general policy of the company is such that everyone else feels comfort-

---

ALL WORK AND NO PLAY

Rising numbers of employees are complaining that the "fun" has gone out of working. An *Industry Week* survey finds that 63 percent say they no longer enjoy their job. About half blame a "dog-eat-dog" climate in their firms. Another 38 percent charge that "initiative-stifling bureaucracy" is the culprit. While fewer than 10 percent complain about low pay, about one-third of those surveyed complain that a lack of praise for their work dampens their day.

—*Across the Board*, September 1991

able with his responsibilities and treatment, that embittered soul remains safely isolated even if he or she is not easily identifiable. (Resentment often wears a cooperative smile—for protection, not out of good humor.) It is when he or she gains an audience that the company itself is in jeopardy. A lone provocateur may be visible and fireable, but a quiet voice reciting his or her complaints to others who also feel helpless or abused can turn an entire department into a cauldron of unpleasant, unproductive, and incorrigible grumbling.

THE SYSTEM PROBLEM

A corporation is more than the sum of its parts. This is true not only in law (the corporation as a ficticious person); it is true in fact. A corporation can have power far greater than the collective powers of all of its employees, executives, and stockholders. The activities of a major corporation can change society, even if no one in or no one who owns the company can do so. Indeed, given the power of business in our society, the activities of any major corporation *will* change society, and the question is only whether it is for good or for ill.

We will discuss the much-debated topic of the social responsibility of corporations in the next part of the book. Here we want to raise a very different issue concerning the workings of the corporation itself. The issue is what we call the "system problem." In short, it is a collective dilemma in which bad consequences follow from no one's doing anything wrong.

The collective dilemma has become an essential feature of contemporary ethics—indeed, it may be *the* main problem of contemporary ethics. A collective dilemma is a situation in which an innocuous action, repeated many times by a great many people, produces results that are intolerable, perhaps even fatal. A moment's thought suggests a great many examples: traffic congestion, pollution, tax avoidance, and energy depletion, to name a few.

LOS ANGELES: THE COLLECTIVE DILEMMA

Every person who lives in this basin knows that for twenty-five years he has been living through a disaster. We have all watched it happen, have participated in it with full knowledge. . . . The smog is the result of ten million individual pursuits of private gratification. But there is absolutely nothing that any individual can do to stop its spread. An individual act of renunciation is now nearly impossible, and, in any case, would be meaningless unless everyone else did the same thing. But he has no way of getting everyone else to do it.

Francis Carney, *Harper's,* 1974

Consider the example of pollution. For hundreds of thousands of years, humans polluted the air with cooking fires and deposited their trash and excretions in nature, without noticing the consequences. We have discovered many more modes of combustion and, of necessity, developed artificial but more efficient ways of dealing with waste. Burning and producing waste are just as natural for an American family in 1994 as they were for an Egyptian family in 3000 B.C., but the collective consequences are very different. Can we say that a person is wrong, therefore, in driving a car that emits an unusually large amount of noxious exhaust fumes or in manufacturing a large number of not-really-necessary, hard-to-dispose-of plastic containers for a fast-food product? Well, yes and no. In terms of the individual action, there is certainly nothing wrong. In view of the collective consequences, we have to say that there is something unethical here. "But my pollution and waste are minuscule, compared to the problem as a whole!" is the inevitable reply. But almost everyone else could say exactly the same.

The examples above concern the collective products of isolated activities of individuals. The power of the corporation, however, is not just the collected effort of hundreds or thousands of individuals. It is the coordinated and carefully controlled activity of an organization. The isolated effort of any one person—even the CEO—may not amount to much, but the collective commercial power generated by even a relatively inefficient corporation is immense. Again, any given employee, manager, executive, or (minor) stockholder can say—probably truthfully—"I don't have any control over what this company does," but, collectively, they all *are* the corporation. The system problem arises when there is a failure of unified vision, when the parts lose sight of the whole.

STINK NOW, PAY LATER

Professor Donald H. Stedman, a controversial University of Denver chemist, is trying to foment a revolution. Even as Congress wraps up a ten-year effort to rewrite the Clean Air Act, Stedman's research is challenging basic assumptions of the law. He believes Congress is about to blunder by making emissions standards tougher and encouraging other fuels. "Modern cars are so clean that tightening standards or switching fuels is a total waste of money," Stedman insists. "Individual dirty cars are the problem."

Stedman's research shows that only a tiny fraction of cars, perhaps 8 percent, account for more than half the pollution. What's more, he believes, annual emission inspections are ineffective—and that using alternative fuels such as methanol to reduce pollution is "a total crock, because methanol can be dirtier in new, clean cars than gasoline."

"Such outspokenness has earned Stedman the enmity of regulators. Yet his agenda is serious. Instead of mandating lower emissions for new cars, which would cost $5 billion, he believes remote sensors that use an infrared light beam to measure the fumes from each car's tailpipe should be used to stop gross polluters. A video camera would record license plates and authorities could then send owners notices to have the dirty cars fixed.

—*Business Week,* October 1, 1990

A decision at General Motors, which may require the input of thousands of employees and consultants and enough information to fill a good-size computer, can multiply small margins of error and uncertainty—or, worse, small margins of faked confidence—to disastrous proportions. Business ethicist Tom Donaldson points out that General Motors, like many large corporations, maintains a distinction between line and staff functions. Both report to the president, but communication between them is vague and often confused. The room for misunderstanding or lack of synchronization is considerable, and tragic errors are possible even when every single employee of the company is doing his or her job correctly.

The system problem is most of concern in ethics when the errors in question have to do with the safety of the product or its impact on the community in general. At General Motors, needless to say, safety is always a major consideration. So is the impact of automobiles on the environment. But there is a very real question as to how much essential ethical issues can be dealt with in a company so complicated. One can deal with specific safety or pollution-control features just as one can deal with any specific features of a car, but not all ethical issues are so specific. In a study of GM in 1970, Peter Drucker declared that General Motors had never yet managed to coordinate its decisions with concern for its environment and compassion for the community. The key word here is "coordinate," for it is not neglect or indifference that is responsible for General Motors' seemingly slow response to urgent ethical concerns. It is rather the system problem, lack of coordination in the system to deal with problems that are holistic rather than particular.

One of the most paradoxical functions of corporate organization, too rarely appreciated by efficiency-minded managers, is to make an organization sufficiently flexible and self-critical—which inevitably means less efficient—to prevent all of those small and possibly undetectable errors from adding up to one gigantic mistake. Ethical problems are typically of this sort. No senior executive orders anything unethical. No middle manager intends anything unethical. No employee does anything unethical. It is not even that everyone is "just a little unethical," bending the rules a bit or slightly cutting corners. And yet the net result is unethical because no one kept the entire system in perspective. No one in a company need discriminate against women or minorities, for instance, in order for the company as a whole to fall far short of a just distribution of jobs and promotions.

As often as not, unethical conduct itself is a function of the system problem. Consider the much-discussed case of B. F. Goodrich, which in the late 1960s had a contract with the Air Force to equip the new A7D planes with air brakes. The executives of the company had decided to go for the contract "at all costs," but there was too little communication between the policy makers who made that decision and the engineers and designers who had to produce the brakes themselves. The time period was too short. Early tests showed that the brakes were flawed. The due date came, and the brakes were delivered to the Air Force. The test plane crashed. An investigation showed that the flaws in the original design had never been fixed, and several otherwise responsible engineers had falsified the early test reports to meet their deadline. They all had done what they thought they were expected to do. Goodrich was another "victim of the system" problem.

We can understand how this happens if we appreciate the extent to which American business is based on the idea of everyone's "just doing his job.'' What gets lost is the overview, the sense of how all of this will add up. No job is itself unethical. It simply consists of getting this contract, designing this product part, doing this market survey, and so on. But we should also ask what questions are *not* being asked, what concerns are *not* being raised by anyone. Are there matters of compliance to ecological and public demands that are something more (or less) than matters of law? What contributions can the company make—over and above the production of a reasonably priced, quality product? And, most difficult, what are the consequences, on the quality of life as well as on the quality of the product, of everyone's doing his or her job? All of those jobs can add up to an ethical embarrassment, just because of the lack of ethical coordination. To take an artistic analogue, one can draw a face with perfect features but nevertheless emerge with the portrait of a monster.

The System Problem

- Can you name a problem that your company has had recently, in which no one is clearly to blame, but nevertheless some serious error in judgment of company performance was in evidence?
- What aspects of the structure of your company (poor communications, lack of coordination among departments, ''too many cooks'') would account for this problem?
- Can you envision a potential problem that might develop in your company, in which no one is to blame but nevertheless some serious error in judgment or performance could emerge?
- What can you do now to prevent this from happening?

CORPORATE PATHOLOGY

Organizations, like people, display predictable, preventable, but sometimes fatal illnesses. Some troubles are easily spotted—unmotivated workers, subversive or ineffective managers, failures of communication, and so on—but the corporation is in real trouble *when no one is to blame.* A new chief executive, a new project or policy, makes no difference. Everyone is doing what he or she is supposed to be doing, and yet something is going very wrong.

In a 1979 study, Evan M. Dudik outlined a general symptomatology of institutions. Some of his results can be adapted to a pathology of corporations. The following symptoms are almost always a sign of the system problem:

1. NO ONE IS TO BLAME. Everyone does his or her job, but the responsibility for failure gets passed up and down the hierarchy.
2. APPEALS TO MAGIC. Incantations take the place of analysis and action. Complaints about "government regulation" or "bad publicity" or "motivation"—though often the names of real problems—tend to become obligatory slogans to block solutions. Outside or abstract factors absorb the blame and make active change impossible.
3. MORAL DEFENSIVENESS. "Everyone does it" or "It would be unreasonable for us to. . ." almost always betrays a system problem.
4. FALSIFICATION. Something more than resistance to criticism, falsification is the attempt to prove the "company's right" at whatever cost to effectiveness or credibility. This too serves to block any possible change and, worse, to muddy the waters so that analysis is impossible.
5. HISTORICAL REVISIONISM. The history of the company, or the industry, gets recast in terms of the present problem. "But we've always done it that way" (when we haven't) or "That's just the way to do it."
6. SELF-FULFILLING PROPHECY. Trouble is magnified by the belief that "There's no way to stop it" or "It's just how our industry is." Negative belief encourages negative results.
7. DOUBLE-BIND SYNDROME. Puts impossible pressure on everyone in the company, and the company itself. An employee can't obey one instruction without disobeying another. A manager can't fulfill one function without betraying another. The double bind is Gregory Bateson's name for the "experience of being punished precisely for being right in one's own view." Such an experience makes commitment impossible, productivity unlikely, and unethical behavior almost inevitable.
8. OPPOSITE-RESULTS SYNDROME. The harder the company pushes

for "results," the worse things get. The push is on efficiency; the result is loss of effectiveness. The push is for better motivation; the result is increased cynicism and indifference.

9. ADDICTION. Defined precisely as "maladaptive dependency on ultra-specific set of circumstances," addiction affects corporations just as it does individuals. The company continues in a practice, as if by compulsive ritual, which everyone knows full well is unproductive or downright destructive. It holds on to a product or a subsidiary despite the fact that the future is hopeless. It holds onto a scheme of management or administration that has long ago proved to be fruitless. And because of the intolerance for falsifiability and the tendency to historical revision and self-fulfilling prophecies, it is impossible to break through the addiction. (Think of a compulsive smoker: "But they've never really *proved* that smoking causes cancer.")

It is our tendency to believe—we would like to believe—that hard work and conscientiousness alone will make a sick corporation better. *Laissez-faire*—in this as in all business matters. But this is no more true in business pathology than it is in medicine, for it is the self-correcting mechanism of the organization itself that has gone wrong. The system problem is ultimately an illness, and one that by its very definition the company cannot get over alone.

BLOWING THE WHISTLE

Because so much of the "business ethics" literature is concerned with moral wrongdoing in business, an inordinate amount of attention has been paid to the relatively rare and controversial employee action called "whistle-blowing." Blowing the whistle means stepping out of the corporation and announcing its wrongdoing to the world—usually to the press or to a government agency. The fact that whistle-blowing is rare does not necessarily mean that most corporations are ethical through and through, of course; a more immediate explanation is that blowing the whistle is almost always catastrophic for the employee. A modicum of historical research shows that corporate whistle-blowers in America have almost always come out impoverished and embittered. They often find themselves locked out of their industry. They don't get hired again, even if there is no conscious or concerted effort to keep them out. They're just "too much trouble" or "too well known." The court cases can go on for decades, and the toll in terms of abuse and contempt from former friends can be terrible. There may be one or two heroes, but they are mostly personal tragedies.

Whistle-blowing is controversial because it throws into conflict the two large obligations of every employee—loyalty to the company and responsibility to society. It is often said that the employee should exhaust every possibility in the corporate hierarchy before going outside, but this reasonable demand usually misses the problem. Few employees who blow the whistle would take such a drastic personal step unless they already felt thoroughly frustrated, if not humiliated, by their intra-organizational efforts. And the fact is that too few corporations make clear to employees what access they have to those with sufficient power to order the appropriate investigations or bring about the essential changes. Indeed, many corporations structurally prevent an employee from gaining such access by locking him or her into the very compartment of the company that he or she objects to. There may be a final and desperate appointment with a senior vice president, when all hope is just about gone. But unless the employee is particularly articulate and persuasive, it is hardly likely that a half-hour audience with upper management will be satisfying or reassuring.

Where a single manager or group is carrying on unethical activity, a corporation has to be downright foolish not to simply fire him, her, or them on the spot, and be sure the dismissals are well publicized within the company. All the potential whistle-blower has then to do is blow the whistle, *within* the company, and possibly emerge as a hero. Where a large part of the organization is engaged in unethical activity, however, it is, first of all, harder to see what upper management can do about it and, second, unlikely that upper management doesn't already know about it. Then the whistle-blower has little hope, except to blow. Some have argued that he or she should simply quit, but this depends, of course, on the seriousness or dangers inherent in the unethical activity. If it is a matter of padding expense accounts or accepting favors from suppliers, it probably makes sense to quit rather than jeopardize one's entire career. But if the problem is shoddy construction of a nuclear power plant near a major city, the moral argument would certainly be that one should do something more than shut up and disappear.

What makes whistle-blowing most problematic, however, is the system problem, the fact that things may be going wrong even though no one is doing wrong. Executives sometimes complain that they have investigated the accusations of a whistle-blower and found no one doing anything wrong. In one sense they are right. In another, important sense, they are wrong. Indeed, the system problem complicates the dilemma of the whistle-blower because not only does he or she fail to specify any particular wrongdoing (and thereby to make a case to upper management) but there is nowhere in the company to go to complain, no level that is safely "above" the level of wrongdoing. The very fact that there is a whistle-blower points to a structural problem in the organization. A company that has an ethical sense of itself and keeps the lines of communication open and receptive will not have whistle-blowers.

Two things are essential:

1. Make sure that potential whistle-blowers have clear and easy access within the company.
2. Make sure that whistle-blowers have little to blow about.

An occasional crank can get hired by mistake, but whistle-blowers are created by the companies themselves.

A Classic Case of Whistle-Blowing: What Would You Have done?

Dan Gellert was a pilot for Eastern Airlines with twenty-five years' experience. In 1972, he went outside the company to report serious defects in the Lockheed 1011, first to the National Transportation Safety Board (NTSB) and finally, in 1978, in a much publicized $12 million lawsuit against Eastern executive officers. The unfortunate circumstances leading up to this were as follows (in brief):

Gellert first realized that there was a possibly fatal defect in the L-1011 in flight simulation. The problem was the automatic pilot, which would disengage without warning about ninety seconds before landing,

FINK? OR LOYALIST?

No one likes a fink—yet our initial revulsion at snitching and our concept of employee loyalty may need serious revision. Clearly the employer has the right to expect a reasonable amount of loyalty from his employees, and to demand confidentiality in everyday business, in contract negotiations, trade secrets, client and personnel lists, and the like. But there are areas of concern to the public—as, for example, uncovering frauds, thefts, and serious improprieties—which require that the informer not be muzzled by employer censorship.

Moreover, the corporate hard-hats holding a "Your company, love it or leave it" attitude are depriving themselves of a useful mechanism for reform, capable of correcting an institution's seemingly unlimited capacity for organized error. Snitchers, in fact, are often a firm's *most* loyal members, for it takes a greater degree of attachment to stay with a firm and to protest than it does to "opt out," by remaining silent or moving on.

Timothy Ingram, *The Progressive*

or two thousand feet from the ground, distorting the instrument readings at the most dangerous part of the approach. He reported this to his management supervisors, who said, "We'll look into it." On December 29, 1972, an Eastern Airlines L-1011 crashed, killing 103 people. Gellert pushed his report to the top of the company. It was ignored. That was when he sent the report to the NTSB. There was a hearing on the crash and a nebulous verdict: "pilot error." Gellert claims that Eastern and the NTSB were "in collusion." Further tests bore out Gellert's diagnosis of the crash, but Eastern once again ignored the reports. (They did, without fanfare, make some of the needed adjustments in the automatic pilot.) In December 1973, Gellert himself was piloting an L-1011 that almost crashed, and he once again contacted the NTSB. Gellert insists, "I thought of myself as a loyal Eastern employee," and sent a copy of his report to Frank Borman. Gellert was demoted, then grounded. His ability to fly was questioned. He went through grievance procedures for seven months, then sued. He won *more* than he sued for ($1.6 million), an expression of indignation by the judge. As a result, he was blackballed from his profession, but he sued again.

He is now a celebrated "whistle-blower." He insists that he never intended to be or wanted to be one, but "couldn't do anything else."

Ethical Hypotheticals

IF I found out that my company was doing something seriously wrong, I would

_____ go to my supervisor
_____ go to the head of the division
_____ go to the head of the company
_____ go to the government regulatory agency
_____ go to the press
_____ quit my job
_____ pretend I didn't know a thing
_____ take advantage of it if I could
_____ collect evidence

My skills for dealing with such a situation are

_____ speaking effectively
_____ writing persuasively
_____ unquestioned loyalty
_____ stubbornness
_____ good mediator
_____ good negotiator
_____ in a position of power
_____ I don't get involved
_____ strong personal values

Name three circumstances in which you would quit your company in protest . . . (If you can't name any, you may be loyal to a fault, or you might have a very bad imagination).

THE INTERNAL ETHICAL AUDIT

Public concern naturally focuses on the impact of corporate ethics—the actions and attitudes of a corporation toward its customers and the larger community around it. But corporate ethics is first of all a concern *within* the corporation, a matter of how executives, employees, and middle managers treat one another and are treated themselves. As in family life, corporate ethics begins at home, and a corporation that emphasizes ethical behavior within the organization is probably going to insist on ethical behavior and a positive impact on the outside community as well.

Evaluating the ethics of one's own company might seem to be as difficult as evaluating the ethics of one's own family, except that one joins a company voluntarily and in the maturity of life. There is no room for "That's just the way we do things." One joins and stays with a company in part because it is ethically acceptable.

It would be a mistake to think that there is a single model for the "moral corporation." Some people and some companies thrive on internal tension, competition, and what would seem to others unreasonable hours, deadlines, and pressures. As a matter of internal ethics, it is not clear that such an environment is in any way "wrong," even if it is unacceptable to many people in business. (Of course, if those pressures also produce unethical or immoral behavior, that is another matter.) What is essential, however, is that one recognize a company's ethical portrait. Obviously, there can be no ethical judgment if there is no ethical awareness.

The internal ethical audit begins and ends with the question "Do you ever feel pressured by your organization to act contrary to your own moral judgment?" If the answer to that question is "yes," then clearly a corporate ethical audit of considerable depth is required. *Why* that pressure? Where does it come from? Is it "real"—or could it be the product of rumor and competition that are in fact inappropriate and unnecessary in the organization? Is it personally worth the cost and risk of staying with the company? Is the unethical behavior sufficiently serious that it demands a formal complaint within the company? Or beyond? But even if the answer to that first question is "no" or "very rarely," an internal ethical audit can be revealing. Since a corporate culture determines, to a large extent, what and who we are, the aim of an ethical audit is, to a large extent, to raise the question "Is this the person I want to be?"—always the ultimate question in ethics.

The basic audit consists of ten questions, only one of which (the final question) involves "right" and "wrong" explicitly. An ethical audit is more a matter of evaluating the corporate context and the culture in which one works, from which one receives not only assignments and responsibilities but expectations and a sense of self-worth.

The questions:

1. Do you consider your relationship with your immediate peers to be primarily one of competition or one of cooperation and mutual encouragement?
2. Does your organization have a "hero"? Who is he or she, and what are his or her virtues? (Any notable vices?)
3. Do you feel that you work in a community, or that you work more or less on your own?
4. Are you rewarded fairly for your efforts and accomplishments? Do you feel that, in general, rewards (and punishments) are distributed fairly in your organization?
5. How important is the hierarchy of status and power in your organization? Are there clear distinctions of rank in everyday working situations? Would you say that status is considered *particularly* important by the members of your company?
6. How friendly are the people you work with? How much emphasis is placed on good humor and warm personal relations in the company?
7. How much emphasis is placed on competition with another company or companies—"them!"? To what degree is that competition benevolent/malevolent? What is the effect of that competition inside the company?
8. What is the general feeling about product quality inside your organization? Real pride? Taken for granted? Some embarrassment?
9. Do you generally work under pressure? Do you ever feel pressed to do more or achieve more than you believe is reasonable or possible? Where does this pressure come from?
10. Do you feel pressured by your organization to act contrary to your own moral judgment? (If so, how seriously, and at what risk, etc.)

A few comments:

If competition is the watchword of American business, then we should expect that competition determines a great deal about a firm's ethical attitudes. A corporation with heavy competition must be expected to condone practices that in a less competitive business would be unspeakable. *But*—there is no competition so severe that there is no established (though not always well articulated) sense of "what is not done." And—a company may be in a highly competitive industry without being competitive *within;* indeed, competition is sometimes the greatest spur to team spirit and cooperation within the company, just as lack of competition in some giant firms seems to bring out the need to compete for status within the corporation (Questions 1, 7).

Executives in PepsiCo expect from the outset that they are more like military officers on the front lines in a war (with Coke, of course) than mere managers overlooking the lines of industry. The head-to-head competition that defines the company's place in the business world translates into a similar competition on the inside; the company makes enormous demands and often pits employees against each other. "The golden handshake" is expected for executives who fail to win battles, no matter how hardworking they may be. How different such a culture is from J. C. Penney, for example, where the company creed is "Do not take unfair advantage of anyone," including customers (who can return merchandise, no questions asked) as well as suppliers and employees. Or consider how Chick-fil-a (an Atlanta-based national chain of chicken sandwich restaurants) stands out among its peers: according to Fortune (October 16, 1996) "turnover of [fast-food] store managers runs 40 percent to 50 percent a year." Turnover at Chick-fil-a, where managers are not just entrenched but rather are judged by "the value they create," is 4 to 6 percent!

Corporate cultures, like people's personalities, can be disordered and at war with themselves. Individual breakdowns in ethics within a company should often be diagnosed in much the same way that one would diagnose a misbehaving person—in terms of impossible and typically contradictory pressures, as a product of vague or unreasonable expectations, as the result of too little feedback (in the form of support or even constructive criticism). But as in the diagnosis of individuals in a family, it is as often as not the structure of the family, or the overall lack of influence or support by the family, that supplies the key to the diagnosis. Unethical individuals reflect structural deformities in the corporation. Pressures encouraging unethical behavior in employees of any rank and status can almost always be explained (and corrected) in terms of the corporate culture.

There has always been a kind of hero worship in American business, as in most other aspects of American life. The fact is that heroes help, especially when an organization is suffering from internal confusion and the kind of contradictions that encourage unethical behavior. But heroes are not only leaders (often they are not leaders at all); they are *paradigms,* examples to emulate and follow, persons to please or do justice to. The philosopher Friedrich Nietzsche once summed up ethics in the question "Who are your heroes?" Is the figurehead of your organization a person who likes to cut corners? Is he or she a devotee of hard work? Or is he or she a person who enjoys the perks of office more than the responsibilities? Is the hero in your organization in a leadership role, or some other? In the inventive electronics industry, for instance, the hero may well be an innovative genius with no executive abilities. In the computer industry, one can find heroes like Jobs and Gates but also men and women in the work force, whose immediate effect on group solidarity and ethics may be just as important (Question 2).

Much is made today of "strong management," but what many businesses need are more heroes—more model examples. Weak management is often invisible management, management without an image. But it should also be said that not all times call for heroes. When industry is staid and stable, heroes may turn out to be tyrants, and corporate ethics may instead call for the nonheroic virtues of courtesy and quiet respect.

Needless to say, nothing corrupts an organization and its employees faster than perceived inequities within the organization—the wrong virtues rewarded (sycophancy, unctuousness, unwarranted self-promotion), or, worse, real merit unrecognized. If a business doesn't play according to the basic rules of the work ethic, its employees are bound to seek out another game. If hierarchy is important, it must be perceived as a function of merit. On the other hand, the more genuine friendliness a company promotes on the inside, the less such status distinctions come to matter, and the more unlikely it is that unfairness will be an issue. As Aristotle once wrote, "There is no need to worry about justice among friends" (Questions 3–6).

Product quality is of no small importance to a company's internal ethics. Pride in a product promotes pride in work and shared self-satisfaction in the company. The sense that one's firm is a purveyor of junk cannot help but poison the whole organization. A sense of product determines corporate ethics in another way, too. A company that makes quality products for the rich (Rothschild, Jaguar) is going to have a different corporate culture, in terms of what (and who) its employees believe to be valuable, from a company that prides itself on making a high-quality product for the general public (Mondavi, Ford). Both of these will be very different again from a company whose business is based on serving the less-well-to-do (bus companies or bargain automobile rentals) or a company whose success is bound to sheer novelty and whose attitude toward the consuming public is somewhat cynical. ("What in the world will they want next?") Compare the unstable values and attitudes of such a culture to those of a company that makes an undramatic but useful product that changes little over the years and requires little or no advertising. (An excellent example is the Calendar Corporation, whose primary product is the inserts for those yearly flip-flop calendars that are on every other desk in the nation.) It is hard to imagine unethical pressures in a company that suffers no pressure itself (Question 8).

Pressures within the corporation are not always the rather obvious pressures to produce. A middle manager may feel intolerably squeezed when confronted with demands that are impossible, accompanied by that horrid threat, "If you can't do it, I'll find someone else who can." But there are other sources of pressure that are harder to identify—and so harder to evaluate. There are pressures to conform, and pressures to be bold (Questions 9, 10).

Risk, for example, is an often neglected or overpraised value of business life that may deeply affect the ethics of a corporate culture. Texas Instruments, in its early years, used to give its employees extraordinarily free range to think and experiment, for theirs is a business that thrives on new ideas and surprises from unforeseen quarters. ITT, on the other hand, is a company pervaded by control and contingency plans for almost everything. "There are no tales of heroism, of sticking bravely to some ill-starred product, like Xerography or zippers, until faith is rewarded. . . . There must be no surprises, no surprises," is the company creed, writes Anthony Sampson in *The Sovereign State of ITT.* Executives at ITT spend hundreds of days a year in meetings, compared with occasional and informal consultations at the young computer companies. Life at ITT is aimed at forecast and control to minimize risk, and the life of an employee is consequently a matter of predictability and company control. Life in the young computer firm is built on uncertainty and surprise; and invention, unlike predictability, is to be found most often in uncontrolled and risky situations.

Perhaps one of the most important sources of pressure—to do good or otherwise—is company *tradition*. In a corporation with an old reputation to maintain, kindness, dubious deals, and tough talk—which might seem necessary to a young, innovative business—may be unthinkable. An executive of a bank is expected to live a certain kind of life and be above suspicion in every ethical sense. An executive in the entertainment industry is expected to live a quite different life. What counts as ethical—even what counts as moral—will be very different (which presents real problems at the intersection of Hollywood and Wall Street, as demonstrated in David McClintick's *Indecent Exposure*).

What counts as "profit," of course, also varies from corporate culture to corporate culture. A reasonable return in one business might be failure in another and scandalous in yet another. However, a publisher can pride itself on a good book published without a profit in a way that a breakfast-food merchandiser cannot pride itself on a clever idea gone unsold. What counts as success depends on the business, the product, and the goals established by the corporate culture, and pressures within the organization to succeed involve not only the *means* to succeed but the nature of the end as well.

Where does one begin an internal ethical audit? Not necessarily with the obvious sources of standards and pressures—the pronouncements of the CEO or stated company policies. Indeed, the most revealing aspects of corporate ethics can be found in the margins of work—in the company's contributions to its employees' leisure time and activities, in the way a company thinks about "wasting time" and hanging around the coffee pot or the water cooler, and, most of all, in the atmosphere of meetings. One might object that such considerations may reflect the ambience and enjoyability of working for a company but very little about its ethics. But the simple fact is that ambience and ethics are often one and the same. A company that is good to be with inspires goodness, too.

Part Four

SOCIAL RESPONSIBILITY: SOCIETY AND THE STAKEHOLDER

WHY SOCIAL RESPONSIBILITY?

The corporation has become, by virtue of its size and scope, more of a public institution than a private one.

Neil Chamberlain, The Limits of Corporate Responsibility

Several years ago, Milton Friedman asked rhetorically, "Do corporations have social responsibilities (over and above their fiduciary obligations to their stockholders)?" The answer, contra Friedman, is "Of course!" In fact, one wonders how such a perverse and narrowminded question could have originated in the first place.

The main reason, of course, is that some people not in business have demanded that corporations respond to problems that have nothing to do with them and have little or nothing to do with their services, products, abilities, or capacities. To insist that corporations *single-handedly* solve the poisonous problem of racism in America, for example, is unreasonable and unfair. Of course one can justly insist that a corporation not contribute to or further racism, but to insist that it set out to solve such a deep-seated social problem is to make a demand that has little justification. Corporations are legal inventions aimed at doing business, producing products and services, employing lots of people, and marshaling together resources for further investment and material progress. To expect anything else of them, it can be argued, is unreasonable and unfair.

But why should anyone have such unreasonable expectations? It is not hard to see why many Americans expect nothing less than miracles from our large corporations—public services at the lowest imaginable

---

RESPONSIBILITY AND SUCCESS

In 1992, John Kotter and James Haskett, two professors at Harvard Business School, once again studied the link between strong ethical culture in a company and economic performance. Among those firms that took seriously their responsibilities to customers and employees (as well as stockholders), revenues were on average four times as much as those companies that did not take their responsibilities to customers and employees as seriously. These companies also expanded on average four times as much and increased their profits by an average of 750 percent and their stock prices by as much as 900 percent.

Figures from *The Economist*, June 6, 1992

---

prices, solutions to social problems that have escaped even the most imaginative and generous government programs. It is ironic that these exaggerated expectations, which are typically used *against* business, are the natural product of the enormous success of businesses in our society in providing cheap public services and solving social problems. Enormous successes breed extravagant expectations.

Another reason for the extravagant demands on and expectations of business has to do with the traditional and natural demands that societies have always made of their richest and most powerful citizens. Wealthy warriors and kings have always been expected to make large contributions to the public good, sometimes because of a sense of fairness but more often because it is considered their duty to do so. It is also in their self-interest. It was Pericles' duty as the leader of Athens to enrich the city and make it the envy of the ancient world, but the fact that he would go down in history as the architect of a Golden Age was surely not distasteful to him. *Noblesse oblige*, it has always been called—the obligations of the nobility. And there is little doubt that in our society the new nobility—the privileged class—is corporate business. Whether measured by visibility, financial resources, or political power, there is hardly another American institution to match it that is not itself another corporation or closely allied with major corporations. (It is not just the "business" of America that is business.)

Social responsibility encompasses an ever-expanding circle of concerns, and this expansion reflects the success and importance of

DOING WELL BY DOING GOOD

Companies making national as well as local grants	$ millions
1. IBM* Gifts in all categories equal (estimated)	118
2. Hewlett-Packard* 87% to education	74
3. General Electric* 58% to education	45.3
4. AT&T 49% to education	35.4
5. Exxon* 48% to health/welfare	22.8
6. Safeway Gifts in all categories equal (estimated)	19.5
7. Eastman Kodak 51% to education	16.2
8. Harris Corporation 95% to education	2.9

*Also make international grants.

Source: Corporate 500; Directory of Corporate Philanthropy. CA: Datarex Corporation, 1995.

business in society. When business represented but a small part of American society, like Adam Smith's "nation of shopkeepers," the social responsibilities of business consisted for the most part in businessmen's doing what they were supposed to do well and honestly—produce quality products and services, provide jobs for the community, and earn a fair return for owners and investors. As industry expanded and technologies became more pervasive, concerns for the environment and conservation of natural resources became essential corporate responsibilities. As consumerism became a central, if not *the* central, identity of the society (the idea of living well and the good life as primarily functions of material well-being and ownership), product safety and consumer relations became responsibilities, and not only because of the need to maintain sales. But, finally, now that

---

SOCIAL IRRESPONSIBILITY

The social role of business is to increase national wealth, and what can be held against bureaucratic capitalism is that it often performs this job poorly. Management's increasing autonomy partially corrupts the logic of private markets, which are supposed to channel investment funds to their most productive uses. In truth, corporate managers control the lion's share of investment capital, and it is not always in their interest to use it most productively. When they don't, we all suffer.

Robert J. Samuelson, *Newsweek*

---

businesses are often the most powerful institutions in the world, the expanse of social responsibility has enlarged to include areas formerly considered the domain of governments: quality of education and support of the arts, funding and facilities for basic research, urban planning and development, world hunger and poverty, hard-core unemployment. There will always be some debate about where the line should be drawn, but this much is clear: The more powerful business becomes in the world, the more responsibility for the well-being of the world it will be expected to bear.

The social responsibilities of corporations depend, quite naturally, on the nature of the corporation and what it can do. A high-tech computer company will probably not play much of a role in solving problems of poverty in third-world nations, but virtually every corporation has its own areas of expertise and wealth where it can do wonders—for itself as well as for the world. The examples may be modest. For example, Trailways Bus Company began a "home-free" program in which they offered free seats to runaway teenagers to get them back where they belong, helping to save many young people from starvation, prostitution, and death in the streets. Helping runaway teenagers is not one of those social responsibilities that gets listed in the textbooks, but it is an excellent example of what good a corporation with a simple, good idea can do.

Another company that demonstrated the wisdom of the social-responsibility concept was Control Data Corporation, led by its founder, chairman, and then-chief executive officer, William C. Norris. Norris, who learned firsthand the problem of economic hardship while growing up on a Nebraska farm during the Great Depression, had long held that the American business community must take an active

---

THE BUSINESS DEBT TO SOCIETY

Suppose that General Motors, Ford, and Chyrsler had to provide the public not only with cars, but with the roads on which to drive them (as the railroads do). Has there ever been a larger government subsidy in the history of the world? Can there be any question whether there are obligations owed in return?

From the lunchtime collection of Tom Stewart

---

leadership role, in cooperation with government and other sectors of society, in transforming the major unmet needs of society into profitable business opportunities. "I think everybody has a responsibility to be socially responsible," he said. "The major difference is that Control Data is willing to take risks and make long-term investments in addressing these basic needs as business opportunities." During 1967, when riots erupted in a depressed area of Minneapolis and St. Paul not far from Control Data's headquarters, Norris responded quickly and constructively. "You can't do business with the town on fire," he explained. "So you stop and think why this happened. It happened because of inequities. The people felt so damn frustrated that this was their way of expressing themselves." Accordingly, in 1968, Norris and Control Data opened a new plant in the riot-torn area and provided employees with a child-care facility, with job training for the disadvantaged and unemployed, with remedial instruction in basic skills for high-school dropouts, and basic courses in computer-related skills. In 1970 a second new plant was opened in a similar neighborhood in St. Paul. Since then, Norris and his company have moved aggressively to address a broad range of unmet social needs that they believe can be converted into profitable business opportunities. These include programs to revitalize urban and rural areas, to create jobs through small-business development, to provide education and training to prison populations, and to meet other basic human needs.

It is unfortunate, however, that the social responsibilities of some corporations become more obvious in the breach. The stories of companies that do not take available precautions in protecting their employees from hazardous chemicals or protecting the environment from the by-products of their manufacturing processes tend to make the headlines, leaving important activities like Trailways' "home-free" program and Control Data's employment efforts to short articles in the

> **ON THE OTHER HAND**
>
> Sometimes companies get bought because the management gets tired of the hassle with local communities. It is sometimes easier to avoid the hassle if you are part of a large, distant company. If communites want to keep local ownership they should show some respect for the people who are managing it. If someone is running a local company and is part of the community but everyone seems to hate you and you are pressured from everyone and every housewife in town seems to have more power than you do, and if the government is changing the rules all the time, and if your children would love you more if you became an ecologist rather than a manager, selling your company seems to answer many problems.
>
> Kenneth Olsen (Digital Equipment Corporation)

back of the business pages while a horrendous pollution scandal takes over the front page. But the social responsibilities of corporations, like the responsibilities of the individuals who work in them, should not be perceived as a burden. Responsibilities are the mark of success, and social responsibilities are the sign of one's importance in society.

"IMPACT" AND THE STAKEHOLDER

In response to the debate over the social responsibilities of business, business ethnicists have introduced the concept of a *stakeholder*. The word is something of a pun on "stockholder," and the point is precisely to replace the overemphasis on the rights and demands of the stockholders with a more general regard for all of those constituencies who are involved with and affected by the corporation. Among the various stakeholders of the corporation are its customers, its employees, and its various suppliers and external contractors and consultants as well as its stockholders. Stakeholders also include the surrounding community, the larger society and, we will add, that often "silent" stakeholder, the environment. The stockholder is indeed a stakeholder, and the company does have obligations and fiduciary responsibilities toward its stockholders. But the stockholders are merely one constituency among many; and there is no fair argument, for example, that employees must always be sacrificed to the interests of the stockholders, or that customers, not the stockholders, must foot the bill for increased taxes or the cost of a liability judgment against the company. But increased attention to the stakeholders of the corporation is not just a matter of morals and social responsibility. It is also good business. Recent research has shown rather conclusively (though not in all cases) that attention to customers and employees and demonstrated concern for the community and environment tends to "pay off" in terms of increased sales, better community relations, improved financial status in the markets, and workplace morale and stability.

The definitive reason that corporations have social responsibilities is one that involves no exaggerated demands or debatable traditions, no questions whether corporations do or do not have obligations to the society that they are part of. That reason can be summarized in the word "impact." Impact is simply what a corporation does to society; what it brings about, causes, changes, creates, and destroys.

Impact, first of all, is a *positive* term. It means that a company is having an effect, making a contribution to society. It is supplying a product. It is satisfying a demand. It may be improving the lives of many people, or at least it may be amusing or entertaining them. Important products change society—the automobile, the electric light bulb, television, the home computer. Only a handful of Luddites (after Ned Ludd, a legendary eighteenth-century antitechnology activist) would say that these things have caused more harm than good. Impact is the whole of those social changes caused by these products. And the corporations that brought them about are—much to their credit—responsible for them.

It is singularly unfortunate that, in most discussions of business ethics, positive impact is discussed so rarely. Ethics consists of virtues as well as of vices, and corporations must be as praiseworthy as they are blameworthy. Indeed, the primary ethical question to be applied to most of business and most businesses is how they contribute to the well-being of society and the happiness of its citizens—through prod-

---

SAFETY FIRST (AND LAST)

California is the safest state for workers and Arkansas is the least safe, according to the National Safe Workplace Institute, a Chicago interest group. The institute rated the states on efforts to prevent workplace accidents, workmen's compensation benefits, and enforcement records.

Top Five in Safety   *Bottom Five in Safety*

1. *California*   1. *Arkansas*
2. *New Jersey*   2. *Wyoming*
3. *New York, Illinois (tie)*   3. *New Mexico*
4. *Massachusetts*   4. *Kansas*
5. *Texas*   5. *North Dakota*

Business and Society Review, Winter 1992

---

ucts or services or employment as well as through a substantial return to the stockholders. The answer in the vast majority of cases is unqualified. That is or should be the main history of business ethics.

Unfortunately, that is not the whole story. There is also negative impact—bad products, harmful by-products, and the disruption or destruction of social life. Even a good and useful product can have negative impact, of course. The producers of the drugs Valium and Quaalude, for example, were undoubtedly producing important and much needed products for a large and proper if nervous and sleepless market. The drugs were thoroughly tested and demonstrably safe. The marketing was contained and distribution carefully controlled. Nevertheless, the social *consequences* of the widespread abuse of those drugs—of Valium through proper but much abused medical and pharmaceutical channels, of Quaaludes through illegal sales on the street and in schoolyards—have been monstrous. And monstrous consequences *always* raise the question, to the corporations involved, *"Were you really careful enough?"* And the hardheaded answer will always be "Given the enormity of the abuses, you must not have been."

When the product itself is faulty, insufficiently tested, or just plain dangerous, there is no question about responsibility. Corporations are socially—and legally—responsible for their products. The questions are when to expect the lawsuit and whether there will be criminal penalties.

Impact involving by-products is a bit more complicated. One ques-

---

CORPORATE CARELESSNESS

Painting clock and watch dials with radium has all but ended in the U.S. today, but scientists from Argonne's Center for Human Radiobiology now say they have found nine breast-cancer deaths in one group of 463 of the former dial painters—more than double the expected rate. Some women who worked at a Luminous Processes plant in Ottawa, Illinois, at various times from the 1940s until the plant closed in 1978 say that safety precautions were almost nonexistent and that workers were constantly contaminated with the radioactive material. In fact, they assert, company officials assured them that radium was safe to handle.

Women at the plant sometimes painted their fingernails with radium paint. Others took pots of radium paint home and painted light switches so that they would glow in the dark. They routinely contaminated their hair, arms, legs and feet with the radioactive material accidentally while they worked, and they wiped paint-covered hands on the front of their work smocks.

Wall Street Journal

---

tion is whether the by-product in question is really necessary to the production of the product (and, if it is, whether the product itself is worth that cost). But if we assume an absolutely essential product (steel or rubber, for instance) in which noxious by-products are unavoidable (given the current state of technology), the question shifts to the responsibility of the company or the industry in correcting the situation. That there is such a responsibility is no longer a matter of debate. The question is rather the extent of such responsibility and how much a company should be expected to put its very existence in jeopardy trying to live up to that responsibility.

Here again, we should notice, we run into the problem of the prisoner's dilemma. It is rare that an isolated company produces pollution, for example; it is usually the entire industry, given that manufacturing methods will be more or less the same. (If a single company is much worse than the others, it can be easily singled out for punishment. If a single company is much better than the others, there will be substantial pressure both inside and outside the industry to share that particular process.) But if an entire industry is responsible for pollution, let us say, it must be the shared responsibility of the industry, not just the responsibility of the individual companies. The prisoner's dilemma lets us see why this must be so. If one company

NORTH AMERICA'S BEST POLLUTERS

The International Organization for Standardization sets quality standards for manufacturing (ISO 9000) and for environmental management (14000).

• Canada's Ford Oakville Assembly Plant was the first North American assembly plant to achieve ISO 9002 certification for quality, and has been ISO 14001 certified. (*Toronto Star*, April 12, 1997)

• Acushnet Rubber (Massachusetts), ISO 9001 quality-certified, was one of the first companies in the United States to achieve ISO 14001 certification. "What we found was that ISO 14001 was just an enhancement of the way a good quality manufacturing facility works." (*Mass High Tech*, March 10, 1997)

• Micron Technology, Inc. was also one of the first American companies to be 14001-certified. "Complicance with state and federal environmental regulations is a minimum. . . . We hope to help shape the standards in environmental management systems." (*Business Wire*, February 18, 1997)

• Lucent Technologies (formed by the restructuring of AT&T) aims to meet ISO 14000 standards at all levels of the organization. "That way it becomes part of the business decision-making process and corporate culture."

—*Eastern Pennsylvania Business Journal*, January 27, 1997

tried to correct its pollution problem alone, the expense of this effort would put it at a ruinous disadvantage in the industry. It therefore becomes essential that the industry as a whole agree to the corrective efforts, whether through mutually binding agreements or through government regulation. However inefficient and against the grain of autonomy, the latter are usually more dependable.

What is most difficult to evaluate is the impact of products that introduce pervasive social changes. We can all agree that the television networks have responsibilities above and beyond their obligations to the stockholders, but once that is said, it is almost impossible to agree on the precise nature of those responsibilities. The head of CBS once insisted that the only responsibility of network television is to entertain its audience—within the bounds of good taste, of course. But what is "good taste"? Does this phrase merely eliminate obscenity and offensive racial, sexual, and religious comments? Or does it also embody an imperative to make programs spiritually uplifting, inspiring, perhaps even (gasp) "educational"? Does it preclude violence? Does it really matter whether it can be proved that violence on TV does or does not cause violent behavior in children? (Does it matter that explicit sexual intercouse in cartoons does not excite six-year-olds?) If millions of people would watch (but might never ask for) nude news on television, would the market justify it? Does television have an obligation to cover the news—or is it just a question of audience shares and good business?

Few corporations are literally as visible as CBS, ABC, and NBC, and few corporations are plagued with that number of ethical questions and implications. But every corporation has impact and so faces questions concerning compliance, contribution, and consequences. Those questions are the essence of social responsibility. There is no such thing as impact without social responsibility, and a company that is without impact is a company that is already out of business.

FRIEDMAN'S PARADOX

> *In a free enterprise, private property system, a corporate executive is an employee of the owners of the business. He has a direct responsibility to his employers. That responsibility is to conduct the business in accordance with their desires, which generally will be to make as much money as possible while conforming to the basic rules of society, both those embodied in law and those embodied in ethical custom.*
>
> Milton Friedman, "The Social Responsibility of
> Business Is to Increase Profits,"
> New York Times, September 13, 1970

Milton Friedman has gone on record with one of the most popular and ultimately most misleading arguments against the idea of the social responsibilities of business. Much of his argument is the perfectly correct insistence that (1) business executives are employed by the owners of a business (the stockholders) and have obligations to them,

---

BIG MAC ATTACK

Advocates of corporate responsibility who argue that business does good only when it departs from its profit objectives are engaging in self-deception. "Doing good" not based on logical self-interest is and should be suspect. . . .

Altruistic programs undertaken by business may make some corporate folks "feel good." And it might make for some good public relations. But, by and large, it makes for better rhetoric than results.

Norman Axelrad (McDonald's Corporation)

---

and (2) it is irresponsible for businesses to undertake social-welfare programs that they are ill-prepared to execute. But the first argument is too often restricted to the claim that executives have only a fiduciary obligation to the stockholders, which simply is not true. Executives are employed for many reasons, *one* of which is their ability to run a business efficiently and make a profit. Executives are also hired—and fired—for the reputation they give to and earn for a company. Executives are expected to make life agreeable for the hundreds or thousands of employees of the company—and not only to increase productivity and avoid lawsuits. And, not incidentally, executives are employed because they are agreeable to their employers. Such nonfiduciary attributes as personal charm, an assuring and unassuming manner, the "correct" political opinions, and cultural interests are of no small importance.

Friedman's second argument, we have already agreed, is arguably correct. Corporations do not usually have the knowhow to solve pressing social problems, and it is irresponsible for them to try to do so singlehandedly; it is as unreasonable to expect them to do so as it would be to expect the Boy Scouts of America to attack the national debt. Moreover, corporations do not generally have the authority to solve social problems, even if they have the resources to do so.

But, this reasonable argument is often taken to extremes that are totally absurd. For example, it is extended to suggest that corporations do not have social responsibilities *even when they themselves have caused the problems in question.* A corporation does not have an obligation to solve a city's employment problem, but it can be argued quite plausibly that it would have such an obligation if, for example, it moved an army of employees into a small town and now contemplates a move elsewhere. Corporations are responsible, like everyone else, for cleaning up the messes they make. Corporations are responsible, like everyone else, for thinking about the changes they make in people's lives and trying to minimize them.

One of Friedman's suggestions is that the corporation as such has no social responsibilities at all. Only the individual does. In the same *Times* article, Friedman writes:

> Of course, the corporate executive is also a person in his [*sic*] own right. As a person he may have many other responsibilities . . . if we wish, we can refer to some of these as "social responsibilities." But in these respects he is acting as a principle, not as an agent. . . . If these are "social responsibilities," they are the social responsibilities of individuals, not of business.

Where impact is concerned, this is nonsense. The executive did not cause pollution as a "person" or as a "principle" but as the manager of the corporation and the agent of the owners. It is the corporation that is responsible, not the individual. Indeed, that is the legal and historical purpose of inventing the corporation in the first place. But if corporations have social responsibilities in this kind of case, it must make sense to say that they have responsibilities in other senses, too. If the corporation is a citizen of society, why should it not have the responsibility to enrich (as well as to avoid harming) that society? Of course, it has often been argued that individuals do not have any obligation to enrich society either, as if it were enough not to cause harm and to leave other people alone. But when one is as powerful as even a minor corporation, it is hard to "leave other people alone," and in any case, we would be a pretty poor society if no one felt compelled except by way of whimsy to enrich society and not just to take from it. Unfortunately, some of the individuals who insist on the magnanimity of corporations are not demonstrably generous themselves in this regard, nor are some of the individuals who insist on leaving charity to individuals.

It is important to note that Friedman insists that making a profit is not all there is to the responsibilities of corporate executives. He adds, significantly, that they should try to make money "while conforming to the basic rules of society, both those embodied in law *and those embodied in ethical custom.*" But this is a loophole in the argument large enough to accommodate the space shuttle. What are our much-celebrated ethical customs in this country if not our willingness to help

---

MAXIMIZING LEGAL PROFITS

Now let's reflect on that [Prof. Friedman's argument] a little. Do you really imagine that an individual, after being told explicitly and by long example that his company has no responsibility to him or to anyone else except insofar as it maximizes its legal profits—do you imagine that such an individual will be of a mind to make a loyal commitment to the welfare and progress of his company, to go to extraordinary lengths in helping it solve its problems? Or do you imagine that such a worker, assuming he is on the shop floor, might be inclined to maximize his own legal profits by stretching out the work so that he can get more overtime—or perhaps even a little Sunday double-time?

J. Irwin Miller (CEO, Cummins Engine Company)

---

other people less fortunate than ourselves, to give generously as we are able without serious sacrifice to ourselves, to support families and communities and culture, to dare into the unknown and explore and investigate, even if no immediate profit appears on the horizon?

Friedman's reputation in the business community rests as much on his paradoxical belligerence as it does on his acknowledged contributions to economics. But not all of that belligerence comes to the aid of business; in fact, his argument has done much to demean both business and businessmen. When accused of being probusiness, he denied it flatly and insisted, "I am pro–free enterprise." Again in the *New York Times*, Sept. 13, 1970, he made socially conscious businessmen out to be dupes.

. . . Businessmen believe that they are defending free enterprise when they declaim that business is not concerned "merely" with profit but also with promoting desirable "social" ends. . . . In fact they are . . . preaching pure and unadulterated socialism. Businessmen who talk this way are unwitting puppets of the intellectual forces that have been undermining the basis of a free society. . . .

Indeed, such language is hardly "pro–free enterprise" either, since the "freedom" in free enterprise presumably includes the liberty to pursue goals other than profits. Friedman mercilessly restricts the freedom of executives to act on the behalf of their companies and their employers in any way that does not directly and demonstrably improve the bottom line, and it must be noted that he also implies a view of

The flaw in Dr. Friedman's statement, rejecting corporate expenditures for social purposes, is the fact that while decrying such action he also acknowledged the right of management to exercise discretion in making some such expenditures (i.e., philanthropy) because it is in the economic self-interest of shareholders to do so. At that point the argument became one of degree rather than principle, and management would seem free to exercise its discretion to make any social expenditures which could be justified on the basis of the long-term economic self-interest of its shareholders.

It is on this basis, in fact, that most such expenditures are made. Management recognizes that its growth and prosperity, and perhaps its survival, is dependent on a healthy society, and it commits corporate resources to help insure a healthy society. . . .

Philip T. Drotning
(director of corporate social policy at Amoco)

business and a view of stockholders that is uniquely unflattering. Good business, Friedman keeps suggesting, is something quite distinct from serving a socially useful purpose, however he may go on to assure us that businesses can and will serve social functions if they show a profit from it. The stockholder, according to Friedman, is something of a monster, a virtual caricature of *Homo economicus*, a person without personality, sex, culture, political opinions, hopes for the future, or faith in technology; an investor pure and simple who cares about nothing but making money. Occasionally this is true: Many investors today play the market without much concern for the nature of the products or the company, for the short term only and a quick profit, perhaps just for "kicks." But short-term, indifferent investors surely are not the "owners" to whom the corporate executive is bound by obligations, except to try (as a by-product of improving the company) to provide a reasonable return on that short-term investment. A good manager is not and cannot be employed primarily to provide short-term gains, and the stockholder to whom he or she is obliged is not the short-term investor but those who really do care about the overall success of the company.

Quite to the contrary of Friedman's insistence on "fiduciary responsibilities," there is an overwhelming argument that an investor who takes so small and narrow an interest in the company deserves little attention in return. The people to whom the managers of a corporation are obliged are those who, like themselves, are concerned with the company and its reputation over the long haul. And you can be sure that for them the social responsibilities of business are much more than just increasing profits.

THE PUZZLE OF CORPORATE RESPONSIBILITY

Most people take the existence and the nature of the corporation for granted. In fact, corporations as we know them are only a century or so old, and with the rise of the corporation come a number of intricate and puzzling problems of responsibility. There is the question of social responsibility: given the fact that some (but by no means all) corporations were created in order to make money and protect the liability of its owners, what "external" responsibilities can and must it be said to have? Our answer, of course, is that it has the responsibility to do the best it can, to be the best it can be, to make a quality product or provide dependable service at the lowest price possible compatible with its doing well for itself. It has responsibilities and obligations to its employees and its customers, but to the larger community too, especially (but not only) where damage or harm has been done. But then there is another dimension and another set of problems having to do with corporate responsibility, an "internal" dimension, especially the problem of assigning responsibility within the corporation. Virtually every function of a company is shared or regulated by a number of individuals, and rarely can praise or blame be laid squarely on the head of one single perpetrator. At the same time, virtually every function of the corporation is under the auspices of the CEO and the board of directors. But are they to be held responsible for everything that goes on in a company, including the daily actions of thousands of individuals and perhaps a million technical details they could not possibly know?

To what extent is a corporation an abstraction? As an abstraction, how can "it" be responsible for anything? To what extent is a corporation a collection or a community of individuals? As a collection or a community, how can anyone in particular be held responsible? In law, a corporation is conceived as a "fictional person"; that is, a creature created by the law but not a "real" person. The purpose of this creation is to consolidate resources, to limit liability, to establish certain obligations, to formalize certain arrangements. But, then, who is responsible for anything, and when something goes wrong, who should get the blame?

What does it mean to hold a corporation responsible? We praise and condemn corporations and corporate activities, and most of us do so without having any idea who the decision makers in the corporation are or how they make their decisions or what they are thinking about. Indeed, even within the corporation, the exact locus of praise or blame may be a matter of mystery or happenstance, although we might well note that there are usually many more people who are happy and willing to take credit and praise for a corporation's accomplishments than there are people who are willing to accept responsibility for a company's failures and misdeeds.

Consider a disastrous decision or mishap of moderate proportions. A middle manager insists that he was "just doing what he was told," and his supervisor claims that she was "just following orders." Her boss in turn was only doing what he thought the top executives wanted done and the executives themselves, even the chief executive of the company, insist that they had no such intention and place the blame squarely on those to whom they had delegated such responsibilities. The board of directors, who are supposedly the overseers of the entire operation, claim to have had no knowledge of what was going on. And the stockholders, who in theory "own" the company, find themselves out of the loop where such decisions are made. Where is the responsibility to be laid? Inevitably, some already beleaguered soul in upper management will be held up as a sacrificial lamb and fired with great fanfare and moral chest-thumping. But such "scapegoating" only hides rather than resolves the difficult problem of assigning responsibility within the corporation.

It is not just figurative speaking that allows us to criticize or compliment a corporation for its behavior, and that is not just shorthand for commenting on the individual officers and employees of the company, individually or collectively. In a case in which a corporation causes serious harm, for example, it is very likely that the majority of the population of the company had no idea what was going on, had nothing directly to do with the harm, and could probably not have done anything about it even if they had known about it. Indeed, sometimes the most serious corporation wrongdoing seems to be no more than the misbehavior or incompetence of a single individual. The Exxon *Valdez* polluted miles and miles of pristine Alaskan wilderness, killing wildlife, ruining the local fishing industry, spoiling the coastline, and costing the Alaskan economy billions in losses and clean-up costs. The fault seemed to lie with one man, the captain of the *Valdez*, who had been drinking heavily and had gone below to "sleep it off." But, then, that means that he wasn't in charge of the boat, so how could he be responsible?

The actual navigation was in the hands of the first mate, who evidently had not been adequately trained for such an enormous responsibility. The ship did not have a pilot, who presumably would have been in the proper position to take over for the captain. It turned out, on investigation immediately after the accident, that the captain had a prior arrest record for drunken driving. Should the personnel people at Exxon have known about that? Should they have done something about it? In any case, shouldn't the company have seen to it that there was more than one person aboard capable of handling the tanker? Moreover, the ship was not triple-hulled, as many tankers now are; and this would have provided the vessel with protection that, in all likelihood, would have minimized if not prevented the damage to both the ship and the environment. Indeed, the more we examine the case and the corporation, the more diffuse the question of responsibility becomes.

There were any number of people within the organization, from those in charge of ship maintenance to those in charge of personnel, who might have done more to prevent such a disaster, but the diffused blame seems to all come together in the office of the CEO. But Exxon's CEO correctly claimed that he could not possibly have known what was happening with a single captain of a single tanker in a corporation that employs hundreds of thousands of people. Should he, nevertheless, have been held responsible? On what grounds? Here some ethicists and legal theorists introduce the notion of *regulative* responsibility; that is, a sort of responsibility that results not from one's direct or "proximate" contact with the case at hand nor does it even suppose knowledge of, much less acquiescence to, the harm in question. It is responsibility that results from one's "position of overall responsibility," from being "in charge." That is, after all, what those extremely high-paid executives are supposedly paid so much money to do, to be responsible for the company—its decisions and mistakes as well as its successes.

Nevertheless, whether or not we hold the chief executive ultimately responsible, it is clear that *the company* must also be held responsible. But, again, what is it to hold a company responsible? One cannot send Exxon, as one might have the irresponsible captain, to prison. A court can fine Exxon, and the Alaskan citizens can sue Exxon for their losses in civil court, but where does that money come from? From the stockholders, who were further away from the mishap and much less in a position to know the situation than the chairman or the people in human resources. Why should they be penalized? And if the fines and settlements are large enough, the cost will be passed on to the consumers at the pump as well. So who is really being punished? And who is really responsible in the first place?

One reply is that no one is responsible; or perhaps a few people are partly responsible, but no blame is really relevant, on this view, and the idea that the company is responsible is simply incoherent. Responsibility belongs to individual agents. Responsibility can be shared, and several persons may be equally and fully responsible for a misdeed they performed together, committing a crime or standing by negligently while some easily preventable disaster was unfolding. (For example, consider four night watchmen playing cards and not paying attention as thieves steal the entire contents of the warehouse they are supposedly watching.) But a corporation, this argument goes, does not "act" at all. Its "actions" are nothing but the decisions and implementations of individuals within the organization. This may include virtually all of them—as in the production of their products and the collected corporate gift to the United Way at the end of the year. It may be a single individual, most likely the chairman, who makes a decision, or it may be a few individuals in the middle of the organization, acting on behalf of the corporation but nevertheless acting alone. But what does this mean, "acting on the behalf of the organization"? How do we differentiate among an employee who does wrong simply as a private citizen, one who does wrong as an employee of the company, and one who does wrong on the behalf of the company? Individual responsibility is part of the answer to any question of responsibility, but it is not the whole answer. Individuals can be held responsible not only alone but in groups, as groups, and as organizations that transcend the individuals who are members of it.

Any large corporation is constantly in flux. People join, people leave.

They retire. They are fired. They take a leave of absence. They are temporarily replaced. The identity of the corporation, in other words, cannot possibly be reduced to the collected identity of all of its employees and managers. It continues despite the change and replacement of its employees. It retains the same legal status, the same name, the same trademark, the same corporate culture, the same basic form of organization, the same way of doing things and making decisions, even though all of the decision-making slots are now filled with other people. In some instances, the people who run the corporation when scandal or disaster hits were not even there when the original mishap occurred. Most pharmaceutical companies, for instance, face lawsuits that stem from drugs sold and taken ten, twenty, even thirty years earlier. The executives who ran the company and approved the sale of the drug, perhaps even knowing the dangers but not telling the public, have long since moved on or retired.

And yet, we blame *the corporation*. How is this possible? The agency of a corporation is determined, according to business ethicist Peter French, by the structure of its "corporate internal decision" (CID) structure (Peter French, Jeffrey Nesteruk, and David Risser, *Corporations in the Moral Community*. Fort Worth: Harcourt Brace Jovanovich, 1992). A corporation, unlike a mob or a random collection of people (say, at a football game), has a formal organization, filled by people who understand that they are engaged in a cooperative enterprise and each of whom knows that he or she has certain specified duties and responsibilities. The corporation can be said to have made a decision when that decision is made by the right people or passes through the designated channels of the "corporate internal decision" structure. Thus corporate responsibility is something more than collective responsibility. It depends on a structure, on a formal organization, and though the individuals who fill the positions in that organization may come and go, the structure itself remains essentially the same. A corporation is responsible for a decision and its implementation if it properly passes through the "corporate internal decision" structure.

The idea of a "corporate internal decision" structure as the key to corporate responsibility allows us to answer a number of troubling questions. First of all, we can understand how we can distinguish an employee of the company who does wrong but only as an individual, not as an employee of the company. He or she acts outside of the corporate internal decision procedure, not going through proper channels, not notifying the proper people of what he or she is doing and not fulfilling the explicit and merely understood duties and responsibilities of his or her job. The corporation may be responsible for hiring such a person, and in some instances should be held responsible for his or her supervision, but if, for example, an employee takes a bribe from a customer in exchange for "looking the other way" during an obviously illegitimate transaction, the responsibility lies with the employee, not the corporation.

Bank tellers, for example, are often in a position to do wrong in this way, but unless it becomes a common practice and the bank does not then implement more secure safeguards, we usually do not blame the bank for such individual malfeasance. Of course, paying bribes may enter into the corporate internal decision process; for example, the chairman of the company (or someone with delegated authority) negotiates a bribe in the name of the company, as in the case of Lockheed in Japan. The idea of a corporate internal decision structure also explains how it is that corporations can be held liable for negligence. It is one thing if a designated employee fails to take responsibility or act competently concerning some event that is one of his or her responsibilities and under his or her control. It is possible that *no one* in the corporation has some particular duty or responsibility, and so no one is responsible when there is a disaster in that area. But nevertheless, the corporation is responsible. It is responsible for that gap in its internal decision structure. To be sure, the uppermost executives will no doubt take most of the heat, but the charge of negligence is not for them alone. The corporation has a responsibility, even if the responsibility in question is part of no one's job.[1]

THE SEVEN DEADLY CORPORATE SINS

In *Business and Society Review,* Larry D. Alexander published a list of "The Seven Deadly Sins of Corporate Doubletalk," a concise study of the most frequent and most "offensive" tactics used by corporations

1. Parts of this chapter have been adapted from *Above the Bottom Line* (Harcourt Brace, 1993).

under fire. Unfortunately, Alexander argues, these almost always "backfire in the long run," even when they initially seem to work. Alexander's study is well worth repeating. Here are the seven deadly sins:

1. *Ignoring Major Social Problems*
   Example: Ford's decision to ignore the hazardous gas tank in its Pinto, saving some $11 per Pinto but ultimately causing dozens of deaths and costing millions of dollars in lawsuits.

2. *Placing the Blame on Someone Else*
   Example: Television networks blamed parents for allowing children to watch violent shows.

3. *Discrediting Outside Critics*
   Example: General Motors made Ralph Nader a national hero when it tried to discredit him and shut him up.

4. *Firing Troublemakers*
   Example: Hooker Chemical and Plastic Company fired the supervising engineer for plant efficiency in New York, who then took his complaint (rebuffed by his superiors) to a local television station, thus triggering the national scandal of Love Canal.

5. *Suppressing Information*
   Example: Equity Funding tried to hide more than 64,000 phony insurance files, but the truth came out, and Equity went bankrupt under a cloud of scandal.

6. *Countering with a PR Campaign*
   Example: A committee formed after the Three Mile Island nuclear power plant accident in 1979 spent $1.6 million on public relations even before the extent of the damage and of the danger was known. Subsequent investigations turned much of the rhetoric into a retrospective embarrassment.

7. *Denying the Charges*
   Example: Firestone denied that there was a problem with its "500" tires, and sold them for half price. When accident reports and lawsuits began rolling in, Firestone took a loss, and an enormous loss in its trustworthy reputation as well.

MERGERS AND ACQUISITIONS: THE ETHICAL DIMENSION

Corporations, like individuals, are dynamic. They grow, they change, they compete, they cooperate, and sometimes they even get married. Marriages are mergers, and as in human marriages of the more romantic kind there can be mergers of convenience as well as mergers of necessity. There are happy but also unhappy mergers. There are mergers made in stockholders' heaven as well as mergers seemingly made by the devil. First and foremost among the more hellish mergers are "hostile mergers," the corporate equivalent of the shotgun wedding or, perhaps, of a kidnapping. In a hostile merger, the acquiring corporation "takes over" the acquired company against the latter's will, often at the end of a protracted, very expensive, exhausting but dramatic battle. And quite unlike the loving spouse, indeed more like the nightmare husband in certain horror movies, the first action of the acquiring company may be physically to dismantle the company acquired, selling off the best parts at a considerable profit, engulfing others and abandoning those that are of no use or commercial value. But as in many bad marriages, the "winning" partner of the merger often suffers its own comeuppance. Several enormously successful takeover companies in the last several years have found themselves in bankruptcy court for literally biting off more than they could chew. The debt incurred in the winning takeover bid nevertheless put the company in an impossible financial position.

But these are the worst marriages, and in any discussion of mergers as with marriages it is only right and proper that we begin with the happy-case scenario. Two companies find themselves competing in a small or diminishing market. One or the other will soon find itself in serious trouble. But instead of competing they decide to cooperate, joining their resources, cutting their operating costs, sharing their expenses, unifying their product lines, and becoming a single profitable company instead of two competing and perhaps unprofitable companies. Or, two companies may find that they complement each other. One, perhaps, makes rubber tires. The other manufactures wheels. They deal with each other all the time. Their various sales and manufacturing people often discuss their mutual needs. They often sell their products in tandem and, not surprisingly, they begin to think of themselves as partners. They decide to formalize their already established complementarity and cooperation, and they merge to form a single company. Again, they pool their resources, probably save a good deal on reduced operating and administrative costs and very likely make their production and marketing methods much more efficient.

Mergers make sense for many reasons. A national or global business that is served by many different small enterprises finds that it could serve more people more efficiently and give them a much wider variety of services if they all joined together as a single operation. Banking, for example, is undergoing such a change in the United States, where interstate banking was until very recently forbidden by law. But anyone who has tried to cash an out-of-state check while traveling knows the disadvantages of such a system, and legislative and other regulative moves are underway to allow more banks to make branches of small local banks and allow them to consolidate their operations and extend to all their customers services that are not now available. Of course, there are dangers to this, but the consolidation of now-independent banking systems seems to be the inevitable trend of the immediate future. Mergers are often major steps toward efficiency and competitiveness, and as such it must be said that they are often good for business.

But bigger is not always better; and mergers are not always good for business, nor are they always in the public interest. The most obvious danger of a merger is the creation of virtual monopolies and the loss of competition in an already limited market; but a more immediate catastrophe, the consequence of consolidation, may be the elimination of many jobs and the shutting down of factories and offices. People are put out of work and whole communities may be destroyed. When the takeover is "hostile"—that is, against the wishes of the current management and often the result of a long expensive court battle—the consequences can be even worse. If the takeover has as its object the liquidation of the company and the sale of its most valuable assets, for instance, the dimensions of the resulting unemployment and destruction can be catastrophic. Not all hostile takeovers have this conclusion. Occasionally, a hostile takeover actually improves efficiency and pays off for both the employees and the stockholders as well as the surrounding community. Unfortunately, this seems to be the exception rather than the rule. There is a special class of cases, for example, in which the conclusion of a purported takeover is not control of the company, but the possibility is so threatening to the current management that it "buys out" its own company, incurring great debt and subsequently has to lay off thousands of its employees and penalize the stockholders as well. Here is where the doctrine of social responsibility and stakeholder theory have their most important implication: against the familiar arguments concerning the "rights of the stockholders" that we heard so often in the 1980s corporations and those who so freely buy and sell them have responsibilities to other stakeholders too.

Perhaps the most subtle and certainly the most interesting consequence of most mergers, even the friendliest and most convenient of mergers, is the mixing of corporate cultures. Sometimes, as in bicultural or multicultural societies, the mix is mutually invigorating, a source of strength rather than a weakness. The vigor of one corporate culture invigorates the other, while the other's congeniality makes the whole company a better place to work. But often cultures do not get along, if only because each is used to doing business in its own established ways. After a merger, there is virtually always a struggle for cultural dominance, sometimes augmented by a personnel battle as well. If one corporate culture has gotten used to a hierarchical, authoritarian structure while the other is a relaxed, consensus-minded egalitarian culture, the immediate results are sure to be marked by mutual resentment. Communication and cooperation will be compromised. One well-known recent example of a merger of corporate cultures yielded the company now known as Morton Thiokol, one of the manufacturers of the space shuttle. Communication and cooperation between its engineers and upper management was troubled by the clash of cultures, and the rest, as they say, is history. "Corporate culture" is not just another cute way of talking about life in the corporation. Culture defines the corporation, and it often determines whether it will be congenial and successful or a hotbed of ultimately self-destructive hostility.

The drama of the hostile takeover, played out on the stage of the business press and involving powerful entrepreneurs, whole teams of highly paid legal and financial advisers, defensive and ambitious managers, anxious stockholders, and thousands of terrified employees, has become part of corporate life. But it can have terrible costs. It elevates insecurity, paralyzes industry, and often rewards outrageous and irresponsible financial behavior. (One recently extremely hostile and well-publicized takeover battle involved high-interest loans of more than $20 billion, not to mention the banking, legal, and consulting fees.) But although such high-stakes financial theater may pay off in entertainment value for the observers and a few of the high-powered participants, there is very little evidence that it is good for business. Mergers may be beneficial and rewarding. It is one of the more recent and now more important questions of business ethics, and of business law too, how we can distinguish the good from the bad and encourage the former, not the latter. The free-enterprise system allows all of this, with some stringent qualifications, but it is clear that the hostile takeover is not what Adam Smith (or any other serious economist) had in mind. The social responsibility of the corporation—and the merger and creation of corporations—is to pay attention to employees, customers, and the community as well as to the price of the stock and the high-level dramas on Wall Street.

LIABILITY IN A LITIGIOUS SOCIETY

Corporate social responsibilities, including responsibility to the customer, are not only a matter of good will and benign corporate strategy. They are now becoming matters of profound concern, even matters of corporate survival. One of the very recent but increasingly threatening concerns of business in America is the dramatic increase in liability suits and punitive damage awards, and, with them, increased legal fees, insurance costs, and executive ulcers. The threat of liability suits has been blamed for blocking the development of new products, for making American industry less competitive and for discouraging foreign investment in American industries. Author Peter Huber raised the issue to crisis proportions with his hard-hitting polemic, *Liability,* in which he blames the litigation industry for imposing a "tax" on goods of $80 billion a year, "more than the top Fortune 200 companies make," plus another $300 billion in "indirect" costs. The President's Council for Competitiveness and then-Vice President Dan Quayle picked up Huber's polemic and his figures and summarized them at the annual meeting of the American Bar Association in 1991. Needless to say, this irritated some of the top legal talent in the nation, who quickly and elegantly defended themselves in the predictable language of "the rights of the citizen, the protection of the little guy." It made quite a media splash.

What is not at all clear, however, are the actual dimensions of the crisis, or whether, for that matter, there is one. The figures and counterfigures fly fast and furiously, and what makes it all so complicated, of course, is that this is an issue in which there is no reasonable measure of the benefits—for example, the expense and suffering saved because potentially dangerous products did *not* make it to the market and did *not* kill or maim any victims. One of the factors behind the crisis mentality seems to be the general dislike of lawyers in our society, the fact that now almost everyone needs one or wants to be one notwithstanding. This is nothing new. The passion for litigation, long court delays, and legal convolutions were described by Charles Dickens in *Bleak House,* and an eighteenth-century French sculptor mocked them in a famous statue in the "Salle des Pas-Perdus" ("Room of the Lost Footsteps") in the Parisian Palais of Justice, where the eminent lawyer Berryer is depicted with his foot on a tortoise. In fact, there are unmistakably contemporary references to the same perverse passion for litigation and legal quagmires in Aristophanes' play *The Wasps,* written in 422 B.C. But it is not just the lawyers who are to blame, and the tentacles of the litigation explosion extend deep into our society.

Part of the problem, again, is the American distrust of big business, the usually unwarranted assumption that corporations care only about profits and not about the quality of the product or the safety of the consumer. But despite this continuing distrust, there is also a shift in expectations. Only a few years ago, one of the few Latin phrases that virtually everyone in the business world knew and often used, whether as consumer or seller, was *Caveat emptor*—let the buyer beware. It was naturally assumed that products and producers were imperfect, that the consumer needed some sense and good judgment and, ultimately, that he or she was responsible for a decision and its consequences. (We are not talking about fraud, negligence, or misrepresentation, of course.) What is new and disturbing on the American justice scene is the apparent expectation that every product be perfect, that human error is not to be tolerated. This view has its clearest manifestation in several much-publicized liability cases. In a speech a few years ago, former President Ronald Reagan mentioned a man who had a fatal heart attack mowing his lawn. His family sued the manufacturer of the lawn mower and won a million-dollar settlement. In another case, a teenage girl decided to sweeten the smell of her decorative candle and so poured some perfume on the flame. The perfume caught fire, the bottle exploded, and the perfume manufacturer was successfully sued for not supplying sufficient warning. Our newspapers, magazines, and contemporary folklore are filled with such stories. Some of them turn out to be apocryphal. Others turn out to be partially true. In one case the jury rewarded a multimillion-dollar verdict but an appeals judge lowered the amount to a few hundred thousand. (Of course, only the first judgment made the headlines.)

Where does the problem lie? Needless to say, every group and participant in the emerging scandal blames the others—the lawyers blame the manufacturers and the insurance companies, and everyone blames the lawyers. The one person who is often absolved from blame is the victim, who may be dead or maimed for life and quite rightly attracts our sympathy. But there are many cases in which the victim is nevertheless responsible for his or her own misfortune and the defendants not at all. Some juries' verdicts should be viewed as proper expressions of sympathy for the victim rather than a judgment about corporate responsibility; but then why do we not separate these two very different concerns, compassion and compensation on the one hand, and blame and punishment on the other? Why punish a corporation for simply doing what it was meant to do? Corporations and insurance companies are too often perceived as limitless resources whose costs are but a few cents per share to the stockholders, and the judgments against them, accordingly, reflect a "deep pockets" mentality (*someone* has got to pay!") rather than a judgment of liability and blame. Indeed, one of the dominant arguments in liability law today is that the purpose of the system is to get those who can afford to take the risk to pay whether or not they are in any reasonable sense at fault in the case. But this wreaks havoc with our notion of justice and it seriously confuses the cost of doing business.

One industry obviously affected by the litigation crisis—but by no means the only one—is the pharmaceutical industry. The unfortunate fact is that every medicine, every vaccine, even the most common and seemingly most innocent, can and almost certainly will cause serious and possibly fatal problems for a small percentage of consumers. A manufacturer can use great care, carry out extensive testing, and thus minimize such problems, but it is the nature of medicine that nothing

---

COSTLY LITIGATION

Executives fear the U.S. legal system is crippling America's ability to compete in the global marketplace. A *Business Week*/Harris poll of top executives at corporations drawn from the *Business Week* 1000 found that 62 percent believe the U.S. civil justice system significantly hampers the ability of American companies to compete with Japanese and European rivals. A striking 83 percent of those polled say the fear of lawsuits has more impact on decision making within their company today than it did ten years ago.

"The American economy can no longer afford this process," says Ronald L. Davis, assistant general counsel at Dow Chemical Co. "The system's inefficiencies are eating away at our industrial base." He says Dow Chemical spends "in excess" of $100 million a year on legal services and liability insurance.

—*Business Week,* April 13, 1992

---

is or can be made perfect. But if the manufacturer of a vaccine, such as the standard childhood vaccine for diphtheria, tetanus, and whooping cough, were to decline to produce it anymore, then all children would be at risk. So, who should compensate the victims?

One of the factors that has not been ignored by the press is that the pharmaceutical industry makes an enormous amount of money from these products, even taking into account the considerable expense of their research and development. Another factor is that society as a whole obviously benefits enormously from such products, even if a few people suffer horribly, and those few people can hardly be expected to handle the consequences themselves. So, should the company be forced, in effect, to spend some of its profits taking care of the unfortunate few? Should the industry as a whole provide a fund out of which they may be compensated? Or should society as a whole take responsibility for the inevitable victims of such misfortunes? The one utterly unacceptable alternative, of course (although that does not mean that it is not often enunciated), is that the victims of such misfortunes should simply be ignored as "unlucky." That is not the way a civilized society works. But, as in so many such issues, the question who should pay is by no means obvious.

Those who attack the litigation industry are not primarily concerned, however, with such inevitable tragedies and the response to them. They are far more concerned with what are called "frivolous" lawsuits. Of course, few cases seem "frivolous" to the person who brings them, but with the emphasis on litigation (for example, in popular TV shows and the press), there is no doubt that such cases have clearly proliferated. Accidents that used to be considered private tragedies are now the basis of lawsuits. The real culprit, one might say, is a social system that encourages some of the worst aspects of all of us, our cultivated avarice and our insecurities and our resentment, as compensation gets confused with greed and reparation gets mixed up with retaliation. A system that only recently rested on the twin virtues of individual responsibility and the obligation of society to provide "protection for widows and orphans" has now become a vicious game of "suffer and sue," of getting even and once in a while profiting enormously. Insurance industry executives now speak wistfully of the days not long gone by when they provided an essential public service, and liability lawyers talk with some amazement about cases that could not possibly have found their way to a courtroom only a few years ago.

Punitive damages can be a valuable tool in the control of willfully irresponsible corporations, notably those who carefully calculate the probable cost of injuries and deaths due to their carelessness or poor

---

NEW FRONTIERS IN LITIGATION

WORKPLACE VIOLENCE. In March 1996 OSHA issued voluntary guidelines designed to prevent violence in the workplace. Implementing these guidelines may also prevent lawsuits against employers: "According to former Secretary of Labor Robert B. Reich, homicides have moved up to the second leading cause of death on the job behind automotive accidents." (*Best's Review*, July 1996)

DOWNSIZING. As experts who have been downsized seek new career opportunities, many will sell their expertise as consultants. The expert flying solo, however, is no more exempt from litigation than the expert flying the corporate colors: hence future prospects for insurance companies in the area of errors and omissions liability coverage.

LITIGOUS CYBERSPACE. The information revolution has caused a lawsuit revolution. Defamation can now be transmitted electronically, and on-going litigation is sketching out the parameters by which "cybertorts" are defined. Additionally, the legal status of e-mail messages and the work place issue of employee e-mail privacy continues to be contested and defined through test cases.

design into the price of a product, but the further addition of "deep pockets" legislation and the lottery "jackpot" appeal of litigation dulls this tool and undermines the essential connection between liability and responsibility. In those cases in which the plaintiff is primarily the victim of his or her own stupidity or carelessness, one would think that the question of liability would be irrelevant, but it is no longer. Some defendants win such cases on a technical point of law. Others win the jury's sympathy and the company pays for their compassion. Many companies settle out of court just to save the expense of the courtroom, knowing all the while that they are innocent of any wrongdoing and not really responsible for the damages in question. In short, the purpose of the liability system has become less and less the compensation of blameless victims and the punishment of those responsible for their plight and more and more a ramshackle, runaway vehicle that tries to take care of all injured persons in the name of a punishment that no longer punishes and only encourages fraud and greed in the name of a "justice" that is just as often revenge. The liability crisis developed as the product of well-meaning intentions to protect the public and punish the irresponsible, but to resolve the crisis we need to understand and distinguish those well-meaning intentions and the perversion of common sense by an overly eager readiness to blame, a greatly exaggerated demand for protection and compensation and no small amount of plain old greed.

FAIRNESS IN THE CORPORATION, JUSTICE IN THE MARKETPLACE

> *Life is never fair, and perhaps it is a good thing for*
> *most of us that it is not.*
> >   *Oscar Wilde*, An Ideal Husband

Justice is to ethics as profits are to accounting—the bottom line. Justice—like profit—may not be an absolute end in itself; the purpose of justice, many social philosophers have argued, is to ensure general happiness and social harmony if not—as other philosophers have argued—to please God. But there can be no ethics without justice, just as there can be no business without profits. In our material-minded society, the ultimate purpose of business—and profits—is justice, and justice is largely concerned with the fair distribution of material goods.

Justice is the ultimate principle of fair distribution—everyone getting (and giving) what he or she deserves. In a monarchy concerned with royal recognition and honors, justice mainly requires the king or queen to distribute privileges and honors fairly, according to the standards of fairness that exist in that society (which lord is next in line, which house has the tradition). In a society dominated by business, commercial, and consumer concerns, justice requires the fair distribution of money and the things that money can buy, according to our very American sense of fairness, especially our sense of *merit*—what a person has *earned*. But what this is is more complicated than meets the eye.

The Dimensions of Justice

1. First of all, our sense of justice is *impersonal*. This does not mean that we don't have personal feelings about it; indeed, our "gut level" sense of justice and, especially, injustice is sometimes overpowering, even epic. (The Boston Tea Party comes to mind.) But it does mean that we feel that justice involves a certain "blindness" to personal interests and attachments. It is for this

> We always worry that a company is unethical because it doesn't pay
> enough. The major temptation on my company's part is that we pay too
> much. If we pay an individual too much, an engineer, a manager, and he
> can't get a job somewhere else because of that high salary, we can
> destroy a man's life.
>
> Kenneth Olsen (Digital Equipment Corporation)

reason that the familiar figure of justice is usually a woman
blindfolded; the particular identities of the people she judges are
not in question, only their actions. Justice demands that two
people doing the same job deserve the same salary, no matter
who they are and whether they are black, blond, male, or female.
Justice demands that a customer who was clearly cheated deserves compensation, whether he or she happens to be charming
and likable or not.

2. Justice, for us, is clearly wrapped up in the notion of *equality*.
This does not mean, as in some socialist theories, that everyone
should get (or give) exactly the same. It does not mean, as few
theorists would be foolish enough to suggest, that all people are
in fact exactly the same. What it does mean is that everyone
counts for something. In Adam Smith's classical view of business,
it means that everyone is part of the market; no one can be
excluded. In more practical (and political) terms, it means that
everyone should at least have a *chance* to compete in the market—what we call "equal opportunity." Ideally, we like to think
that anyone, through education, experience, and hard work, can
make his or her way in the business world. In fact, of course,
there are obstacles for many people that close the doors to both
education and experience and which no amount of hard work will
make up for. We were all brought up to believe that "any
American child can become president"—or, we might add, the
CEO of General Motors. The fact is that the majority of children
in America have as much chance of becoming president or CEO
as they do of becoming the next Shah of Iran. Is this unjust? But
equality is not the only consideration in justice.

3. Justice means *entitlement*. A person can be entitled to wealth and
privileges that are not available to anyone else, that he or she did
not earn in any sense whatever. If the village idiot is left a fortune

IN A CLASS BY THEMSELVES

The salaries of U.S. executives are in a class by themselves. An international executive-search firm says that an average American CEO makes $932,040 a year, counting base pay, bonuses, stock options and other forms of payment. By contrast, it is said, the average total pay for a French CEO is $586,004, for a German $494,483, for a Japanese $453,546 and for a British $491,698. In Germany half the board members at most big firms are workers' representatives, which puts a powerful brake on any temptation to raise CEO salaries at the expense of workers' pay. In Japan, board members are mostly other executives who are less inclined to give mega-raises to CEOs than are U.S. boards, which are often dominated by outside directors, most of them high-paid CEOs themselves.

—*Chicago Tribune,* September 2, 1996

Average wage and benefits for U.S. workers rose a scant 2.9 percent during 1995, according to the Bureau of Labor Statistics, the smallest increase in 14 years. Nationwide, chief executive officers of the 20 companies with the largest announced layoffs last year saw their salaries and bonuses jump by 25 percent, according to Business Week. Total CEO compensation at 30 major U.S. companies soared to 212 times what the average U.S. worker earned in 1995, up from 44 in 1965. Some researchers have concluded that high CEO pay can be linked to higher turnover, lower job satisfaction and lower quality products. A 1992 study of nearly 100 companies found the companies with the bigger pay gaps between the CEO and hourly workers produced lower quality products.

—*Houston Chronicle,* June 9, 1996

by a dying wealthy eccentric (who is not idiotic), the village idiot is (probably pending appeal) *entitled* to the money by virtue of the old man's will. A wife, husband, son, or daughter is generally entitled to the assets whether or not (or in whatever sense) he or she helped earn them. A person is entitled to a salary because it was promised at the beginning of the job—whether or not, in retrospect, it seems excessive. Contracts, in general, establish entitlement. The traditions and expectations of society also mark out entitlements, whether or not there is an explicit contract (for example, a will) and, again, quite irrespective of merit. The eldest son of a feudal lord was entitled to lead the army and inherit the castle; the CEO of a major corporation is entitled to a salary considerably larger than that of anyone else in the firm. This doesn't necessarily mean that he works any harder, shoulders any more responsibility, or even improves the company in any significant way (though then we can be sure that he will not long keep the job). But most important in a free-enterprise system is the demand that a person is entitled to the money he or she makes, quite apart from questions about how the money was made (assuming, of course, that it was made legally and ethically). A man who makes a million on a lucky gamble in the stock market is as entitled to that money as the man who slaves away for years. "Unearned income" is just as just as earnings. But a person can also be entitled to compensation because of what he or she did *not* earn. A person who has been discriminated against or cheated out of earnings has an entitlement claim in our society.

(The hardest question: What entitlement does an entire *group* have in the case of historical discrimination? What do we do when their entitlement conflicts directly with the entitlements of an already advantaged group? A black man applies for a promotion; a Caucasian with slightly better credentials applies for the same job. The one has a history of racism behind him; the other can claim to deserve the job on the basis of his superior achievements. Is there *any* conceivable solution to this problem?)

4. Justice is based on *merit*. In the well-known Marxist motto, "From each according to his abilities, to each according to his needs," there is no mention of merit—that is, what a person has *earned*. In our sense of justice, however, a person's merit is a primary consideration in deciding what he or she should be paid. However important we find the concept of equality, we are offended when one manager—who is productive, extremely hardworking, and has made significant improvements in the department—is paid exactly the same as the local slouch, who puts in well-timed appearances but is generally a drain on everyone around. Equality is always important, but it is rarely everything.

5. Justice means recognition of *need*. We agree with the Marxists at least this much: People who cannot take care of themselves financially deserve some kind of help and attention from the rest of us. Of course, there will always be considerable debate about how such "welfare" is to be taken care of—through charity or government agencies, for example—but what is beyond debate is the belief that a civilized country will not allow some of its citizens to starve in the streets while others live in luxury.

THE TOP-PAID CHIEF EXECUTIVES

	1996 salary & bonus	Long-term compensation
1. Lawrence Coss Green Tree Financial	$102,500,000	none
2. Andrew Grove Intel	3,003,000	97,590,000
3. Sanford Weill Travelers Group	6,330,000	94,157,000
4. Theodore Waitt Gateway 2000	965,000	81,326,000
5. Anthony O'Reilly H. J. Heinz	2,736,000	64,236,000

For 1996, CEO pay gains far outstripped the roaring economy or shareholder returns. The average salary and bonus for a chief executive rose a phenomenal 39 percent to $2.3 million. Add to that retirement benefits, incentive plans, and gains from stock options, and the numbers hit the roof.

CEOs' average total compensation rose an astounding 54 percent [in 1996], to $5,781,300. That largesse came on top of a 30 percent rise in total pay in 1995—yet it was hardly spread down the line. The average compensation of the top dog was 209 times that of a factory employee, who garnered a tiny 3 percent rise in 1996. White-collar workers eked out just 3.2 percent, though many now get options too.

—*Business Week,* April 21, 1997

These five standards of justice do not form a harmonious whole. They clash and conflict and cause enormous problems for the business person who wants to be ethical and think ethically. Let's take an example. One theme that is common in the American press is the challenge to the luxurious salaries (and more) of top American executives. "Are they worth it?" is the continual question, and "Why should the chief of the company make so much more than anyone else?" the continual complaint. The replies by business, on the other hand, are sporadic and often inarticulate. The accuser is using a standard of justice that turns on the idea (a) that justice is a matter of what one earns and (b) that justice requires that all people be treated (paid) equally. But the salary of a CEO is rarely a matter just of worth, and to give in to a pure equality standard is immediately to admit that corporate society is the very height of injustice, in which the gap between the executives and the workers on the line of a company is not much better than the gap between lord and serf in feudal times. Knowing how to answer such accusations is a key part of business

FLYING INJUSTICE (SINCE GROUNDED)

[Before folding] Braniff International increased the salaries of 864 management-level employees by 11.4 percent, just when the firm was imploring 11,500 employees covered by union contracts to accept a 10 percent salary cut to keep the airline flying.

Mark Green, *The New Republic*

ethics. Not knowing how to answer them contributes to the suspicion of business in many people's minds today.

The justice of high salaries for executives must be defended in terms of entitlement based on status and responsibility but not as a matter of personal merit or abilities alone. Then again, there is iconoclast Robert Townsend refusing to accept a salary from Avis any larger than an ordinary manager. In a system that depends on competition, entitlement cannot be everything. Indeed this is one of the oldest running battles in capitalist ideology—whether merit is more important than entitlement or vice versa. Our society is founded on the idea of individual merit, hard work, and initiative, and it is hard to see how business could prosper unless everyone—from top to bottom—is rewarded on the basis of merit. (Indeed, it is the lack of such incentive that is the primary flaw in most socialist economies.) On the other hand, it is clear that some very unworthy people profit handsomely in business while others who are clearly deserving, by virtue of a lifetime of hard work, do not. This does not strike us as fair, but to correct it would interfere with another of our most cherished values—freedom. It has been persuasively argued by some classic liberal economists (Friedrich von Hayek, for example) that only entitlement, independent of merit, preserves freedom, since giving anyone the authority to decide merit (whether it is a government agency or a commission of some sort) would clearly infringe on individual liberty.

The clash between standards of justice is of immense practical importance in business. Business is a matter of supply and demand; it is also a matter of *fair* dealing, and justice is fair dealing. Half of the ethical problems and accusations encountered by business are a matter of fairness, and thinking and talking in terms of justice is the only way to deal with these. This is true when dealing with an irate customer, supplier, or employee. It is true when making speeches about the benefits of free enterprise. Being able to clearly define the basis of a decision according to the standards of justice is an essential part of business ethics. To recognize when equality is at stake, or when a privilege is a matter of entitlement rather than of merit, can solve (or at least set the stage for solving) a great many business complaints. Not to see these differences, or to blabber carelessly about "justice" as some grand but impractical abstraction, is a sure way to fuel those complaints rather than settle them.

THE TRAGIC ANTAGONISM BETWEEN LABOR AND MANAGEMENT

The customer gets most of the attention in classic capitalism, but it is the employee, and in particular those workers who fall under the general rubric of "labor," who have become the primary stakeholders in the corporation—and the most often ignored. For example, many countries (and our own civil service) have fairly strong laws requiring that the firing of any employee specify certain reasons, but in the United States, a great many workers are employed strictly on an "at will" basis and, even when the firing is unjustifiable or illegal, many employees find that they have no legal recourse. Executives and managers get raises while workers take pay cuts and are let go. Safety conditions are ignored until (and often after) a lawsuit threatens. Unskilled workers can be easily replaced from the pool of millions of unemployed and often desperate workers, and even skilled workers regularly feel the threat of discharge. Given the importance of work in our society, both as a means of survival and a source of identity, this sense of powerlessness can be devastating. It can also be devastating to the company.

Labor unions and management have been at odds with one another since the formation of the former. The history of this conflict is a fascinating chapter in its own right, but let us just point out the obvious here. Labor unions in this country grew out of the desire of working people to have more say and more power in their working lives. Although such organizations were ruthlessly attacked in their early days, particularly by those employers who did in fact exploit their workers and took full advantage of the ease with which they could be fired, labor unions are not only compatible with economic efficiency and prosperity but essential to democracy as well. Powerlessness in the workplace is antithetical to the autonomy required of citizenship.

Labor unions are often treated as an obstacle or worse, a betrayal of the capitalist economy, in part because of the original alliance of some labor unions with socialist causes and the communist party. Indeed, unionists are still sometimes tarred with the now out-of-date epithet "Communist," even though such charges are no longer intelligible. The truth is rather that labor unions originated not in opposition to capitalism but as a necessity to maintain the American business system. The rights of workers to be protected against the reprisals of their employers was established with the passage of the National Labor Relations Act, the Wagner Act, in 1935, during some of the worst days of the Great Depression. The central concern of Congress in its passing of the Wagner Act was the low wages of workers, who thereby had little purchasing power, as well as the frequent disruption of industrial production caused by strikes. The Wagner Act was an attempt to rehabilitate the free market by making labor a stable and dependable factor in production.

Under the Wagner Act, it is illegal for an employer to interfere with or discriminate against workers who are trying to form such a union. The act encourages collective bargaining, the process by which a contract covering all workers is negotiated and administered. Acting together in contractual cooperation with industry thus assures stability. Arbitration further stabilizes the process, as "wildcat" strikes get replaced by discussion motivated by mutual interests.

The Wagner Act also establishes the framework within which unions can come to represent previously unrepresented workers, although it is a misunderstanding that unions simply come in and "take over." When 30 percent of the workers in a company or an industry "show interest" in establishing or joining a union, an election is held under the auspices of the National Labor Relations Board, the federal agency set up to administer the Wagner Act. If 50 percent or more of the employees vote for a union, the shop becomes "union" and is so represented. Some employees may object, but this situation is no

---

UNIONS AND DEMOCRACY

One thing to keep in mind about the future of American unions, when
we look at Solidarity in Poland, or when we look at what happened in
China . . . is the demand of workers for the right to unionize. Which is
the *sine qua non* of whether a political system has any democratic
features. And those who believe that unions are passé or that unions can
disappear and managers can manage their workers best without union
representation are talking about an autocratic totalitarian state. This
country will never survive as a democracy without free trade unions.

—Jerome M. Rostow, president of the Work in America Institute, in the Los
   Angeles Times

---

different from any other democratic decision procedure that depends
on majority rule.

Arbitration has a privileged position with industrial relations. Especially since 1960, when the Supreme Court ruled in three different
decisions concerning the steelworkers union, arbitration can now be
judically enforced. Again, the aim is industrial stability while at the
same time settling disputes and satisfying the demands of both workers
and management. Arbitration helps avoid the two most costly and
disruptive forms of dealing with such disputes: strikes and "slow-
downs," on the one hand, and prolonged litigation on the other.
Indeed, since 1960, the tendency in the courts is to assume a "no
strike" clause in favor of arbitration, even where there is no such
explicit clause in the union contract. But as even arbitration has
become more and more expensive and time consuming (although not
nearly so much as litigation), mediation has tended to become a first
and often final step in coming to agreement. It has also cut down on
the adversarial nature of the labor-management relationship. In the
face of increasing international competition, cooperation and not mutual antagonism is obviously in the best interest of all concerned.

The union is the exclusive bargaining representative of all employees, including those who have decided not to join the union. But there
are some obvious problems here, and the history of labor relations has
a few bloody episodes in the development of this curious situation.
With the ascendancy of the unions after the passing of the Wagner
Act, many industries had "closed shops"; that is, in order to obtain
employment in a particular company or industry, one already had to
be a member of the appropriate union. There were also "union shops,"

COUNTDOWN

Unions are down to 10.4 percent representation in the U.S. private sector. Charles Baird, professor at Cal State Hayward, says unions will drop to 7 percent of the private sector by the year 2000, and pick up most of their gains in the future in the government sector.

—*Oakland Tribune,* September 1, 1996

---

which did not require prior membership but did require joining the union once on the job. Closed shops, in particular, made possible a new form of discrimination and arbitrariness, not at the hands of employers but at the hands of the union. And some trades and occupations quickly became exclusionary, for if you could not get into the union, you consequently could not get a job. Both of these have gone out of practice; the former now prohibited by law, the latter depleted in substance.

What has taken place is the "agency shop," in which an employee cannot be compelled to join the union but, because he or she benefits from union representation, can be compelled to pay the union the equivalent of union dues; that is, the proportion of dues that pay for bargaining and administrative costs. There are advantages for some individual workers in not joining a union. For example, although he or she cannot get involved in internal union matters, he or she is not subject to union discipline either. In case of a strike, the nonunion member is not compelled to join but may nevertheless enjoy the benefits won from the strike. According to the provisions of the more recent Taft-Hartley Act of 1947, however, employees have the right to work in a union-represented workplace even without paying dues, although, again, they are still covered by union benefits. Such "right-to-work" laws even entitle a nonunion member to be personally represented by the union in case of unjust discharge, without reimbursing the union for its services.

Traditionally, the ultimate weapon of labor unions has been the right to strike. There is power in collective bargaining, and there is considerable power just in collective thinking and cooperation among union members, but when all else fails, when management will not listen or refuses to agree to what seem to be reasonable demands, there is nothing more effective, in terms of threatening management and gaining public attention, than a strike. Of course, this right has sometimes been abused; indeed, it has been used even when it did not exist, for example in the air controllers' strike in the early 1980s, which was clearly prohibited by their federal contract. Then-President Ronald Reagan summarily fired them all and they have not been able to work (as air-traffic controllers) for over a decade. In other countries, notably England, France, and Australia, strikes routinely paralyze public services, showing quite clearly that the strike is a weapon that should be used with care and caution.

But the right to strike has been limited severely, at least in America, and today's labor practices include the right of the employer to replace a striking worker, making the act of striking a particularly dangerous one. (Technically, the employer is required to offer the replaced employee his job back after the termination of his replacement, but this could take many years or even decades.) This renders the right to strike all but empty and leaves labor without its ultimate weapon. In these days of cutbacks and high unemployment, it remains to be seen whether the management of most major industries take seriously their role and responsibilities as "stakeholders" to their employees or whether they use this as license to return to the same old forms of exploitation.

A new cooperative relationship is being forged between management and labor, not because of any grand conciliation but because of necessity. A country that cannot work together can no longer compete in the world market, nor even, in many cases, in their own markets. One of the efforts that has made some headway in the past decade or so is a cooperative arrangement known as "quality circles." It is part and parcel of some programs in "Total Quality Management," and the

---

NAFTA: A NEW UNION-BUSTING WEAPON?

Since the North American Free Trade Agreement took effect, U.S. employers have routinely threatened during union elections to close plants and move production to Mexico or elsewhere, says a new study commissioned under NAFTA. . . . The report, based on union elections from 1993 to 1995, indicated half of the employers threaten to close plants when facing a union vote. Labor loses nearly half the time when that happens, vs. 33 percent when no warnings are issued. When employers lose, 75 percent go ahead and close the plant, triple the level in the pre-NAFTA 1980s.

—*Business Week*, January 27, 1997

WORKING FOR THE JAPANESE

Unlike U.S. blue-collar workers, who generally praise their Japanese bosses, many U.S. managers working in these businesses say they aren't allowed to make decisions or fully use their talents. Japanese concepts of *nemawashi*—consensus building—and *ringi*—shared decision making—frustrate American managers accustomed to individual responsibility and recognition. Aggressive, ambitious Americans feel out of place.

In addition, American managers typically complain about a lack of feedback from their Japanese superiors. Even when the work is exemplary, some managers contend, they aren't promoted, simply because they aren't Japanese. Many quit in frustration—reinforcing a belief among Japanese that Americans are ready to jump ship when a better offer comes along.

—*The Wall Street Journal*, November 27, 1991

Japanese are often taken as exemplary in their practice of shared expertise and decision making. The basic idea is utterly right: bring employees into decision making and use their knowledge of the products they work on and their own situation to improve not only production but design and marketing as well. Break down the antagonism between labor and management and give the workers not only a piece of the action but a voice in the company as well. There is no question but that it improves morale, and stimulates loyalty and productivity.

Quality circles should be approached with some scrutiny, however, even as they are to be applauded. In Japan, for example, the circle may well encourage input from everyone in the project, but make no mistake: the scope and range of the comments and opinions is strictly dictated by the culture and by the manager in charge, and the harmonious consensus that Americans so understandably admire is by no means a matter of egalitarian agreement. The delicate balance between democracy and chaos depends on much more than mutaul discussion, and until American companies have their priorities in order—cooperation rather than antagonism in labor relations, loyalty and mutual respect instead of "every man for himself"—quality circles as such will not be the magic bullet for productivity and competitiveness. What is worse, however, is that quality circles are sometimes used to aggravate and abuse labor relations even further by becoming a new technique of exploitation. Some of what goes under the name of "employee empowerment" and the like, according to the National Labor Relations Board, amounts to no more than "sham unions," a new way for managers to enter into and interfere with employee relations. Meanwhile, union organizers are using such programs as a new way of organizing, thus increasing rather than decreasing the traditional antagonism with management, according to the national Chamber of Commerce. In the name of cooperation, the disruptive antagonism is getting worse. And then we wonder why we can't keep up with the competition.

EQUALITY AND EQUAL OPPORTUNITY

> *All animals are equal, but some are more equal than others.*
>
> *George Orwell*, Animal Farm

Equal opportunity is the premise of American capitalism. We can easily imagine (and find) societies that are based on competition for markets and products but in which it is clearly understood that only a certain class of people is allowed to enter the competition in the first place. We take it to be part of the justification of the market—and a key element of justice—that the free-enterprise system gives everyone a chance to compete. There is no legally privileged class. There are, strictly speaking, no classes at all. But there is, of course, a privileged group of people in the American business world—the people who are already there, and their children. There may not be social classes in America in the sense that it is considered inappropriate for a person to have ambitions and to "rise above his station." But it is a plain matter of fact that a bright MBA from Boston Business College does not have the same opportunities as a no more able or accomplished MBA from

---

REVERSE DISCRIMINATION

Even if contemporary treatment programs which contain quotas are wrong, they are not wrong for the reasons that make quotas against blacks and women pernicious. The reason why is that the social realities do make a difference. The fundamental evil of programs that discriminated against blacks or women was that these programs were a part of a larger social universe which systematically maintained a network of institutions which unjustifiably concentrated power, authority, and goods in the hands of white male individuals, and which systematically consigned blacks and women to subordinate positions in society. Whatever may be wrong with today's affirmative action programs and quota systems, it should be clear that the evil, if any, is just not the same.

Richard Wasserstrom, "Racism, Sexism and Preferential Treatment," *UCLA Law Review*

Harvard, and a bright and uneducated black teenager from Prairie View, Texas, does not have the same opportunities as his white, wealthy counterpart in Houston. But whether or not we do or can have equal opportunity in this country, it is enough that most Americans believe that we *ought* to. And that means that lack of opportunity will be treated not as misfortune but as betrayal. It will be greeted not with resignation but with resentment—and sometimes with violence.

Equality is not considered to be an essential or desirable feature of justice by many people in many societies. Plato designed his "republic" according to a rigid hierarchy of classes. A person was born into a class and stayed there for life, doing what the members of that class were supposed to do (farming, fighting in the army, making shoes) and living in the style appropriate to that class. The majority of societies in the world still operate on the assumption that some people are "naturally" superior to others and deserve more power, more status and respect, and more wealth and luxury than the rest. We do not believe this. We believe in equality. But it is important to be clear about what we believe and what we do not.

We believe, first of all, that everyone is equal "before the law." This means that the law plays no favorites, that the president of the United States or of the Ford Motor Company is just as bound by the 55-mph speed limit as anyone else. A millionaire who murders his wife should get exactly the same trial and treatment as the poor fellow who has been out of a job for ten months. And in business, equality means that the most powerful corporation in New York is bound by the same laws as the most modest shop in Modesto. The failure to declare a third of the year's income would be just as illegal for Metropolitan Life Insurance Company as it would be for Marina's tortilla stand. Of course we all know that Metropolitan Life has considerable tax advantages with its complex corporate structure and its army of accomplished accountants while Marina struggles each April to fill out a 1040E by herself. And it is not likely that the president's limousine will be stopped for a speeding violation. But it is of no small importance that we believe that the same laws should apply to peasants and presidents alike, and that

THE TOP TEN FOR WORKING MOTHERS

Every year, in the October issue, *Working Mother* publishes a list of the best companies in America for working mothers. The top ten in 1996 were:

• Barnett Banks (Florida's largest bank)—three on-site child care centers in Florida; a $1.2 million Family Center opened in 1996.

• Eli Lilly (one of the world's leading makers of prescription medicines)—FMLA leave for childbirth plus 156 weeks, with 6 weeks full pay.

• Hewlett-Packard—ongoing redesign of work schedules to provide more flexibility.

• IBM*—funds near-site child care centers in 28 locations; 2 weeks paid paternity leave.

• Johnson & Johnson*—covers 50 percent operating costs of on-site child care centers, and 100 percent of sick-child care at these sites.

• MBNA America Bank—operation of the three on-site child care centers is contracted out, but MBNA takes an active role to ensure that caregivers are paid decent wages and receive benefits.

• Merck* (one of the world's leading makers of prescription medicines)—online database that allows employees to make confidential searches for potential job-sharing partners.

• NationsBank—pays up to 50 percent of sick-child care for low-income employees; free on-site snowy day child care in seven locations.

• Patagonia (designs and distributes outdoor wear)—all new parents (including those who adopt) are entitled to eight weeks of paid leave, followed by eight weeks of unpaid leave.

• Xerox*—under LifeCycle assistance program employees earning less than $50,000 a year are eligible for up to $1,750 annually in child care subsidies.

*eleventh year on the list

the tax rate *ought* to be the same for any company of any size, and, at least in the letter of the law, it is.

We believe, secondly, that *irrelevant* differences should not interfere with a person's ability to get ahead. We also believe that a great many more differences are irrelevant than most societies do. A person should not be barred from a job because he or she is Catholic or Jewish. A person should not receive a lower salary because she is a woman. A person should not be blocked from promotion because he or she is tall. What is relevant sometimes varies with the context. We do not think that it is unjust that a Jew is not allowed to become a bishop or a cardinal or that a Catholic is turned down for the position of rabbi. We will not object if a person is rejected from the basketball team because he or she is too short. But in every case, we believe that a person should not be blocked from advancement for reasons that are not relevant to the job to be done. In some cases, this is controversial. To what extent should a person's personality influence his or her opportunities? That depends. In a research position, not much. In a managerial position, considerably. To what extent should a person's attractiveness determine his or her success? When are "looks" relevant to a

---

WAGE GAPS

[In 1995] black households posted bigger income gains than white households, but Hispanic households lost ground. On the whole, blacks still earned less than whites, but the gap narrowed.

—Knight-Ridder, September 26, 1996

A study of U.S. census data concluded that "even for those Mexican immigrants with education of skill levels comparable to native workers, wages are lower and the progress toward parity slower. . . . Overall . . . wage parity for immigrants has been falling steadily in the past 20 years because of lower education and skill levels. For immigrants from Central America and Mexico, average wages were 25 percent to 40 percent lower than natives' in 1970; by 1990, the differential had grown to 50 percent."

—*Los Angeles Times*, July 3, 1996

In 1994, women working full time earned 76.4 cents for every dollar earned by men. [A] female attorney made 74.1 percent of her male counterpart's weekly earnings. Female physicians earned 76.7 percent and engineers 86.5 percent.

—*Colorado Daily Sentinel*, July 28, 1996

DESERVING POOR

The typical image of the poor—as an isolated "underclass" separated from the mainstream by negative attitudes about work, tolerant attitudes toward teenage pregnancy and welfare use, and high rates of school dropout and crime—is inaccurate and a hindrance to waging an effective war on poverty, says Urban Institute researcher Patricia Ruggles. The lead witness in a series of hearings on poverty chaired by Rep. Stephen Solarz (D-N.Y.), Ruggles adds that more than 85 percent of the poor in the United States are either under 18, over 65, disabled, or working. The leading cause for the excessively high poverty rates, concludes Ruggles, is stagnant or declining real earnings of low-income workers and a lack of effective federal assistance programs.

—*In These Times*, Aug. 21–Sept. 3, 1991

---

job and when are they not? When is a woman better (or worse) qualified for a job because she is beautiful, and when is she being considered for attributes having nothing to do with the job? Are there *any* jobs for which a woman cannot be as qualified as a man?

Third, we believe that two people who are equally qualified deserve the same chance, and two people doing the same work deserve the same rewards (or penalties). This is the most obvious sense of equality, and also the most likely to cause a furor when it is violated. It is not always obvious when two people are equally qualified or doing the same job, of course, but taking equality seriously means being extremely conscious of such similarities. If we did not believe in equality, it would not bother us when people of similar abilities were treated very differently; in fact we probably wouldn't bother to ask whether they had similar abilities. But it does bother us, and we do ask. Believing in equality means treating equals as equals.

We also believe, although this is much harder to specify, that everyone is equal in some sense as a "human being." Whatever our superficial abilities, qualities, and advantages, "deep down" we are all the same—all metaphysically naked human beings before God.

We do *not* believe, however, that all people are equal in the sense that they all have the same native abilities. To believe that they do is not idealistic; it is just plain stupid. Some people are too dense to do a job that requires careful thinking and problem solving. Some people are too frail to do a job that requires considerable strength and endurance. One might feebly suggest that we all share the same beginning as infants, but even that dubious equality ends the moment

---

AN OPEN PLAYING FIELD

Five years ago prestigious venture capitalists rarely received proposals from women starting high-technology businesses. Today Patricia Cloherty, president of New York City-based Particof & Co., says that 15 percent of the new business proposals she gets come from women. At a San Francisco–based venture capital outfit, 5 of the 40 companies in its portfolio have female executives. "In the tech industry people don't care how old you are, what color you are or what sex you are," [says] Christina Jones, who cofounded Austin, Texas's Trilogy Development Group. . . . Why are so many women making it big in high-techland? "There is more mobility because there isn't a man with 20 years' experience in line for the job ahead of you."

—*Forbes,* December 30, 1996

---

one baby is swaddled in silk, another in a soiled sheet. Indeed, some people have more advantages from the very moment of conception, and no amount of social engineering or egalitarian blindness will alter that fact. What we can do is to insist that those advantages contribute to the well-being of all.

The fact that we believe in equality *and* believe that those who contribute more should get more means that the concept of equal opportunity is all the more important to us. We need not pretend that everyone has equal abilities in order to insist that people with similar abilities should have similar chances to use them and to reap their rewards. We do not have to defend what Milton Friedman sometimes calls "pure and unadulterated socialism" in order to recognize that some people in our society do not have even the most elementary opportunities to develop their talents or prove their worth. If people who clearly could contribute more to society are not allowed to do so, it not only diminishes the prosperity of the whole society but also breeds justifiable resentment on the part of those who know they could do more but aren't permitted to. It also marks as hypocrisy the proclamation of equal opportunity. Perhaps it is unimaginable that a society could ever have totally equal opportunity—the children of the rich starting on an equal footing with the children of the poor. But the justification of the free market ultimately depends on its working toward the ideal of equality as well as the ideal of prosperity. Our ethical ideal as a nation is not just that everyone should be materially comfortable but that everyone should have the chance to do what he or she can do, so that, for almost everyone, enjoying the wealth of the nation is also the reward for contributing to it.

LEGAL RIGHTS, CIVIL RIGHTS, HUMAN RIGHTS

> *Everyone, as a member of society, has the right to social security . . . and a standard of living adequate for health and well-being.*
>
> *United Nations Declaration of 1948*

> *We hold these Truths to be self-evident, that all Men are created equal, that they are endowed by their Creator with certain unalienable Rights, that among these are Life, Liberty and the Pursuit of Happiness.*
>
> *American Declaration of Independence*

If justice is the bottom line of ethics, respect for rights is the measure of its currency. The writers of our Declaration of Independence puts "Rights" at the top of the self-evident truths on the basis of which they broke away from England and founded their own society. The United Nations today takes respect for rights to be the hallmark of civilized society. The U.N. Declaration of 1948 begins:

> Whereas disregard and contempt for human rights have resulted in barbarous acts which have outraged the conscience of mankind, and the advent of a world in which human beings shall enjoy freedom of speech and belief and freedom from fear and want has been proclaimed as the highest aspiration of the common people. . . .

Human rights are the basic demands and expectations of every human being. In a business context, rights represent the limit beyond which no business enterprises—no matter how prosperous—can go. To say that an act violates a person's rights is—in law and in ethics—to say that it is forbidden, absolutely.

Rights are entitlements with trump status. A company with a contract has a right to have that contract fulfilled. An employee with a grudge has a right to speak, however unreasonable his claims may be. An elderly recluse has a right to her rundown property, even if a local

FIVE BASIC EMPLOYEE RIGHTS

1. The right to privacy
   (in your office or locker, your files, your telephone conversations, your home, your personnel data)
2. The right to your own outside activities
   (political, social, cultural, and economic, so long as you don't compete with or hurt your own company)
3. The right to conscientious objection
   (the right to refuse an order that violates your religious or moral principles; e.g., fudging in the figures in a profit statement, sleeping with the boss, or price-fixing to make a profit)
4. The right to (qualified) free speech
   (to complain, to "commit the truth," even to blow the whistle and go outside the company*) not, however, to slur the company
5. The right to due process
   (a prompt, impartial, and fair hearing; "where civil liberties and constitutionalism in business should start")

David Ewing, *Freedom Inside the Organization*
*In a recent poll of *Harvard Business Review* readers, only 14 percent backed an executive who fired a complaining employee (who then sued), "a pretty impressive sign that the times are changing."

real-estate developer knows that he can build a spectacular apartment complex and, not incidentally, make a huge profit. A customer or a supplier has a right to be dealt with fairly by a company, no matter how large or small his claims.

A basic question in every business decision is, "Will this violate anyone's rights?" Most of the time, the answer is no. One does not violate anyone's rights by entering into business competition. It is one of the premises of the free market that no one has exclusive rights to a product (not even telephone service). Anyone who can manufacture an automobile has the right to do so. No one has exclusive rights to a customer. A person who wants to buy a radio has the right to buy any kind or brand manufactured. Indeed we believe that it is the right of the consumer to buy whatever he or she wants (within somewhat controversial bounds of morals) at the cheapest price possible, and that in turn is the justification of the free market and the freedom of anyone to supply that market if he or she is able to do so. One need not be Ralph Nader to advocate consumer rights. The idea that the consumer has rights as well as desires is the starting point of the business world. (Adam Smith even called the consumer "sovereign.")

There are different kinds of rights. Knowing what kind of right is involved is as important as knowing that there are rights claims involved in a business decision.

First, there are *contractual rights,* rights by virtue of an individual contract or promise. An employee has certain rights in a company just because he or she was promised a specific position, with a specific title and carefully stated duties and a specified salary at the beginning of the job. The supplier of rubber hoses has a right to be paid exactly $43,000—no more and no less—because that is the amount that was agreed on and specified in the contract. The company has a right to the land by the river because, years ago, the owner signed an agreement that, on his death, the company could take over. Contractual rights are the heart of business. Without them, our concept of a business transaction would make no sense.

There are also *legal rights.* I don't have to have a contract with the government in order to have the right to free speech. That right is already in the Constitution. A Buddhist doesn't have to extract a promise from a local grocer to have the right to buy his produce. There are already laws against discriminating against customers on the basis of religion. If our elderly recluse does not want to sell her property to the developer, she has a legal right not to do so and not to be forced to do so. Businesses are protected by legal rights; they are also limited by other people's legal rights. Every right protects somebody and limits somebody else—which is to say that rights guarantee liberty, but they also specify its limits.

Legal rights vary with the laws. A person has a legal right to drink beer while driving in Texas but not in Massachusetts. A person has the right to sell pornographic photographs in Los Angeles but not in Bakersfield. But some rights do not depend on specific laws and so don't vary from place to place; they are so basic to the very conception of the society that they can be claimed everywhere, even in communities or states that do not accept them. We call these *civil rights,* and

---

The idea of full, unlimited, private ownership of anything, is now and always has been largely fiction.

A. M. Honore (professor, Oxford University)

among them are the various freedoms that are legally protected in our Constitution. But they would be rights even if they were not guaranteed by the Constitution, for our very conception of our country is that it is a land where all have the freedom to say and believe what they wish.

Finally, there are *human rights*. Freedom to make fun of the president is one of the more amusing as well as basic rights in our society, but it is not in Iran. Having the freedom to dress immodestly and provocatively is the right of every woman in our society; it is not in Iraq. But there are some rights that we consider so basic that we do not want to limit them to our own society. They belong to every human being—everywhere. The right not to be tortured or thrown in jail for no reason whatever are such rights. The right not to starve to death when there is food readily available is such a right. Because they apply to all humans everywhere, these are called "human rights." (They used to be called "natural rights.") It does not matter if the laws or customs of a society do not recognize such rights; we feel perfectly justified in criticizing the violation of those rights anyway. *We* recognized the rights of Jews in the former Soviet Union, even if the government of that country did not. *We* despised the use of torture to extract information from suspects in the Philippines, and it did not much matter if the government there thought that this was justifiable.

When we ask "Does this action violate anyone's rights?" is it important to ask as well "What kinds of rights?" A business plan that violates someone's contractual rights can be pursued by renegotiating the contract in question. A company may not want to continue to pay a rate of interest that is now several points higher than the going rate. But by making other promises and adding a few incentives, it might be able to obtain a reasonable reduction. On the other hand, if someone's civil rights are violated, it is not as if one can negotiate a special deal. A company can always challenge the law that defines legal rights in court, but where human rights are concerned, it would be hateful even to try. (A company might fight for the right to administer lie-detector tests to its employees in the wake of an epidemic of in-house thefts; it should not even raise the question of the right to torture them for the same information.)

The most flagrant violations of rights usually involve interference with a person's freedom or well-being—for instance, physically preventing a man from speaking or persecuting him for his religion. We might call these "freedom rights," and they generally amount to leaving a person alone. In business, the basic freedom right is often exclaimed in French: *laissez-faire,* "leave us alone!" It is one of the

---

THE RIGHT TO LIFE?

Every year thousands of Americans are killed or injured where they
work. . . . The OSHA (Occupational Safety and Health Administration)
recently calculated that the steel industry could annually save the lives
of several hundred of its coke workers if it invested in equipment to
control coke fumes. The cost per life saved would be $4.5 million. Is this
too much money?

Leonard H. Orr, *Business and Society Review*

---

undebatable presumptions of our society that a person—or a corporation—has the right to do whatever he, she, or it wants to do so long as
it does not harm or violate the rights of others or break the law. We
believe that freedom is the way to a prosperous society, but even if we
did not, we would probably still recognize the right of everyone to live
as he or she wants to.

There is another kind of right, however, that is much more difficult
to circumscribe and defend, although almost everyone would agree
that there must be some such rights. These might be called "positive"
rights or "entitlement" rights, for they do not just insist that a person
be left alone. They are demands, claims that society *owes* a person
something besides benign indifference. For example, most people
would agree that everyone has the right to eat, even if he is incapable
of feeding himself. Most people would agree that children deserve an
education, even if their parents can't pay for it. Some people would
insist that everyone deserves the best medical care available without
having to pay for it. A few zealots have claimed that everyone has a
right to almost everything, demonstrating not (as they think) the
ubiquity of rights but rather the absurd extent to which rights can be
abused as well as violated.

Entitlement rights are in part the product of a basic precept of
justice—that people ought to have their basic needs taken care of even
if they cannot contribute to the society. They are in part a presupposi-
tion of our belief in equal opportunity, since a person cannot possibly
compete in the marketplace without decent health and a reasonable
education. Part of the importance of entitlement rights is that they
ensure that the advantages of prosperity will extend at least a little to
everyone, and they provide a "safety net" underneath the sometimes
brutal competition of the market. But while it is clear that businesses

---

EMPLOYEE RIGHTS, CLEARLY EXPLAINED

Everybody but Sam had signed up for a new company pension plan that called for a small employee contribution. Unfortunately, 100% employee participation was needed; otherwise the plan was off. Sam's boss and his fellow workers pleaded and cajoled, but to no avail. Sam said the plan would never pay off.

Finally the company president called Sam into his office. "Sam," he said, "here's a copy of the new pension plan and here's a pen. I want you to sign the papers. I'm sorry, but if you don't sign you're fired." Sam signed the papers immediately.

"Now," said the president, "would you mind telling me why you couldn't have signed earlier?"

"Well, sir," replied Sam, "nobody explained it to me quite so clearly before."

Bits and Pieces

---

have an inescapable obligation to respect and not violate the freedom rights of individuals (and other companies), it is not clear what it means for businesses to respect and not violate the entitlement rights of individuals. It is clear that no business, no matter how powerful, has the right to take private property away from an unconsenting individual, and it is clear that no company has the right—under penalty of law—to silence an employee who wants to exercise his or her right to free speech. But what is the obligation of a business when there are people poorly housed in the community, or children who are not getting a decent education? Indeed, what is the obligation of a reasonably well-off citizen of that same community? We may well agree that people have entitlement rights, but what one ought to do to satisfy those rights is a matter of serious contention.

In business ethics, rights are fundamental. But in business, rights are often misunderstood. Not all rights are legal rights, and a company will not find itself in good ethical standing just because it obeys the law. This need not mean that every corporation should take on itself the entitlement rights of the poor and disadvantaged, but it certainly does mean that business must be aware of and attentive to such rights and help out when and where it can. A company does not have the obligation to hire workers it does not need. But when there are American workers unemployed and the firm exploits cheap foreign labor instead, the accusations of "unethical behavior" will be fast in coming.

Furthermore, habits and expectations are not the same as rights. The fact that a business has been free from regulation may be a matter of good fortune rather than a right, just as the infamous expense-account "three martini" lunches should be seen as a privilege of affluence and a controversial tax loophole rather than as a God-given right. One can enjoy privileges, but claiming them as rights casts a dark shadow on one's ethical sensibilities and invites equally irresponsible demands in return.

THE RIGHT TO DIGNITY: "HARASSMENT" AND SEX IN THE OFFICE

First and foremost among human rights, indeed the foundation for all other rights, according to many theorists, is the right to human dignity—a right to basic respect, a right not to be humiliated, and in the workplace a right to do one's job without compromise to one's integrity and innermost self. Of course, there are deep philosophical and cultural ambiguities surrounding this formulation. Some scholars would ask: Does not work itself touch our innermost being? Why should we think of "what we do" as merely superficial, and should we not see an unchallenging or merely menial job as itself a violation of our dignity? Does our insistence on human dignity conflict with the very idea of the hierarchical corporation and employee-employer relationships? Some egalitarians would say so. Indeed, some people would say that even the idea of having to work for pay—no matter what the job—is a violation of one's dignity, a form of prostitution. Are there not actions and modes of behavior that constitute, in effect, giving up the right to dignity? Well, perhaps, but always within certain limits. Making a fool

---

SEX RIGHTS: SEXUAL HARASSMENT GUIDELINES (EEOC)

Under these guidelines, sexual harassment is defined as unwelcome sexual advances, requests for sexual favors, and other verbal or physical conduct of a nature which constitutes harassment when

- submission to the conduct is either explicitly or implicitly a term or condition of an individual's employment;
- submission to or rejection of such conduct by an individual is used as the basis for employment decisions affecting that individual; or
- such conduct has the purpose or effect of unreasonably interfering with an individual's work performance or creating an intimidating, hostile, or offensive working environment.

Included in the area of offensive behavior which may constitute sexual harassment are:

- Deliberate assaults or molestations.
- Explicit or implicit promises of preferential treatment in return for sexual favors (*e.g.,* high grades, good performance evaluations, promotion, better work schedule, special favors).
- Explicit or implicit threats that the individual's scholastic or professional career will be adversely affected if the sexual demands are rejected (*e.g.,* low grades, poor performance appraisal or recommendation, non-promotion, reassignment to a less desirable position/schedule).
- Deliberate, repeated, unsolicited verbal comments, gestures or physical actions of a sexual nature (*e.g.,* unnecessary touching, pinching or patting another person). . . .

---

of oneself in public may seem to be a matter of throwing away one's own dignity, but this surely does not mean that one has given up the right to be treated as a human being, with some sympathy and understanding at the very least. Even a vicious criminal retains the right not to be tortured and abused, although he may well through his actions have given up many of his other rights. The minimal violation of the right to dignity is *harassment*. Of course there are more serious violations—physical assault and murder, for example—but harassment covers a large area of subtle and not-so-subtle abuses. Sexual harassment gets the most press coverage, but it is one part of a more general violation, most instances of which have little or nothing to do with sex or gender.

The always-pressing question, especially in a free-enterprise system, is what one can be hired to do, what can be sold or for sale, and what rights and entitlements an employer has vis-à-vis the employed—and vice versa. The notion that an employee can be treated in any way that the employer wishes, for example, is intolerable. It is reminiscent of those awful institutions, slavery and indentured servitude. Central to our idea of dignity is freedom and, in particular, freedom of choice. A job is a contractual arrangement, and although there are many and difficult questions about what counts as coercion and compromise of one's ability to choose (the difficulty of getting employment elsewhere, a desperate need for money, and so on), we are generally agreed that the fact that one person (or organization) hires another imposes obligations and duties only to the extent of the job itself.

A person is hired to do a particular job, to have particular responsibilities, and though these may have many aspects and far-reaching consequences, even dangers, every job involves a contract, real or implied, that limits what one person can expect or demand from another. In corporate life (and in almost any career or profession), of course, the demands of the job will also include all of those "favors" and "supplements" that will (one hopes) lead to promotion, and some of these may seem very much like a violation of the right to dignity. (Just think of the stereotypical corporate flunky.) We do not consider these "harassment" only because we also consider them voluntary.

Expectations may also change with time. Twenty years ago, it was simply understood that a stenographer or typist would also make coffee as a part of her or his duties. For good reason, many women—who held most of these office positions—found such an expectation demeaning, a not-very-subtle reminder of their lowly status in the office and their inferior prospects. Today, accordingly, such duties are no longer understood to be part of the routine office contract, but—where it is not simply a matter of mutual courtesy ("whoever gets here first turns on the coffee pot")—it is something to be negotiated quite independently and explicitly. Harassment in the workplace begins with demands that people do more than they were hired to do, although what they were "hired to do" almost always remains an open question.

The arena in which such rights have become most controversial and most widely and heatedly discussed, needless to say, has been the realm of sexual privacy. However else we want to draw the line between a person's job and his or her private life and "innermost

PREVENTING HARASSMENT: WHAT EMPLOYERS CAN AND SHOULD DO

A program for prevention and a formal system for investigation of complaints can go a long way toward avoiding the economic and emotional costs of sexual harassment in the workplace, according to Equal Employment Opportunity Commission guidelines and Los Angeles attorney David Kadue.

Before employers can implement comprehensive sexual harassment policies, they must understand the scope of the problem. The stereotypical case of a male supervisor harassing a female employee is only one example of sexual harassment. Such discrimination may involve other patterns as well. EEOC considers the following points in identifying these cases:

- *The victim or the harasser may be of either sex.*
- *The harasser does not have to be the victim's supervisor.*
- *The victim and the harasser need not be of the opposite sex.*
- *The victim does not have to be the person to whom the sexual advances are directed.*
- *The victim does not have to complain to the harasser or inform the employer.*
- *The victim need not suffer a concrete economic injury as a result of the harassment.*

Once an employer has a clear understanding of what sexual harassment is, "prevention is the best tool" for its elimination, say EEOC guidelines. As part of an effective preventative program, EEOC advises employers to do the following:

- Implement an explicit policy against sexual harassment.
- Regularly and clearly communicate the policy to all employees.
- Affirmatively raise the subject with all employees.
- Express strong disapproval for sexual harassment.
- Develop appropriate sanctions for harassment and explain them to employees.
- Implement a procedure for resolving sexual harassment complaints that encourages victims to come forward, protects confidentiality to the extent possible, and guards against retaliation.

Reprinted with permission from "Sexual Harassment: Addressing the New Realities of the 1990s," published by BNA Communications, Inc. A free single copy of the report may be obtained by writing to BNA Communications, Inc., a subsidiary of The Bureau of National Affairs, Inc., 9439 Key West Avenue, Rockville, MD 20750.

self,'' that line is sure to fall somewhere between the work and a
person's body. To be sure, jobs that involve regular and intense
epidermal contact—dance partners or professional wrestlers, for instance—may involve a more subtle set of signals and protections of
privacy, such that even the most intense shared physical activity
remains merely physical and does not become sexual or intimate. So,
too, medical personnel, masseurs, and masseuses learn very delicate
distinctions between even the most intrusive techniques and movements and sexual or romantic suggestiveness. But in the realm of the
usual corporate office, such subtleties are not particularly relevant to
the question of sexual harassment. What is relevant is a line that is
usually much more obvious. And in the current atmosphere of hyper-
sensitivity and excessive mutual suspicion, not to mention lawsuits,
the best advice is probably summed up in the warning *"don't touch,"*
which used to be found mainly on works of art and dangerous machinery.

Sexual harassment is not just a matter of touching, of course. An
off-color joke, a not-so-subtle suggestion, a comment, or a look can be
sexual harassment as well. If one wanted to catalog the different looks,
words, jokes, and gestures that might count as sexual harassment in
some context or other, one could concoct a virtually endless list, but
that isn't the point. The idea that one could have such a guideline is
itself part of the problem, that people want to insist on a precise list of
"don'ts" rather than exercise *sensitivity* around and toward other
people. Indeed, some people (and some cultures) are very physical.
Hugs and slaps are commonplace and completely innocent. Other
people are very reserved, and even a casual compliment might be taken
as provocative or pregnant with meaning. Sensitivity, as opposed to
some objective legal policy or criterion, depends upon communication
and awareness, mutual respect, or at least a decent distance. Nevertheless, the issue cannot be left up to sensitivity, for the obvious reasons.
People are very different, and they don't (usually) wear their attitudes
as a uniform. The old (male) ethic seemed to be "they'll get used to it.
They have to." The new, more sensitive ethic is that sexuality is
explosive and intrusive, so be careful, cautious, and when in doubt—
don't.

But because we are a morally Manichean people who would rather
believe in black and white than a more colorful moral universe, we
have tended to move too far in the opposite direction, toward the total
prohibition of in-the-office romances and sexual suggestions of any
kind. Given that most of us spend most of our adult waking lives in the

office and that many people do in fact meet their marital partners on the job, this total prohibition—whether by way of company policy or by just "common knowledge"—is unreasonable and, I would argue, itself a kind of harassment, a refusal to treat employees as whole people, with sexuality and romantic desires. So where does one draw the line? Once again, the answer will be discomforting to those who want clearcut objective criteria. The antidote to sexual harassment is not prohibition but good judgment and sensitivity.

Romance in the office is not only a fact of life. It is one of those experiences that makes the workplace human. It gives some people something to hope for. It gives everyone else an opportunity to guess and gossip, two social activities that may well be as necessary and as natural as sex. But it would be a mistake to underestimate or leave unstated the problems that usually accompany even the most discreet relationships. There is a potential problem in any relationship between nonequals, a problem of equity and fairness. There is always the danger of coercion, even if unintended, and humiliation, if things don't "work out." There is also a problem of equity and fairness in the office itself, and it is for good reason that many corporations insist on transfer when a romance or a marriage interferes with the routine division of labor or rewards in the same office. Office romances are by their very nature explosive and disruptive, but they are the kind of danger and disruption that most of us celebrate as well as tolerate and, in terms of office morale and morals, it is as much of a mistake to forbid them as uncritically to encourage them.

Sexual harassment is not a form of romance, of course, but rather a form of rape in which the explicit abuse of power is a crime. When a supervisor makes sexual submission by a worker a condition for a promotion or for keeping her or his job, that is extortion, backed up by the power of the organization. And when the organization refuses to withdraw that power, by firing the offender or otherwise ending the harassment, it is a full party to the crime.

The process by which harassment charges can be made and established is a matter of considerable dispute, but it seems obvious to most of us, since the Anita Hill–Clarence Thomas hearings in 1991, that the familiar mythology of "his word or hers" is by no means the end of the issue. There are, no doubt, casual comments and one-time propositions that are just as well forgotten. There are encounters that, however inappropriate or traumatic, are not subject to verification. But experience suggests that sexual harassers are compulsive repeaters and usually devoid of much sense of discretion. They are typically known to just about everyone and are the talk of the office. Several victims, not just one or two, are ultimately in a position to testify to the abuse. It is a travesty that so many corporations still refuse to utilize such cumulative evidence and tend to protect the alleged harasser with far more conviction than they protect the harassed. In any such process, there will be abuses and injustices, and surely we would all endorse the principle that people are innocent until proven guilty. But where good judgment and sensitivity fail in the individual, corporate integrity is on the line as well. It is therefore the responsibility of the corporation to protect the dignity of its employees.

THE ENVIRONMENT: THE SILENT STAKEHOLDER

Concern for the environment has become an inescapable concern for the free-enterprise system. Thirty years ago, it was at most a marginal aesthetic issue for most industries. Today it is or should be part of every corporate mission. In current business ethics terms, the environment has become a "stakeholder" in the corporation, one of its sources of obligations and responsibility.

The environment does not have a voice or a vote in running our society. It is not a stockholder and has no say in the running of our corporations. Nevertheless it provides the atmosphere, many of the resources, the very ground and climate within which all business and all human activity takes place. It is, therefore, the silent stakeholder of every corporation, or rather, the precondition for every corporation's very existence. For many centuries, the impact of the relatively small and not-yet-industrialized humans on the earth was not sufficient to notice, except, perhaps, in towns with very concentrated populations. To be sure, there was some air pollution because of the many fires that were used to cook food and warm houses, and there was always a problem of waste disposal, which was not always delicately handled and whose importance for community health was slow to be appreciated. But it is only recently that we have had to worry about the problems of massive carbon monoxide poisoning of the air due to millions of internal combustion engines in motorcars and toxic chemicals spewed into the air by thousands of factories, not to mention the particularly deadly wastes of nuclear plants. It is only recently that we have managed to pollute not only a few local streams and dirty our local rivers but literally kill entire lakes and poison the oceans, that we have managed to release enough dangerous chemicals into the air and damaged the surface of the earth to such an extent that we have endangered the atmosphere and the climate of the planet. In the Scriptures, our ancestors are famously promised "dominion" over the earth. But those were the days when the entire human population wouldn't fill the average American suburb and almost all refuse and pollution were, by their very nature, "biodegradable." And as the population of the planet continues to grow—from two billion to five billion in only a few decades—there will be more pollution, more environmental damage, more mouths to feed and vehicles to power.

Like all noble causes, environmentalism invites self-righteousness. All too often, environmentalists demand too much and refuse to compromise, and otherwise responsible corporations feel forced to take a much more reactionary "anti-environmental" position than they would or should. A false and extremist dichotomy has arisen between what I call "reverential" attitudes toward the environment (the environment as a holy and untouchable object of worship) and merely "utilitarian" attitudes; namely, "how can we *use* the environment?" So, too, the distinction between "corporate self-interest" and altruism/sacrifice is exaggerated and turns possible solutions into impossible choices. There is the predictable insistence on self-sacrifice, which in the corporate context translates into giving up profits or even accepting losses for the sake of a sometimes dubious environmental gain. There is the familiar attitude problem among the environmentalists: Greener if not more Tao than Thou. Or, perhaps, who is a "deeper" ecologist. Environmentalism can be taken to extremes: the preservation of species becomes an absolute rather than one more moral consideration. Pollution becomes an evil rather than an undesirable by-product of progress, and thereby it becomes immune to negotiation and compromise. Indeed, a few Earth Firsters and some of their counterparts have said that humanity is the problem, and we hear praise for the AIDS virus and the reappearance of smallpox.

Against such virulent antihumanism, there is a predictable reaction.

Reject environmentalism. Dismiss the whole movement as extremist. But this response, like the absurdity that provoked it, is wrongheaded and offensive. Environmental consciousness has become a necessity, but sensible planning and negotiation is also necessary. Environmentalism presents new restrictions but also new challenges and new opportunities for business. Cooperation is the key. Those relatively few developers and business spokespeople who insist on challenging and "baiting" the environmentalists do the entire business world as profound a disservice as those environmentalists who simply assume that each business and every corporation is an enemy and environmentally irresponsible.

The United States is, in fact, well ahead of most other countries in its efforts to fight pollution and clean up the planet. Nearly a third of the trees in Germany's romantic Schwartzwald are dead from the pollution along the Autobahn. Most of Eastern Europe's rivers, including the historic Danube (which hasn't been "blue" for decades) have become cesspools of chemical waste. The air in Tokyo and Mexico City is so bad so much of the time that citizens are warned not to go outside, or to wear gas masks if they do. We still do not know how extensive and long-lasting the damage may be from the breakdown of Russia's Chernobyl reactor. And the intentional damage done to the Red Sea and the entire atmosphere of the Middle East by Saddam Hussein during the Persian Gulf War of 1991 has still not been fully evaluated, much less cleaned up.

But, of course, we are not innocent in this regard, and much of our own apparent good fortune has to do with the fact that our messiest industries are often shipped overseas, where environmental restrictions and protection laws are far more lenient. A chemical pesticide factory owned and operated by the American company Union Carbide leaked its deadly contents one night and killed thousands of people in Bhopal, India, leaving many more thousand with chronic ailments and illnesses. It is, perhaps, a matter of luck that our nuclear mishaps due to negligence or faulty design have thus far had little impact. And, of course, the Exxon *Valdez* disaster is not far behind us, and there have already been similar disasters with comparable environmental damage.

It is the nature of environmental pollution that, unlike most mistaken policies or ill-designed products, the results cannot be simply revised or recalled. Environmental damage is often irreversible, and it can last lifetimes. Environmental damage often cannot be contained, and the damage caused in one part of the world may quickly and unstoppably affect another. For example, the production of "acid rain" does not recognize international boundaries, say, between the United States and Canada or between Germany and Switzerland; and the damage that is being done to the atmosphere, by way of depletion of the ozone layer and the "greenhouse effect," for example, does not just affect the countries most responsible for causing it. The smoke and pollution from Iraq's oil fires spread beyond the Persian Gulf to much of the planet within a few months. The destruction of the rain forests in South America and Southeast Asia is felt in the industrialized countries of Europe and North America, and the cultivation of cattle for the beef industry, according to environmentalist Jeremy Rifkin, is wrecking the planet.

Our industries produce millions of tons of potentially harmful substances, some 70,000 different compounds, and at least several hundred of these can be seriously argued to present serious health or environmental risks. To complicate matters, substances that seem to be harmless can later be shown to pose serious dangers. For example, asbestos, which only a few decades ago was being celebrated as a fibrous wonder that could (and did) reduce and eliminate the danger of fire, proved to be extremely toxic and has been blamed for many deaths. So, too, with the elements lead, mercury, and radium and the compounds dioxin and benzene. But as so often, the damaging effects of such substances, in addition to not being predicted beforehand, may take decades to develop. Even smoking tobacco, which comes as close as possible to cumulative or delayed causation of fatal damage to the human body, takes decades to develop and leaves enough room for argument about the specific mechanism of the cause for industry defenders to insist that "the connection has not been proved." Even where the damage is immediate and visible, there may be good arguments of the cost/benefit variety that conclude that the product in question is worth the cost to the environment—but worth it to whom, and who will pay that cost?

Virtually every industrial product has some pollution, some noxious or seemingly unusable substance, as its by-product. Some industries are relatively clean—the computer software business, for example. Others are notoriously "dirty"; in fact, so polluting that it has become a real question whether we are willing to tolerate them on our soil, even at the cost of becoming dependent on foreign-made products. The steel industry is a prime example, and it should not be surprising that many of our largest and once most-successful steel companies have been diversifying in part in order to avoid the enormous costs it would take to clean up their industry. The result, an increase in our dependency on steel from abroad, where environmental standards are often much lower—not a healthy alternative.

The production of paper is a particularly messy business, and the recycling of paper, we should add, is as well. But only a few extremists have seriously suggested that we should give up paper and its manufacture, although the cost of paper production is pollution. But pollution admits of degrees, and there are always new technologies that decrease and limit pollution in the paper business. The problem is, technology can be very expensive. If a paper company buys and installs the new technology, its costs of production increase significantly. That means, presumably, that it will have to charge more for its product. But now suppose, just for the sake of simplicity, that there are ten paper manufacturers competing with the same product in the same market. If one of them installs the new technology but the others do not, that one environmentalist hero will soon find itself unable to compete with the others. Its product will be the most expensive in the industry. Now suppose that all but one of the companies goes for the new technology. That one environmentally irresponsible holdout will in fact capture much of the market, assuming that people will tend to buy the least expensive product. One might like the ten companies to get together and agree that they will all install the new technology and all raise prices together, but, first of all, this is illegal, as "collusion." And, second, what is to prevent one or more of the ten from cheating on the others, refusing after the agreement to in fact install the new technology and then beating the others on prices?

The first and most preferable, according to the most sacred canon of capitalism, is that the consumer should mandate corporate concern for the environment by buying or refusing to buy products from corporations on the basis of their environmental impact and sensibility. Consumers can refuse to buy paper from companies that pollute more than is necessary, for example, but that also means that they must be willing to pay higher prices for "cleaner" products and their production. Unfortunately, what people say they would do or would like to do is not always what they do, and it is not altogether clear to what extent consumers are willing to use their "sovereignty," particularly when they are not convinced that others will "vote" along with them. Consumer boycotts have had spectacular results in certain industries, resulting in not only improved products but also increased market share and profits for those companies that are quick to respond.

In many industries, of course, consumers remain more concerned about low prices than about the effects on the environment. In many others, information about production and pollution is not readily available. Consumers can only find out so much, and in many cases, the details of production and the chemistry of the process may well be beyond the grasp of any but the most educated scientist or industrialist. And most consumers buy and use hundreds if not thousands of products in a few months or years, and they cannot possibly be expected to keep abreast of the production processes of them all.

Where consumer pressure is inadequate or not well-enough informed to pressure companies into pollution-free technologies, government regulation may be to everyone's benefit. Most people would probably not voluntarily spend the extra several hundred dollars it costs to reduce the exhaust emissions on their automobile, and many people would not buy fuel-efficient cars if the price of gasoline remains cheap enough. The result is that everyone pursues their own interest, and everyone suffers. So, too, a few overly cost-conscious or ambitious companies can retard innovation throughout an industry. By refusing to research or develop new technologies, they can undercut their competitors and inhibit their willingness to do so as well, even though the whole industry will be hurt in the longer run.

When the government steps in, it can be to the benefit of the industry as well as the society in general. Of course, that presupposes that the regulation is truly regulative and not punitive, that it appeals to the cooperative and community sentiment of corporations rather than simply treats them all as likely criminals, that it depends as much as possible on self-regulation and minimizes the administrative burdens. It is not regulation that deserves the bad name it has earned in business, but burdensome and often pointless regulation, regulation that assumes guilt instead of voluntary compliance, regulation that serves to empower only the bureaucracy and not those whom it is supposed to serve.

When government requires of the paper producers that they all conform to a uniform standard, every company in the industry can install the new pollution-reducing technology, grumbling no doubt about government interference, and each of them will raise their prices knowing that the others must do so as well. The consumers will pay the difference because, if they want paper, they have no choice. But they will also have a cleaner environment, whether or not they notice the difference. So, too, when the government mandates emission standards and fuel efficiency, the industry growls, automobiles get more expensive, but the air also gets cleaner. This is one area where "protectionist" legislation is or ought to be unobjectionable to free-market advocates. Imposing standards on the basis of health and safety is not the same as interfering with free-market forces on the basis of local advantage alone.

Perhaps, given the choice, some people would prefer cheaper, bigger, more polluting cars. But do future generations, who will find their cities suffocating, have a voice in the matter? Should all of those who do not want bigger cars and are willing to pay the price for a (relatively) pollution-free environment have to suffer for the preferences and choices of a few? The question of choice here is critical, because it is on the basis of free choice that the very idea of the free market is founded. What if people do not care about the environment or worry about pollution? But here the hard-to-calculate question of future generations and other nonconsumers (e.g., infants) comes into play, and here we need a larger vision, which it is the job of government to provide, to see beyond the sometimes narrow focus of individual consumers. This is a touchy point. People may well say, indeed insist, that the environment be protected, the air cleaned up, but when left to their own personal choice they prefer to leave that burden to others. Here the government acts on the basis of one choice and frustrates another. But where the environment is concerned, this split willfulness, the demand for a healthy environment, on the one hand, and the demand for a dubious individual freedom to pollute, on the other, is all too common.

From these examples, and many more like them, we can appreciate the fact that much of the pollution in the air and water caused by industry must be blamed not on business alone but shared with the consumer and the citizenry at large. And it is the government—so often maligned for its role in regulation—which must sometimes come to the rescue. In the 1950s and 1960s, the Detroit automobile industry (then unchallenged) designed and built enormous and unnecessarily overpowered cars because consumers demanded them. With the growing awareness of the environmental problem and stiffened emission standards, consumers began to change their tastes, but it must be said that Detroit was disastrously slow in responding. Japan and Germany, however, were quicker off the mark, and by the 1980s the demand for small, fuel-efficient cars was such that it was not just the environment that was at stake. It was the American auto industry. Given the new awareness of the fragility of the planet, consumer and citizen demand for cleaner, healthier procedures and processes, even at somewhat greater cost, will continue to have a strong voice in the market. Indeed, one of the growth industries of the 1990s, it seems, is the environmental

BIG SPILLERS

The nine largest U.S. oil companies as listed in the Fortune 500 spilled 6,922,928 gallons of oil in the years 1984 to 1988, according to researchers at the Center for Study of Responsive Law and Essential Information. In all, 83,402,112 gallons of oil and gas spilled in and around U.S. waters. Spills from the nine biggest companies represent 8.2 percent of that total. Listed by company, here are the number of gallons spilled over the five-year period:

Chevron	2,800,000
Amoco	1,300,000
Texaco	926,000
Exxon	843,869
Shell	536,768
Mobil	495,696
Arco	22,222
Tenneco	15,374
Occidental	375

protection industry—hazardous waste and trash disposal, clean-up processes, antipollution devices.

The concern for the environment, like so many public issues, has too often taken an unjustified toll by way of increased attacks on and suspicions of business. But, again, one should be cautious about leveling blame and assigning responsibility, and focus the accusations where they are deserved. Many companies are laudably conscientious about the environment and the effects of their production methods. They should be held up as models and supported with enthusiasm. Some are irresponsible. They provide one of the tests for the most essential claim of the free market. Will the consumers and the government representing them take the long-term and broader view, or will they take the same short-run, ultimately disastrous point of view that so many of them so readily find objectionable in some corporations? When business claims that they are only giving the public what they want, that is not just an excuse. It is also a rightful sharing of the responsibility. Lack of cooperation and mutual hostility between business and environmental advocates produces stalemate, slows productiveness, and forces the government to intervene with often hasty, politically motivated regulation, further hurting business and rarely

---

GRASSROOTS GREEN

A Time/CNN poll in January [1995] reported that 55 percent of those
asked would increase government spending on the environment, 1 percent would decrease it and 27 percent would keep spending the same.
Other polls show strong environmental support among suburban Repub-
licans and blue-collar white males, who are furious that business is
pushing environmental cuts.

—*Time,* April 24, 1995

---

helping the environment. Environmental regulation, properly conceived and worked out through sensitive negotiation with business as
well as environmentalists, can be a boon for both business and the
environment. But the best regulation is self-regulation, and better yet
if it becomes part of the profit-making plan of the corporation.

The problem in environmental debates, as in so many real-life,
practical philosophical disputes, is an excess of polarization of the key
ethical terms. There is the harsh distinction between altruism and self-
interest—yielding some fascinating sociobiological arguments but
clouding the issue. There is the self-righteous rejection of all "utilitarian" arguments for the environment in favor of what one might call
"reverence" arguments. And there are two competing conceptions of
nature, as a mere resource "out there" for the taking, albeit to be
conserved as any finite necessity, and as precious in itself, filled with
the wisdom of homeostasis and a "balance" of nature that is visible
only to the shortsighted or the poetic.

Whatever else it may be, environmentalism need not and should not
include a rejection of the human perspective. It should be an appeal to
what is best and most human in us, our aesthetic and spiritual sensitiv-
ities, our ability to step back from our narrow projects and our
prejudices and appreciate and empathize and cooperate in a world that
is bigger and grander than ourselves. Such polemical distinctions as
the love of nature versus the exploitation of nature ("reverence" and
"utilitarianism") distort and disguise the complex issues of environmentalism and make mutual understanding and cooperation impossible. "Deep" ecologists who wage war against one another and reject
all conceivable technological solutions to environmental problems do

THE MONSANTO PLEDGE

St. Louis–based Monsanto, the nation's fourth-largest chemical producer, has adopted the following pledge:

- Reduce all toxic releases, working toward a goal of zero.
- Ensure that no Monsanto operation poses undue risk to employees and communities.
- Work to achieve sustainable agriculture through new technology and practices.
- Ensure groundwater safety—making our technical resources available to farmers dealing with contamination, even if our products are not involved.
- Keep our plants open to our communities, bringing the community into plant operations. Inform people of any significant hazard.
- Manage all corporate real estate to benefit nature.
- Search worldwide for technology to reduce and eliminate waste from our operations, with the top priority being not making it in the first place.

the environmental movement no favors but only isolate environmentalism from the very possibility of cooperative reforms (e.g., *The Ecologist,* Vol. 18, no. 4/5, 1988). It is in response to such divisive polemicizing that the reactionary accusations of environmentalists as "elitists" gain plausibility (e.g., William Tucker, *Progress and Privilege,* New York: Doubleday, 1982). Competition for the high moral ground is not the way to environmental reform.[1]

There is another way. The Environmental Defense Fund, originally formed in the late 1960s as an advocate of the "Sue the Bastards" approach to corporate pollution, embarked on a new strategy, under Fred Krupp, of acting in cooperation with those same corporations, encouraging market-oriented solutions. In 1990, they convinced and then helped McDonald's to get rid of their styrofoam packaging and become an environmentally sensitive company. They are now working with General Motors to get pollution-belching old clunkers off the

1. Some of the material in this section has been adapted from my essay, "Environmentalism as a Humanism" in *Entertaining Ideas* (Buffalo: Prometheus Books, 1992) and reprinted with minor changes from *Free Inquiry,* 1992, with thanks to Tim Madigan, and from my textbook, *Above the Bottom Line* (Harcourt Brace, 1993).

road. This does not mean an end to adversarial proceedings and protests, to be sure, and there is still plenty of room for Greenpeace and the Sierra Club. But the new message is that the environmental issues do not belong to them alone, and the more cooperation and involvement from the corporations themselves, the better.

NOBLESSE OBLIGE:
BUSINESS AND CULTURE

> *Supposedly we despise the rich. In fact we emulate them faithfully. When they are good and interesting models, civilization flourishes. When not, not. At various times the British gentlemen, the landed European knight and the classical Athenian citizen have been worthy models. These days, for good or ill, well-off Americans are models for the world. So far, our best are only medium good and medium interesting.*
>
> Stewart Brand, Whole Earth Catalog

Society as a whole is a stakeholder in every corporation, and one of society's central interests is what is often called its "quality of life." There is no question that corporations have social responsibilities; insofar as corporations affect society and have "impact," they, like anyone, are responsible for what they do. Like any citizen, insofar as a corporation reaps the benefits of society, it owes something in return. And like any other ethical enterprise, business of necessity has a concern for justice, a sense of equal opportunity, and respect for rights—contractual rights, legal rights, civil rights and, especially, human rights. Businesses do not have a *special* obligation to help the

WHY THE ARTS?

I would like to lay to rest the notion that business should support the arts because support of the arts is "good for the image of business." When the products of business really work, when business is known to step up and accept responsibility . . . then I think the image of business will change for the better. Well then, why should business give to the arts? [Because] the artist at his best helps each of us to discover what our best might be, helps us truly to see our neighbor, helps him to see us. I think such an America might be a very good place for any business.

J. Irwin Miller (CEO, Cummins Engine Company)

poor, end racism and unemployment, or improve the environment, but, like anyone, they should want to do so if they can, and they will be expected to do so when they can. But what of those concerns that are not at all within the province of business, that are not even remotely related to the products or services in which a business specializes? What about art and culture? What about education, not just the business schools but the humanities—literature, history, classics, philosophy? What about the sciences, not the technological innovations that aid industrial research and produce new products but knowledge for its own sake? What about the quality of life? What can and should the corporation do?

The familiar argument is that business has no responsibiliites or obligations in these matters because (a) they have nothing to do with business and (b) they have nothing to do with the expertise of business people. But anyone advancing such an argument ought to be aware of the obvious consequence, which is that people who do consider such matters to be vital to the life of society quickly and naturally fall back to the long-standing conclusion that businessmen are, by their own admission, philistines. ("Business has nothing to do with the finer things of life. People in business do not know and do not care to know about art, music, literature, and ideas, since there is nothing in business that prepares them to do so.")

It does not have to be said again that the historical portrait of the businessman is not at all flattering. Charles Adams, himself a successful businessman, once complained, "I have known and known tolerably well a good many 'successful' men. . . . A less interesting crowd I do not care to encounter." Theodore Roosevelt similarly remarked:

CORPORATIONS IN SUPPORT OF PUBLIC TELEVISION

American Telephone & Telegraph
Atlantic Richfield
Chevron (Standard Oil of California)
The Chubb Group
Danskin (Esmark)
Exxon

Ford Motor
General Electric
Gulf Oil
Mobil
J.C. Penney
Xerox

> I am delighted to show any courtesy to Pierpont Morgan or Andrew Carnegie, but as for regarding any one of them as I regard Professor Bury or Peary the Arctic explorer—why I could not force myself to do it, even if I wanted to, which I don't.

And all of this in the country whose business is business, according to several presidents. One doesn't have to look far into other cultures or earlier into history to find an army of enemies of the stereotypical, uncultured, uncouth businessman. The ironic thing is that, especially in this country, the arts and education—even what good there is on television—virtually exist because of the efforts and generosity of business, from Texaco's sponsorship of the Metropolitan Opera to the latest exhibit underwritten by IBM at the Whitney Museum.

Instead of the self-defeating argument that business has no business getting into the arts, let's look at and appreciate the simple fact that business *is* in the arts—in music, in education, in ideas. The philanthropists who built the great American art collections and museums were almost all businessmen—Rockefeller, Getty, Whitney, Mellon, Carnegie, Frick, Morgan, Astor. The most spectacular and popular art exhibits of the last few years have all been sponsored by major corporations, and most of the music and dance companies in the country are supported by local businesses. On a smaller scale but in greater numbers, for better or worse, most of the contemporary art that is being bought today is being bought by businesses—adorning professional offices and the great lobbies of the largest corporate headquarters. Businessmen who are particularly anxious to detach themselves from this wanton display of cultural involvement might perhaps rationalize these activities as investments or public relations, but the fact is that not only does art in America depend upon business but business obviously welcomes that dependency and the opportuni-

HOW TO GIVE (EFFECTIVELY)

The following guidelines could prove useful in developing a program that serves both the company and the public:

- Is the task worth doing? Too many corporate charitable activities are designed to gain favor instead of making a significant contribution. The first step is to make sure the effort is worthwhile. Just "helping the homeless" isn't good enough. An example is the Rampathon program initiated by the Remodelers Council of the Builders Association of Greater Boston. It decided to build wheelchair ramps, free of charge, at the homes of disabled persons who could not afford them.
- Make charitable support an extension of a company's normal business activity. That is what the forestry and specialty products division of International Paper Co. has done with a program to save the endangered Red Hill salamander in southern Alabama. The multinational corporation offered its resources to make it possible for small landowners, from whom International Paper buys its lumber, to create a habitat for the creature.
- Stick with the commitment. Many charities have become cynical about corporate support that is "hit-and-run" and 100 percent self-serving. Companies have inundated a worthy activity with dollars, then left as soon as the news value had been milked dry.

—*USA Today,* January 1995

ties that come with it. Is this true "responsibility of business"? That isn't much of a question. When one willingly and enthusiastically undertakes an enterprise, what would it mean to say that it is not one's responsibility? And when one gets involved in matters of taste, obviously one ought to have the good sense (whether or not it is also a responsibility) to acquire (or hire) some good taste.

Why should businesses and business people get involved in the arts? One reason is that people in business are cultured human beings who cater to other cultured human beings. However successful they may be in terms of pure wealth, people in business are ultimately liked and respected for the same reasons that anyone else is, because they are part of a culture, because they are involved in improving society in intangible as well as tangible ways. Indeed, it would be hard to find a more central theme in nineteenth-century American literature than the nouveau-riche businessman who is excluded from society because of his "vulgarity." And in contemporary corporate life, it may not be mentioned in the same breath as managerial experience, but a candidate's literacy—or illiteracy—is carefully noted. It may not be on a par with "Thou shalt not steal," but participation in, and knowledge

---

STANFORD STUDENTS JOIN DREAM

In 1981, industrialist Eugene Lang launched his "I Have a Dream" program in which he guaranteed elementary school students at his alma mater in East Harlem that he would pay for their college education if they made it through high school. The program inspired many others across the country to do likewise. One of the latest efforts was mounted by students at the Stanford Business School, who banded together to help third and fourth graders at the Flood School in predominantly black East Palo Alto.

The idea of MBA student David Michael, the project has involved some twenty students at Stanford. They have agreed to serve as tutors and advisers to the grade schoolers right through their high school years. They also raised more than $400,000 from alumni, students, faculty, and corporations, which will assure each of the grade school students a scholarship of $4,800 for college. The Stanford students put up $22,000 themselves.

They hope to have the same success Eugene Lang experienced. In a school with a 75 percent dropout rate, 85 percent of his adopted class went on to receive their high school diplomas.

WITE-OUT SNIFFS OUT PROBLEM

Corporate social responsibility doesn't have to hurt the bottom line. Just ask Chairman Archie Douglas of the Beltsville, Maryland, Wite-Out Corp. He was disheartened to learn that his popular correction fluid was being sniffed by teenagers for a cheap high, with some dying as a result. Douglas ordered that a new formula be developed, without the intoxicating solvent trichloroethylene—also known as methyl chloroform—which promotes fast drying.

Fortunately, that's not the end of the story. The revised product, called For Everything, works on everything from fax copies to ink, greatly increasing the sales potential. Says Douglas, "The social concerns that prompted this research will enhance both market share and profits."

—*Business Month,* September 1990

CORPORATE GIVING TOPS $5 BILLION

According to preliminary figures, charitable contributions by corporations topped the $5 billion mark for the first time in 1989. That was the word from the Council for Aid to Education, which received data from 356 companies responsible for about one-third of all corporate giving. The Council said complete figures for 1988 showed that corporate giving represented 1.5 percent of pretax profits. A little more than 40 percent of the charity dollar went to education.

and support of, the "finer things" that a culture has to offer is an essential part of business ethics.

The second reason that business people are involved in the arts and support the arts goes back to ancient times. As the wealthiest citizens in society, they are in the best position to support the arts, and because they can, they are expected to. This is not picking on business, and it has nothing to do with the particular expertise of business institutions or business people. The role of cultural overseer has variously been filled by warriors, statesmen, church prelates, and aristocrats. Supporting culture is the obligation of those who can: *noblesse oblige.*

It is a matter of indifference whether businesses (or warriors or statesmen or church prelates or aristocrats) support culture because they believe that it is also in their self-interest, because it will increase long-term profits, or because it will improve the public image of the corporation. The Medici did not support the arts out of a pure sense of either aesthetics or obligation; they were quite clear about the fact that they were, by hiring such consultants as Raphael and Michelangelo, assuring themselves a kind of immortality. Most cultured New Yorkers know the names Frick and Guggenheim only because of their support of the arts. So, too, Texaco may be remembered, long after oil is depleted or obsolete, for its contributions to the arts. Such a reputation is not unenviable, and it does not matter if the original purpose was only to sell more oil. The point is that they did it and they do it. Culture has never depended on the selflessness of the rich; it has depended only—and always will—on their financial support.

THE SOCIAL-RESPONSIBILITY AUDIT

It is often said that the problem with ethics is that its values are so intangible, while it is not the least virtue of cost/benefit analysis that its terms are measurable—literally—to the penny. But lack of precise measurement does not render a value mysterious, and the fact that one cannot put a dollar amount on virtue and vice does not make them any less real or less accountable. One can carry out a social-responsibility audit just as one can audit any other aspect of a company's performance. One part of that audit—one of its key factors—will be profitability. A project that is guaranteed to lose money has one fatal strike against it, while a project that will at least break even and possibly earn a considerable income has a strong argument on its side from the very beginning. But profitability is not the only argument, and there are forms of liability not directly evident in profit-and-loss ledgers. Furthermore, there is a "price" to be paid by every business just for being permitted to operate in the first place. This is not the sort of cost that gets entered directly in the books as an operating expense. It rather allows the possibility of having books in the first place.

A 1974 study by the Committee on Economic Development distinguished three different categories of corporate social responsibilities, much as we have in the preceding chapters.

1. legally required activities
2. voluntary activities (nonprofit)
3. socially useful activities for profit

There is a tendency among ethicists to discount 1 and 3 (see, e.g., Norman Bowie, *Business Ethics*, p. 108). But one of the troubles with business ethics is that critics too easily dismiss all of those ethical activities that are also in a company's own interest, leaving only those that are not. Ninety percent of business ethics is simply good business. In carrying out a social-responsibility audit, this is no small consideration.

Like any audit, a social-responsibility audit has an asset side and a liability side. On the asset side are all of those activities that the company should have done and did do, as well as some possibilities that were tempting and potentially profitable that the company rejected for ethical reasons. On the liability side are those activities that the company should have done but didn't as well as those that it shouldn't have done but did. The fact that an activity was legally required or forbidden certainly adds to its weight on one side or the other, in financial costs as well as responsibility credits. So too the fact that an activity in the interest of the company (or an activity left undone that was not in the company's interest) is of no small importance financially, but it should not be ignored in terms of responsibility. There is nothing wrong with doing right when it is also in your own interest, although there may not be much to crow about.

One need not manufacture dollar amounts in order to get a clear picture of credits and debits. Some authors, for example David F. Linowes in *The Conference Board Record* (1972), have tried to fix a dollar-amount statement of costs and benefits for such activities as training minority and handicapped workers, setting up day-care centers for employees' children, installing safety devices, and so on. Expenditures, of course, can be counted by straightforward dollar amounts, as can fines, legal fees, and publicity costs. But it is not always easy to measure the benefits created by training minority or handicapped workers, for example. The contribution of the employee to the company might be measured but it is hard to measure the extra contribution generated through gratitude and goodwill, difficult to calculate the more general advantages gained by a company with a reputation for such efforts, impossible to weigh numerically the simple humane virtues of allowing an otherwise wasted life to become productive and happy.

Figures don't always tell the truth in such matters, and the fact that there are no hard-and-fast dollar amounts does not mean that one can't make a hardheaded, rational decision about the costs and benefits of social responsibility. A purely voluntary activity that will promote an important social good but certainly cause bankruptcy is not obligatory or desirable. An activity that will aid an important social cause without cost to a company is obligatory and desirable, even if it is not legally required. (An individual is not legally required to help a person in trouble, but when he or she can do so and does not, we consider that the height of everyday irresponsibility.) The fact that most socially responsible activities are minimal in additional cost and often have benefits that may not have been anticipated. The point of a social-responsibility audit is not—as it is sometimes suggested—to keep a corporation "in line." It is rather to reinforce what many people already know—that there is much good that business can do *without* sacrificing from the bottom line, and very likely even improving it.

There is, however, one feature of the social-responsibility audit that cannot be put into quantitative figures at all. That feature is *morality*, including *justice* and respect for people's *rights*. Injustices and violations of rights may receive a dollar value, of course—when they are brought to court. Immoral behavior may be punished by law or exile from the business community. Such costs are, from a human perspective if not from the financial point of view, equivalent to bankruptcy. But small matters of morality (propriety or good taste) must realistically be matched even if they cannot be measured against concerns of profit. If it is an established fact that sexual innuendo sells both soap and cars, it would be a bit priggish to insist that morality forbids the use of such a connection in advertising. So, too, small violations of justice and rights may be negotiable; an employee who is never given a raise he deserves because he never asks for it may be a victim of an injustice, but it is not an unambiguous matter of immorality on the part of an employer who reasonably resists giving raises until necessary. But this is emphatically *not* to say that matters of morality are less important than questions of profit. It is rather to insist, once again,

AN UNRESOLVED CRISIS: CAN BUSINESS HELP?

The following is excerpted from a speech by U.S. Senator Bill Bradley (D-N.J.), delivered on the Senate floor more than one month before the 1992 Los Angeles riots:

Slavery was our original sin, just as race remains our unresolved dilemma. The future of American cities is inextricably bound to the issue of race and ethnicity. By the year 2000, only 57 percent of the people entering the work force in America will be native-born whites. That means that the economic future of the children of white Americans will increasingly depend on the talents of nonwhite Americans. If we allow them to fail because of our penny-pinching or timidity about straight talk, America will become a second-rate power. If they succeed, America and all Americans will be enriched.

To say to kids who have no connection to religion, no family outside a gang, no sense of place outside the territory, no imagination beyond the cadence of rap or the violence of TV, that government is on their side rings hollow. Their contact with government has not empowered them but diminished them. To them, government at best is incompetent—look at the schools, the streets, the welfare department—and at worse corrupt—witness the cops and building inspectors on the take, the white-collar criminal who gets nothing but a suspended sentence, the local politician with gross personal behavior. And replacing a corrupt white mayor with a corrupt black mayor won't make the difference.

In such a world, calls to "just say no" to drugs or to study hard for sixteen years so you can get an $18,000-a-year job are laughable. Instead of desires rooted in the values of commitment and service to community as expressed through black churches and mosques, desires, like commodities, become rooted in the immediate gratification of the moment. Television bombards these kids with messages of conspicuous consumption, and they want it now. They become trapped in the quicksands of American materialism. The market sells images of sex, violence, and drugs, regardless of their corrosive effects on hard work and caring—values formerly handed down from an older generation. And with no awareness of how to change their world through political action and no reservoirs of real self-knowledge, they are buffeted by the winds of violence and narcissism.

that such matters must always be taken into account, even when they are small enough to be overridden.

An In-Process Social-Responsibility Audit

Given any planned activity:

- Who is affected? How?
- Who might be affected?
- What criticism might be expected? By whom? Is it justified? How can it be avoided?
- Who could be helped by the plan? Who could be helped by a slight change in the plan?
- How much would that cost?
- Is the planned activity one which you would be willing (even happy) to publicize and make known to the community? Are there social aspects of the plan that would be well worth your publicizing?
- If not, why not?
- Does the activity involve (or encourage) any immoral activity?
- If so, how could this be avoided?
- Are the net effects of the activity just and fair? Will anyone be cheated out of something rightfully his or hers (land or its value, royalties, credit, dignity, health)?
- Are there any laws likely to be violated in carrying out the plan?
- Are anyone's rights likely to be violated?
- Are there valuable social institutions that could be served by the action?
- Are other people's customs or ways of living likely to be violated?

Part Five

THE NEW WORLD OF BUSINESS:
A MACRO-ETHICAL VIEW

IS THE FREE MARKET FAIR?

*Marxism has failed, but the realities of exploitation
and marginalization remain in the world.*
                                                        Pope John Paul II

In 1989, in the wake of upheaval in Eastern Europe, Pope John Paul II
issued what is generally considered to be the most positive and praising
evaluation of the free-market economy in the history of the Catholic
Church. But in it, he warned that the fall of communism should not
distract the capitalist nations of the world to the injustices of their own
system. The Pope, who is Polish, warned that while "the free market
is the most efficient instrument for utilizing resources and effectively
responding to needs, there are many needs which find no place on the
market." He distinguished the "fundamental and positive role of
business, the market, private property and the resulting responsibility"
from the moral vacuum that can result from deregulation, exploitation,
ignoring consumer and community rights, and a purely "negative"
notion of human freedom. The encyclical (entitled "The Hundredth
Year") updated a similar major papal statement by Pope Leo XIII
addressing the poverty of the industrial working class, which he called
"the yoke of slavery," and attacking "the inhumanity of employers
and unbridled greed of competitors." That was in 1891. Pope John
Paul II did not, like his predecessor, attack the market system but
rather praised the role of profit and self-interest, "initiative and entrepreneurial ability in the mobilization of human resources, and the
courage of business people." He attacked socialism, which had not,
he said, eliminated "alienation"—the lack of real meaning in life—but
rather increased it, betraying economic inefficiencies and an inability

---

THE BOTTOM LINE

Buckminster Fuller once noted that not until 1907 could 9 percent of the world's population be said to live under conditions of adequacy; by 1970, it was perhaps 40 percent. Without modern wealth invented in the West, all would still be poor; life expectancy would be about thirty years; nine of every ten human beings would be consigned to a short and hard life of unremitting toil.

Carl Madden, "Forces which Influence Ethical Behavior," *The Ethics of Corporate Conduct*

---

to provide even the most basic necessities. Nevertheless, he too raised the issue of widespread poverty, of those whom the market did not reach and those to whom it was not "free" but closed, of destructive competitiveness and the "web of false and superficial gratifications called consumerism." With an eye to the future and his concern firmly focused on the issue of global fairness, he warned: "In our time, there exists another form of ownership which is becoming no less important than land: the possession of know-how, technology and skill. . . . The fact is that many people, perhaps the majority today, do not have the means which would enable them to take their place in an effective and humanly dignified way within a productive system in which work is truly central." Many cultures are marginalized by the new technology and their own lack of education and training. And yet, "unable to compete," they are "allured by dazzle of opulence which is beyond their reach" (*New York Times*, May 3, 1991).

What the Pope is pointing to is one of the undeniable facts of our times. Capitalism is no longer a socioeconomic system that can be confined to certain societies or contained in certain parts of the world. It is, by its very nature, global, and, as such, it has global responsibilities as well as social responsibilities within particular societies. What this means, however, is by no means clear. Overpopulation and chronic poverty are the curse of many nations in the world. Gross inequalities between rich and poor are evident even within the most "advanced" free-market societies, and on the world stage they are so enormous as to be mutually incomprehensible. This is the challenge for the free-market system in the coming new century. Can it transform the world as a whole and share the prosperity it has provided for a relatively small number of people and nations? Can it expand the notion of "social responsibility" to encompass not only the local community and the larger society but the whole of the world's peoples?

SPINOZA'S WORM

The seventeenth-century Dutch philosopher Baruch Spinoza once asked us to consider what it would be like to be a tiny, wormlike organism, living on a corpuscle in the bloodstream of some great creature. Our world, in a sense, would be the day-to-day world of the corpuscle. We would be aware of the movement of the corpuscle, perhaps at times the power of the rush of blood in which we were transported. But it would only be with a special effort that we could get any idea of our real place in the organic scheme of things; that is, of the nature of the beast in whom we played a minor (but let's assume beneficial) role. What does the beast do? Is it good or bad? Is there a world in which the creature plays a part, in which it is as small as us worms? As we work along in our wormlike duties on the corpuscle, what are we really accomplishing? What kind of creature are we part of?

For Spinoza, the great creature was God. For our purposes, we can reduce our cosmos to the secular world, the business world in particular. Each of us plays a role—or a number of roles—in which our function is to serve an enterprise much larger than ourselves. We can see, almost regularly, the progress, setbacks, and immediate impact of the firm or department we work in (the corpuscle). With some effort, or in times of urgency, we can get a sense of the larger currents of the business world, sweeping us along quickly to a future not yet clear. But it is only with great difficulty that we can see beyond our small sector of the business world to appreciate the great creature—dubbed "capitalism" in the last century—in whom we play a small but, let's hope, beneficial role.

One could, to be sure, fulfill most of the functions of the corpuscle and live well (as a worm) without ever knowing or even asking what the great creature itself might be doing. But the meaning of life—the meaning of business life—involves the big as well as the little picture. Spinoza insisted that the worm that achieved the total vision found bliss most divine. More modest and more secular, let us just suggest that it is in the larger picture, and not just in the small victories and failures of business life, that the meaning of success and ethics in business is to be found.

ECONOMICS AND ETHICS: AN UNTENABLE DUALISM

> *The modern age is unique in that economics is allowed to override every other value.*
> William Gomberg *(emeritus professor of management, The Wharton School)*

The name of the beast is economics—*macroeconomics*, to be precise. Economics has been called the "dismal science," not because it has put so many students to sleep but because one of its key inventors, Thomas Malthus, spoke far more of tragedy and disaster than he did of good fortune and happiness. But it is economics, whether we like it or not, that defines the life of the Western world today. People may praise religion, but they work and pray for money. They argue politics, but they "vote their pocketbook." And in a society whose primary value is money, economics, inevitably, turns out to be ethics.

Ethics is always more than economics, but it would be a mistake for us to let stand the impression that economics is a science—dismal or otherwise—that is wholly detached from ethics. The language of the market and the balance sheet may sometimes sound more like physics than like a discourse on justice and happiness, but, nevertheless, there is more ethics to economics than we are usually led to believe. Economics without ethics is blind; ethics devoid of economics is empty.

The problem of appearances begins with the fact that economists insist on thinking of their subject as a pure "science." Not that there is anything wrong with that honorific label; it means only "systematic knowledge." But economics (from the Greek *oeconomicus*, "household trading") is and always has been part of the humanities—the sympathetic understanding of people and what they want. At least at the "micro" level, economics presumes participation as well as observation. You know what people want and how they will behave because you (think that you) know how you would behave in similar circumstances. It's not like organic chemistry. You don't have to enjoy the company of ketones or sympathize with an aldehyde.

Economic theories, like all theories by people about people, are self-distorting. Suppose a social scientist tells you how he thinks that you should behave; whatever you do is in part a response to what he has told you, even if you decide to ignore him or rebel against him. People, unlike molecules, have the annoying habit of changing their behavior when they hear a theory. Linus Pauling didn't worry that the chemical-bond market would change as soon as he published his theory. Henry Kaufman or Joe Granville used to utter an oracle on "Wall Street Week" and it would change the situation that very day. Economics changes what it explains; indeed, it may occasionally be the determining factor in those changes.

Economics is a human activity, and its theories are part of our economy-minded culture. It is not an academic exercise, although anything can be made into an academic exercise, and the post-Keynesian field of macroeconomics lends itself to academicization better than virtually any discipline (except perhaps literary criticism). It invites formalization, mathematical models, and grand equations. It is not threatened by the problem-solving threat of experimentation, for there has never been an economist powerful enough to "experiment" on that scale of international magnitude. It therefore demands tinkering and retrodiction—largely by way of esoteric and again unprovable explanations about why a hypothesis provable with certainty on the computer turned out to be a bust in the real world. In a religious society, there will be theologians. We have economists.

What Adam Smith presumed between the lines, what "science"-

> Why do economists disagree? A truncated answer: They begin with
> political positions and develop their economic theories to conform to
> those positions.
>
> *Business Week*

minded economists have rejected, is the essential role of ethics in the
"dismal science." Economic language consists of advice concerning
what *ought* to be done as well as predictions about what will happen.
Disagreements between economists are just as often about who *should*
be hurt or helped as they are about what the market in fact will do.
The key to our economic thinking is fair exchange. Supply and demand
are not just quantitative categories; they are measures of *value*. Monetary theory is not just numbers; it is a measure of trust and what
people think their time, effort, goods, and money are *worth*. We teach
our students about the *free* market as if it were a piece of machinery
rather than an ethical commitment and a daring experiment. We
analyze international exchange rates and leave out dissatisfaction with
the local dictator. Then we get annoyed when "politics" (a popular
revolution or a consumer revolt, for example) interferes with our
fraudulently neat mathematical curves.

Science tells us how the world is. Economics, on the other hand,
tells us how the world ought to be, in the opinion of one or another
economist. The free market isn't a datum for economics (as the
existence of a planet is a datum for astronomers); it is an ethical
viewpoint, a vision of how the world ought to be and how people ought
to behave. Lester Thurow has pointed out that it is only in economics
that a theorist will suggest the elimination of one or another "market
imperfection" when there is a disagreement between the model and
reality. "If wages do not fall with higher unemployment, it is due to
the market imperfection of monopolistic unions. In contrast, no astro-
physicist recommends the elimination of a planet he has observed
because it doesn't fit his grand scheme of the universe." In economics
we change or bend reality to fit our conception of how the world ought
to be.

Economics without ethics is a discipline without substance. It is
possible to formulate and tentatively answer abstract questions about
taxes, employment numbers, M-1, and GNP, but without some basic
understanding of the people behind the numbers, no predictions are

plausible and no theories have much meaning. Economics itself is part of the market—and economists "sell" their ideas in much the same way that the practitioners of "micro" they talk about sell their wares, according to their ability to advertise and get promotions from people in power, according to the readiness of the public and those in power to accept one viewpoint rather than another. In reaction to this unpalatable commercialism (economists like to praise the market, but most of them don't like the idea of being in it), there has arisen the mistaken idea—which is too easily confused with the ideal of "science"—that an isolated, abstract, and conscientiously amoral discipline has something to say about human reality. But that isn't economics. Never was.

WHY BUSINESS?

In many discussions of business ethics the most obvious virtue of business is ignored: its success. That does not mean the success of this or that industry, nor even the undisputed power that business and the market have in the daily lives of (almost) every American. Business is successful because it has earned the fidelity of the society as a whole. The poor may complain of inequities, but they do not complain about the ready availability of comforts and luxuries that would have been unthinkable in a nonbusiness society. Economy travelers pass through the first-class cabin with some resentment, but, in the words of one much-traveled journalist, "It's nice to know that it's there." Even Marxist critics are ideal consumers in our society, complain as they will about "commodity fetishism" and the evils of capitalism. The free-enterprise system may not be a suitable object for worship— as some would suggest—but it is business that has made possible American life as we enjoy it today. If business is successful in America, it is because business gives America what it wants.

CAPITALISM AS PHILOSOPHY

They went for a walk that afternoon, following the gravel road down into the valley, then branching into the forest along a broad, pitted track lined with felled timber. All the time, Fiedler probed, giving nothing. About the building in Cambridge Circus, and the people who worked there. What social class did they come from, what parts of London did they inhabit, did husbands and wives work in the same Departments? He asked about the pay, the leave, the morale, the canteen; he asked about their love-life, their gossip, their philosophy. Most of all he asked about their philosophy.

To Leamas that was the most difficult question of all.

"What do you mean, a philosophy?" he replied. "We're not Marxists, we're nothing. Just people."

"Are you Christians then?"

"Not many, I shouldn't think. I don't know many."

"What makes them do it, then?" Fiedler persisted: "They must have a philosophy."

"Why must they? Perhaps they don't know; don't even care. Not everyone has a philosophy," Leamas answered, a little helplessly.

John le Carré, *The Spy Who Came in from the Cold*

What does America want? It has been argued, persuasively, that many of America's wants are created, not only satisfied, by American business. And, indeed, it is true; what child would have the imagination to want blue, transparent toothpaste if television advertising had not squeezed it out so appealingly? How many Americans would really care about or notice the difference between a Bud and any other beer if the status of the brand had not been so touted over the generic brew as such? Would a Cadillac represent luxury if it were not said to do so? Would we worry about armpit odor if we were not told to sniff and panic? Business advertising makes us want products, which business happily sells to us.

So?

The argument is sound and persuasive, but—its deleterious effects on an adequate understanding of Adam Smith aside—it begins in the middle of the case and misses the point. What makes us susceptible to advertising in the first place? Why should we care about product status? Material comforts, luxuries, and status were not invented on Madison Avenue. It is doubtful that a jingle could convert us to asceticism, and it is just as doubtful that the equation between what one buys and who one is could have been formulated in the Marketing Department of the Wharton School.

Advertising substitutes the factors of an equation that is already deeply ingrained in our way of thinking. Business may manipulate but it does not and cannot create supply and demand. Business is successful not because it has put one over on us but because it does indeed satisfy desires that are very real and very human, the frivolity of some products aside. (Who ever said that frivolity isn't an essential part of being human?)

Why business? That is the ultimate question of macroeconomics. One can complain about the vulgarity of a business society, its lack of "depth" and its single-minded concern with money. But one hasn't worked at the criticism until one also asks "Why, then, does it succeed so?"—and it is a cynical answer indeed that says that Americans are basically vulgar or single-minded. The fact that most Americans are in business and welcome what business can give them has to be balanced by the fact that most Americans also have a healthy amount of skepticism about money and business and are willing—in economics as in politics—to accept the "lesser of the evils" or the flawed candidate who seems the best of the lot. And in economics, the best candidate has proved to be business, what we simplistically call the free-enterprise system. Whatever might be said against it—and there is much to say against it—it tends to maximize individual freedom and multiply the material benefits and the pleasant varieties that make our lives so enviable. Perhaps it can be said, and rightly, that this isn't enough. But only a person who is already enjoying those benefits and that variety can usually say that.

Why business? Because business works for us. It doesn't follow that it will work for everyone. It doesn't follow that it works equally for all of us. It doesn't mean that there are no flaws or that the freedom of the business world can prevent the prosperity of a number of repulsive characters and shady businesses. And it doesn't mean that whatever is part of or allowed in the business world is equally legitimate as business. There is the *point* of capitalism—to serve the prosperity of the nation—and then there are its *possibilities* (to make a fast buck, to acquire an ailing company just as a show of muscle). But not all possibilities are faithful to the point, and not everything permitted by business is part of its essence.

We say, "Business works." But there is no way of doing a cost/benefit analysis of capitalism itself, since capitalism as a conceptual

TWO CRITICAL QUESTIONS

To talk of the business corporation as facing a "crisis of legitimacy" does not imply that there exists any significant controversy as to whether it should exist; there is none. Rather it is to suggest that corporate leaders are being confronted with two basic questions:

- By what right do you who manage these huge corporations exercise your power?
- And what means do we have to insure that corporate power will be exercised in accord with some generally accepted notion of the public interest?

John Clark, *The Ethical Basis of Economic Freedom*

system *defines* the measures of costs and benefits and one would be hard put to find an objective measure that would serve as well. One can argue that capitalism is more efficient than other economic systems, but, of course, efficiency is not considered a virtue in most other economic systems. One can argue that capitalism is more productive than other economic systems, but, again, productivity is the point of capitalism; it does not follow that it is the point of every economic system. Indeed one can point out that economics itself is not a critical element in all social systems, and reading symbolic status rituals as economic functions has been the error of many a Western anthropologist. (See Annette Weiner's *Women of Value, Men of Renown*.) It has also been the error of a great many economists trying to explain putatively economic behavior in this country. It can be argued—convincingly—that capitalism provides the fairest distribution of goods in a society, but it should also be clear that the standards of justice and fairness invoked will inevitably be those peculiar to capitalism. Finally, it can be argued that the economic *laissez-faire* of capitalism is basic to a free society. But the concept of economic freedom is also a value intrinsic to the capitalist view of the world, and it has yet to be demonstrated—though it has often been assumed—that economic freedom is the sine qua non of all freedom.

Why business? Because, ultimately, we *are* business. We see the world in a businesslike way, and, given that we want something out of life, the American business world has proved to be the best framework in which to find it.

THE JUDGMENTS OF HISTORY: THE ASCENT OF FREE ENTERPRISE

> *He who has enough to satisfy his wants and nevertheless ceaselessly labors to acquire riches, either in order to obtain a higher social position, or that subsequently he may have enough to live without labor, or that his sons may become men of wealth and importance—all such are incited by a damnable avarice, sensuality, or pride.*
>
> *Fourteenth-Century Schoolman*

It is too often supposed that business is one of those essential human activities—like eating, drinking, sleeping, having sex, and watching television. The truth is that the business world as we know it is less than two centuries old, or, if we are being more precise, two decades. Throughout most of history such basic business enterprises as lending money with interest and making a profit have been condemned as "usury" and "avarice" respectively, and, until very recently, the businessman has almost always been considered something of an outcast in civilized society. The past is not everything, of course, and a dubious history need not be an obstacle to self-respect today. But one learns a lot about the place of business in the world by looking at the great difficulty with which business and businessmen gained respectability. (Businesswomen were all but unthinkable, the "world's oldest profession" aside.)

Working and trading, of course, are as old as human existence, and with work and trade the ethics of justice have always been in evidence. We have evidence of extensive and surprisingly sophisticated marketing mechanisms in ancient Sumeria and Phoenecia. Many of the marvelous hieroglyphics or "picture writing" of the ancient Egyptians are in fact account ledgers and inventories. The Middle East was one enormous market years before Christ chased the money lenders from the temple and two millennia before Adam Smith formulated the gospel of supply and demand. The old Arab merchants knew all about that, though the "invisible hand" would have meant something quite different to them.

But as long as there has been business, there has been prejudice against business. Aristotle launched one famous attack more than three centuries before Christ, at the same time earning himself a place in history as the first theoretical economist. Aristotle tried to develop a theory of fair exchange, according to which a doctor and a farmer, for example, might fairly exchange their goods and services. Money is the medium, he says, but only as a matter of convenience. The idea that one might use money itself to make money horrified him, and he attacked merchants in general as "parasites" devoid of virtue and social sense and able to produce nothing of value. It is worth noting that Aristotle had no notion whatever of what we call the "market." "Fair price" depends entirely on the value of the things or services traded and not at all on the process of trading itself, the supply of the product, or the demand.

Merchants, in Aristotle's view, were worse than peasants, who at least produced food. Wealth belonged to the military and the statesmen. Wealth followed power, in other words, and it was all but unthinkable that a man could become powerful by virtue of his wealth. Indeed, most merchants were literally outcasts—Jews, Orientals, and other "barbarians." They did business not because it was an honorable calling but because there was nothing else that they were allowed to do. The notion of the businessman as a "pillar of the community" was as plausible as the idea of a peasant-king in that aristocratic society.

After Aristotle, the role of the businessman did not become much more enviable. Jesus displayed the antagonism between money and spirit far more convincingly than some of the current-day Christians who try to equate them, and virtually every Christian spokesman from St. Paul and Augustine to St. Thomas Aquinas and Martin Luther had the same thing to say about avarice (the "profit motive"): It was a damnable sin. The historian R. H. Tawney summarizes the whole of the Middle Ages in the twin assumptions that (1) economic interests are always subordinate and antagonistic to the real business in life, which is the salvation of one's soul, and (2) economic behavior is absolutely bound by the rules of everyday morality, which forbid almost any business transaction other than a plain, simple, equal trade of goods and services. "Usury" meant not just *high* interest rates but *any* interest rates at all, and was punishable by excommunication. St. Thomas Aquinas applauded the idea of a society that had no need of businessmen whatever, and the very idea of selling something or some service for more than it was worth was considered to be sordid if not disreputable.

The guilds, which are often viewed as the precursors of our trade unions, had as their main function the prevention of competition of any kind as well as making sure that none of the guild members made more than he ought to. As late as the seventeenth century, laws dictated the conduct of business to the number of threads allowed in a piece of cloth. (Talk about regulation!) A successful business was not one that prospered or grew; in fact, a *growing* business would have been viewed as a monster that would have to be destroyed. Business was, at best, a necessary evil—and most thinkers weren't so sure about the "necessary." Looking back at business as late as 1650, it is almost unthinkable that business would ever become a respectable and powerful practice. If *laissez-faire* meant anything at all, it would have meant "leave the bastards alone." Freedom *from* enterprise seemed to be the rule of civilized society, from the temple in Jerusalem to the better streets of Paris, which certainly would not demean themselves with the presence of a bank or a shop.

The change in the fortunes of business, ironically, followed some dramatic changes in religion. The world had to change, too. The change in religion came with the Reformation, not with Martin Luther (who retained the age-old prejudices against business) but with John Calvin in Switzerland in the next century. Calvin was an advocate of hard work and its material rewards. His theology consisted of the harsh thesis called "predestination," which meant that a person's salvation or damnation was a matter already settled. Life was no longer, therefore, the pursuit of salvation, and it could well be the pursuit of wealth that, not coincidentally, might be taken as some indication of one's fortunes in the hereafter. Calvin taught the novel virtue of *thrift*. Investment, for the first time, became a matter of ethics. The medieval assumptions were turned upside down. Business became not only respectable but downright ethical, and began to determine the more general rules of ethics besides.

It is with Calvin that we begin to understand the profound change from the ancient view that man is a "social animal" to the modern view that he is an *economic* creature. Maximizing one's own individual interests, quite apart from working for the interests of the whole community, now becomes respectable. Money became a tool for personal advancement, not just a convenient medium of exchange. But still, the idea of the free market, bound neither by tradition nor by law but determined by individual and corporate self-interest, remained an outrageous idea that no sane social thinker would ever have suggested.

> If you want to know what is new in the modern world, it is the modern corporation.
>
> James Coleman, *Power and the Structure of Society*

The Very Idea of a "Free-Market System"

In *The Making of Economic Society*, Robert Heilbroner asks us to imagine ourselves as consultants to a "developing" country:

We could imagine the leaders of such a nation saying: "We have always experienced a highly tradition-bound way of life. Our men hunt and cultivate the fields and perform their tasks as they are brought up to do by the force of example and the instruction of their elders. We know, too, something of what can be done by economic command. We are prepared, if necessary, to sign an edict making it compulsory for many of our men to work on community projects for our national development. Tell us, is there any other way we can organize our society so that it will function successfully—or better yet, more successfully?"

Suppose we answered, "Yes, there is another way. Organize your society along the lines of a market economy."

"Very well," say the leaders. "What do we then tell people to do? How do we assign them to their various tasks?"

"That's the very point," we would answer. "In a market economy, no one is assigned to any task. In fact, the main idea of a market society is that each person is allowed to decide for himself what to do."

There is consternation among the leaders. "You mean there is no assignment of some men to mining and others to cattle raising? No manner of designating some for transportation and others for weaving? You leave this to people to decide for themselves? But what happens if they do not decide correctly? What happens if no one volunteers to go into the mines, or if no one offers himself as a railway engineer?"

"You may rest assured," we tell the leaders, "none of that will happen. In a market society, all the jobs will be filled because it will be to people's advantage to fill them."

Our respondents accept this with uncertain expressions. "Now look," one of them finally says, "let us suppose that we take your advice and allow our people to do as they please. Let's talk about something specific, like cloth production. Just how do we fix the right level of cloth output in this 'market society' of yours?"

"But you don't," we reply.

"We don't! Then how do we know there will be enough cloth produced?"

"There will be," we tell them. "The market will see to that."

"Then how do we know there won't be *too much* cloth produced?" he asks triumphantly.

"Ah, but the market will see to that too!"

"But what is this market that will do these wonderful things? Who runs it?"

"Oh, nobody runs the market," we answer. "It runs itself. In fact there really isn't any such *thing* as 'the market.' It's just a word we use to describe the way people behave."

"But I thought people behaved the way they wanted to!"

"And so they do," we say. "But never fear. They will want to behave the way you want them to behave."

"I am afraid," says the chief of the delegation, "that we are wasting our time. We thought you had in mind a serious proposal. What you suggest is inconceivable. Good day, sir."[1]

CLASSICAL CAPITALISM: ADAM SMITH

> *He intends only his own gain, and he is, in this, as in many other cases, led by an invisible hand to promote an end which was no part of his intention. . . . By pursuing his own interest he frequently promotes that of society more effectively than when he really intends to promote it.*
>
> *Adam Smith,* The Wealth of Nations

Adam Smith's *Wealth of Nations* appeared in 1776, a year of considerable significance for the United States and the future of the business world. It is a book that is often misunderstood as an essay in econom-

---

[1]Robert L. Heilbroner, *The Making of Economic Society*, 4th ed., © 1972, pp. 26–27. Reprinted by permission of Prentice-Hall, Inc., Englewood Cliffs, N.J.

ics. But it is also one of the most powerful theories of ethics of modern times.

Before he wrote *The Wealth of Nations*, Smith had already become famous in Great Britain for his earlier book, *The Theory of Moral Sentiments*, an unabashedly ethical treatise in which he defends the importance of "sympathy" and fellow-feeling, those quiet passions that hold society together and make the social world a decent place in which to live. That people are not essentially selfish is the theme of his theory. It is a thesis we had better keep in mind whenever we talk about his *Wealth of Nations* and the alleged "virtue of selfishness."

Much of *The Wealth of Nations* is devoted to an attack on existing economic theories and policies and, as such, is of little interest to the modern business reader. Yet one of Smith's most profound and revolutionary theses appears in the very title of his great book—that of the "wealth of the nation." According to the outdated policy he spends the most time attacking—"mercantilism"—the wealth of a nation is its state treasury, often measured by the king's ability to raise an army and attack his neighbors, take their colonies, and further increase the treasury. It is the first principle of Smith's ethics that the wealth of the nation is not to be so measured but is rather to be counted as the material comforts of its citizens, not only businessmen but everyone. Thus the concern with distributive justice enters into classical economics not as an afterthought but as its basic premise.

The Wealth of Nations is not a work of science so much as a celebration of material well-being. Much of *Wealth* is devoted to the explanation of the "mechanism of the market," although it is essential to keep in mind that for Smith and his contemporaries, it is a mechanism based on a sense of fair play, individual responsibility, and the very human character of economic life.

> The natural effort of every individual to better his own condition, when suffered to exert himself with freedom and security, is so powerful a principle that it is alone . . . capable of carrying on the society to wealth and prosperity.

The familiar explanation breaks down into two general components, a micro component and a macro component. The micro component is the law of supply and demand, which applies not only to products but, more important, to services and in particular to labor. The macro component is the assurance that the net effect of this law, exemplified thousands of times every day, will be the overall prosperity of every-

> If we examine, I say, all those things . . . we shall be sensible that without the assistance and cooperation of many thousands, the very meanest person in a civilized country could not be provided, even according to what we very falsely imagine, the easy and simply manner in which he is commonly accommodated. Compared indeed with the more extravagant luxury of the great, his accommodation must no doubt appear extremely simple and easy; and yet it may be true, perhaps, that the accommodation of a European prince does not always so much exceed that of an industrious and frugal peasant, as the accommodation of the latter exceeds that of many an African king, the absolute master of the lives and liberties of ten thousand naked savages.
>
> Adam Smith, *The Wealth of Nations*

one, the "invisible hand" that coordinates a multitude of small, selfish actions into the wealth of the nation.

The "law" of supply and demand has become an all but unchallenged tenet of current economic thinking; it affirms that prices rise to bring purchases into line with the available supply and fall to absorb available production and labor. When there is an excess supply, prices and wages will fall until everything is sold and everyone is employed. It is a simple and persuasive theory. It is also, when we turn to the macro aspects of the theory, an article of faith. We can see this in our current economic dilemma, in which the faith is defended by any means whatever, including a redefinition of the terms and a rejection of plain facts. For example, "full employment" gets redefined as "fewer than 6 million people unemployed" plus an uncounted several million teenagers. Idle factories in the face of unfulfilled demand are explained away as "aberrations in the market." Of course, Adam Smith didn't have to defend the faith; he was just trying to define it.

The law of supply and demand is undeniable in a system of rational consumers and competitive producers. Unfortunately, the idea that people are rational in the sense required is not even an article of faith; it is a flat falsehood of great importance to modern business: a status product purchased in a high-class showroom at twice the price; a smaller profit in return for an enviable reputation. This is emphatically not to say that consumers are irrational; it is only to say that buying products at bargain prices and selling them for a "killing" isn't the whole of life. The law of supply and demand explains most people's

---

Q: WHAT IS CAPITALISM?

Volumes have been written on what capitalism "is"—a market system, a system of economics and political freedom, a system of wage labor and exploitation. But all these different interpretations have one central area of agreement: It is that the life of capitalism is its incessant and insatiable drive to accumulate wealth. Ask Adam Smith and Karl Marx to name the first necessity of the system they both analyzed, and they would answer from their widely different perspectives that it was *accumulation*—using the capital created by the system to build more capital. Ask any businessman, and his answer will be the same: The first necessity is expansion, growth. Capitalism is a system that cannot stand still.

Robert Heilbroner, *New York Times Magazine*, August 15, 1982

---

behavior about as much as the ideal gas theory explains a suspicious smell in an elevator.

Adam Smith's capitalism presupposes a large number of small producers in competition for an already-established market in which none of them have dominance. Accordingly, the competitive model envisioned by Smith, whether or not it was applicable at the end of the eighteenth century, is as dated as Clausewitz's rules of war (formulated in the 1830s). Corporations may be competitive, but they determine the market as much as they supply it. A corporation faced with low demand for its product will more likely lower production and fire workers than lower prices. Indeed corporations blow the classical theory right out of reality. As Lester Thurow argues in a 1983 book attacking price-auction economics *(Dangerous Currents)*, "Economics has a supply-and-demand theory of price determination for competitive markets and complete monopolies, but it has no theory of price determination for oligopolies—the most prevalent form of industrial organization." Smith dismissed corporations in a few paragraphs as aberrations in his "nation of shopkeepers," and he complained that "people of the same trade rarely meet together, but the conversation ends in a conspiracy against the public." Business has outgrown simple supply and demand.

It is worth noting that Smith did not take competition itself to be a moral virtue, much less as the proof of one's manhood—as we find in some his present-day interpreters. The market wasn't a "jungle"

(Darwin wasn't even born yet), and Smith would have been appalled by the metaphor. He saw the world of business as a civilized and respectable bustle of busy bourgeoisie and laborers, all pursuing their interests but not at all to each other's disadvantage. And however central self-interest may be, Smith says, it is never to be divorced from the ethical qualities of sympathy and compassion. Indeed, these sentiments, writ large, provided the ultimate justification of capitalism. Today, the ethical argument that affluence for the richest produces benefits for the poorest is criticized as the "trickle-down effect," but in 1776, it was a radical suggestion that the needs and desires of the poor were just as much a measure of the economy as the size of the treasury. Today, too, it is the nature and the mission of the business world to increase the general prosperity, even to provide, in Smith's words, "universal opulence even to the lowest ranks of people." We may be increasingly confused about our own economic system, but its ultimate purpose and measure of success are not in question.

THE MARX BROTHERS: QUESTIONS THAT WON'T GO AWAY

> *The less you eat, drink, buy books, go to the theater, go dancing, go drinking, think, love, theorize, sing, paint, play sports, etc., the more you save and the greater will become your capital. . . . The less you are, the more you have. . . . So all passions and all activity are submerged in greed.*
>
> *Karl Marx*

> *Man exploits man and, sometimes, the other way around.*
>
> *Woody Allen*

Karl Marx did not leap into the world with full beard and dogma, the self-appointed champion of the proletariat armed with the iron laws of history. He was, in fact, a humanist who came out of the same liberal tradition as Adam Smith, in which individual freedom and the well-being of everyone were the two basic tenets of any acceptable ethical system. But where Smith envisioned a rosy future of progress through business competition, Marx and his lifelong friend Friedrich Engels perceived ever-increasing differences and antagonisms between rich and poor. They saw monopoly, not competition, as the natural outcome of free enterprise. They saw resentment and revolution as the outcome, not general satisfaction and prosperity. Many of Marx's ideas are now outdated, but then so is the model of capitalism that he was attacking. Many of Marx's most radical proposals are now routinely incorporated into both the Democratic and Republican platforms. And there is little question that he would have found recent regimes that call themselves "Marxist" as repulsive and unethical as we do.

Marx's strength and influence can be attributed to one talent that businessmen would be well advised to follow: Whereas capitalism has tried to defend and explain itself in ever more "scientific" and impersonal language, Marx at his best was thoroughly aware that effective criticism is *moral* criticism. Smith talked about "gain," Marx about "greed." Smith formulated the "mechanism of the market"; Marx talked about the "exploitation of our fellow man." So too today, the neo-Smithian Milton Friedman complains about the monetary policies of the Federal Reserve; third-world Marxists scream about justice, equality, and "foreign oppressors." Which kind of argument, we can ask rhetorically, is more likely to inspire enthusiasm, even drive men and women to the barricades?

Marx's own "scientific" account of the workings of capitalist markets are technical and debatable, but the ethical vision of the life of capitalism provides a challenge that to this day must be an essential concern for any ethics of business. If business ethics is about the good life, there is no avoiding Marx's challenge. It has two parts, a micro thesis and a macro thesis. The micro thesis is that the business emphasis on money and profits threatens to destroy all other values and reduce everything to a commodity to be bought and sold. The macro thesis is that capitalism does *not* succeed in making life better for everyone. Productivity and wealth may increase in general, but workers are exploited and dehumanized and the distribution of wealth becomes less equal, creating a class of the superrich and tens of millions of poor people.

Both Marx and Adam Smith accepted what is often called the "labor theory of value"—the idea that the value of a thing is the work it takes to produce it. But where Smith placed his emphasis on the commercial value of the product in the market, Marx emphasized the process of production itself. It is often argued that the problem with Marxism is that, unlike capitalism, it does not emphasize the work ethic. This is not true for Marx. He took work to be the meaning of life, essential to being human. The ultimate society might be classless, but it would assuredly not be workless. Marx attacked *degrading* work, *meaningless* work, *boring* work, work for which the worker was not adequately rewarded. He was not against incentives; indeed he insisted that good, productive, meaningful work is its own incentive. Working for a living is what work is all about, but selling one's soul for a salary is quite a different matter. "Alienated labor"—Marx's central concept—is just this sense of unsatisfying, insufficiently rewarded work. "Exploitation" ultimately refers to being forced to do such work in order to survive. And, it is not sufficiently noted, this applies just as much to harried middle managers as it does to line workers and semiskilled labor.

Marx's ultimate objection to capitalism is an aesthetic one: The market tends to devour all other values. (Indeed, this voracious metaphor permeates his writings.) Artistic values become market values. Sex becomes a commodity like any other commodity (indeed, prostitution becomes a general condition of life; selling or sacrificing one's personal values for what the market will pay for them). Adam Smith assumed that profits were a means to satisfy material needs; Marx sees that profits can become ends in themselves, instruments of economic power that ultimately can redefine or strangle every value, including the individual freedom that classical capitalism presupposes. What he envisions, accordingly, is not a society with a different economic system so much as a society with *no* economic system—at least in the sense that we use that term. Not surprisingly, his vision of this alternative is left famously obscure.

Marx is always presented as the enemy of capitalism, but this isn't quite right. In his most belligerent book, *The Communist Manifesto*, he and Engels insist on the point that it is capitalism that has made possible—for the first time in history—a humane and creative standard of living for everyone. If "capitalism digs its own grave," as Marxists are fond of saying, it would be because of its enormous success, not because of its failures. But where capitalism will inevitably fail, according to Marx and Engels, is in its tendency to create masses of unemployed, in part because of the inhuman supply-and-demand structure of the labor market but also because capitalist technology will reduce

THE CONQUEST AND CRISIS OF CAPITALISM

The bourgeoisie, during its rule of scarcely one hundred years, has created more massive and more colossal productive forces than have all preceding generations together. Subjection of Nature's forces to man, machinery, application of chemistry to industry and agriculture, steam-navigation, railways, electric telegraphs, clearing of whole continents for cultivation, canalization of rivers, whole populations conjured out of the ground—what earlier century had even a presentiment that such productive forces slumbered in the lap of social labor? . . .

[But now] there is too much civilization, too much means of subsistence, too much industry, too much commerce. . . . The conditions of bourgeois society are too narrow to comprise the wealth created by them. And how does the bourgeoisie get over these crises? On the one hand by enforced destruction of a mass of productive forces; on the other, by the conquest of new markets, and by more thorough exploitation of the old ones. That is to say, by paving the way for more extensive and more destructive crises, and by diminishing the means whereby crises are prevented.

Karl Marx and Friedrich Engels, *The Communist Manifesto*

the need for labor itself. The historical conflict between the haves and have-nots will explode in a revolution, the nature of which is never entirely clear. Or, in Marx's words, "The material forces of production in society come into conflict with the existing relations of production." These relations then "turn into fetters, and then comes the period of revolution." What is clear is that the market mechanism will be abandoned and an explicit rule of justice will take its place: "From each according to his ability, to each according to his needs." But this will not involve, Marx assures us, overwhelming authority in the government. Indeed, "The state will wither away," he says (a phrase he borrowed from the liberal German playwright and poet Friedrich Schiller).

The warnings in this macro-ethical portrait have been well heeded in the twentieth-century business world—one significant reason that the "inevitable" revolution has been indefinitely postponed, at least in the advanced capitalist countries where Marx insisted it must come. In his early writings, Marx supposed that the misery of the proletariat would increase absolutely—and this would be the cause of the revolution. Later, in *Capital*, he revised and weakened this view such that the

> We hired workers and human beings came instead.
>
> Max Frisch

misery of the working class would increase only relatively to the capitalists, even though the absolute standard of living might improve considerably. Even in the harsh days of the sweatshops, the business world knew full well that its success could not be built on a foundation of misery. And today, when most American workers continue to dream of owning their own homes and sending their kids to college, when skilled laborers make more than middle managers and the public is much more concerned with consumer rights than with exploitation, the security of capitalism—the national deficit aside—seems ensured. But if Marx was wrong about the inevitability of revolution, he was surely right about the ethical demands on capitalism. Business is not an eternal verity, thriving and surviving by Divine Right. It is a historical institution that has existed for two short centuries and continues to exist today because it recognizes that the prosperity of the society as a whole and in particular the well-being and satisfaction of its own workers are not only its social responsibilities but its own prerequisites. Either the business community recognizes values other than its own bottom line and supports interests other than its own or it will be, in the unsentimental eyes of history, a memory, like the feudal lords of the eleventh century.

AN ETHICAL VIEW OF CAPITALISM: COSTS AND BENEFITS

> *If the U.S. is the greatest place in the world to live,*
> *why are so many people unemployed, underedu-*
> *cated and unhappy?*
> Second-grader Brandy Stanton in
> Scholastic News, June 1984

Within the business world, certain values can be taken for granted—
for example, the desirability and justice of one person's making an
overnight fortune in the commodities market just on the basis of a
hunch. We can easily find societies, on the other hand, that would
consider such unearned sudden wealth both undesirable and unjust
(reflected in the government's ravenous attempt to take it all in taxa-
tion). Within the business world, we simply accept the importance of
hard work, high finances, competition, negotiation, strategy, hierarchies of power, status, and salaries, and large differences in pay and
perks between workers and executives. These are, in fact, our values.
They determine our sense of justice, our sense of what society should
look like, our sense of how we, as a society, should live.

But it is also important, if only for a passing moment of reflection,
to ask ourselves how these values might themselves be evaluated. How
do they stack up on some larger, even cosmic scale of considerations?
What ultimate system of values keeps us capitalists? (It is sheer
historical ignorance to think that capitalism and communism are the
only possible alternatives.) What are the ultimate values of the business world?

One can find any number of societies in the world and in history that
cultivate their values without central dependence on economic concerns. Of course, everyone has to eat, but we slip too quickly from the
fact that everyone has certain basic material needs to the idea that
everyone is "really" a materialist who wants nothing more than a
Cadillac and a condo. Most of the cultures in history have found
religious and other spiritual values of far more importance than material gains. Most societies in the world today still take national and
cultural concerns to be prior to economic development, the latter

serving the former, not vice versa. The numerical predominance of such cultures need not cow us into doubting our own values, but they do indicate the need to look at our own values with an appraising eye.

The ultimate values of capitalism might be summarized in three terms:

1. prosperity
2. freedom
3. justice

It is important to see what these values preclude as well as what they mean. There is no mention of spiritual values. Though a capitalist can surely be religious, even devout, such spirituality is not dictated by our economic values. There is no mention of artistic values. A capitalist may love and support the arts, but good taste is not dictated by capitalism. Indeed, it is a common objection to business in the arts that the market has no taste, or, worse, that it guarantees the success of bad taste. Finally, there is no mention of cultural and nationalistic values. A capitalist can be a patriot, but the values of capitalism overflow ethnic and national boundaries. Indeed, it has been argued that the main promise of peace in this century lies not in nuclear deterrence (which is highly debatable) but rather in international business, which puts mutual satisfaction of needs and negotiation ahead of mutual hostilities, isolation, and fears.

The three key value terms of capitalism are, to a certain extent, defined by capitalism. Our sense of "prosperity" is a distinctly material sense of prosperity. It means not only that, ideally, everyone gets enough to eat and a comfortable place to sleep but also enjoys certain luxuries such as cars, video recorders, air-conditioning, and reclining chairs. It is a very different kind of prosperity from the "art cultures" of the South Pacific, for example, where wealth is measured not in purchasing power but in symbolic totems.

So, too, our notion of freedom is particular to a business society. It is often argued that the foundation of all freedom is economic freedom—that there could be no freedom of speech or religion if it were not for, first of all, the freedom of the marketplace. This is not at all clear. It is true that freedom of the marketplace is one of *our* essential freedoms, but it is not at all obvious how this is *prior* to freedom of speech or religion. The great fear, of course, is that a government with the power to determine the production and exchange of goods also has the power—and will use it—to interfere with free exchange of ideas and expressions of faith as well. In terms of political reality, this is no doubt true. But the value of these other freedoms does not therefore depend on economic freedom. Rather, economic freedom depends on freedom of speech, freedom to gather together, and freedom of religion—not least the faith we have in the market and the belief that unregulated competition and the scramble for profits is a good thing with good results.

"Justice," too, has different meanings in different cultures, as we have seen. In the world of business, justice is largely a matter of entitlement, then a matter of merit, finally a tenuous matter of equality—but only equal opportunity, not equality of results. Indeed, capitalism would be unimaginable if everyone were guaranteed equal reward, independent of luck, skill, or effort. Some societies put equality first; others would eliminate questions of merit altogether, leaving matters of wealth and power "in the hands of God"—in other words a matter of inheritance and the occasional interference of luck or calamity.

What are we to say of capitalism, of the business world as a whole? Does it in fact maximize its own values? And should it have other values as well, even other values of overriding importance? This last question is almost impossible to answer categorically; most people will agree that there is at least some value that is as important as the three values of capitalism. But there will be little agreement what that is. Some people say religious values. Most will agree that moral values are at least as important as prosperity, freedom, and justice, but most people in business will also point out, quite rightly, that there is no evident contradiction among these; indeed they reinforce and define one another. Some people will put good taste and elegance above business values, whereas others will insist that culture and national heritage are of primary importance. None of these disagreements leads to an ethical crisis, however, until one group insists on imposing its values on the others—or until one insists that business values should be the *only* values, leaving religion, art, patriotism, and culture mere pawns in the marketplace, matters of "market value."

With regard to its own inherent values, however, one group can and must make an effort to evaluate capitalism in its own terms—in effect a cost/benefit analysis. We know what the benefits ought to be: prosperity, freedom, and justice. It is worth noting that, as so often in ethics, only the first of these can be measured in dollar amounts, though even there it can be argued that prosperity is not just a matter of wealth but also of health and happiness, and these can't be measured in dollars. Nevertheless, we think that there is considerable justification for the proposition that capitalism—the business way of doing things—has achieved more prosperity for more people in the past two hundred years than any other value system ever imagined. Of course, this is taking "prosperity" according to capitalism's own understanding, taking for granted that material comforts and luxuries are indeed desirable (whether or not they are the most desirable things in the world).

What are the costs of prosperity? That might sound like an odd question, but there are indeed costs, whether or not we usually think of them. First and foremost, there is the enormous amount of work and worry that goes into business. We may approve of hard work and take worry to be an essential part of life, but, nevertheless, they are very costly indeed—in terms of time, energy, even health and happiness. Even if the payoff for most people is worth it, business is, in terms of time and energy, an expensive way of doing things.

Second, a considerable cost of capitalism is *envy*. Envy is the emotion that covets—other people's luck, other people's wealth, other people's happiness. In a society with absolute equality (if such could be imagined) there would be no envy. In a society that really accepted the idea of "God's will" or "What will be will be" there would be no envy. But in a society that stresses competition, equal opportunity but unequal results, luck, and comparative wealth, envy is a considerable emotional and social cost. It emerges in economic terms by way of our extraordinary crime rate (which has harsh emotional costs, too). It emerges internationally in terms of resentment, protectionism, and America's unenviable position as the Great Satan in some of the poorer countries of the world.

Finally, we might mention again that one cannot stress one value without threatening others—and the more importance we give to endless prosperity, the less attention we can pay to values that don't "pay." What's more, there is that ancient but still wise observation that too much comfort and luxury blinds a person to not only the harsh realities of life but also much of its beauty. A whole society, like a pampered child, can be "spoiled"; spoiled, that is, in its ability to face and appreciate life as it is. Perhaps we would not, on that account, give up our prosperity, but it should certainly dampen our self-righteous sense of entitlement.

In terms of economic freedom, it is indisputable that capitalism maximizes freedom—if only because capitalism is *defined* in terms of such freedom to enter and operate in the marketplace as one can.

Restricting ourselves to economic freedom, it would be pointless to ask whether freedom is good, since it is one of those values by which we understand everything else. But we can ask whether economic freedom promotes other freedoms, and there the matter is debatable. And we can point out that, in addition to being a benefit itself, economic freedom helps promote prosperity and is an essential part of our conception of justice.

Does freedom have costs? Of course it does. First of all, there is the uncertainty and anxiety of freedom—the need to make hard decisions, the absence of any benign and wise power telling us what would be best for us and what we ought to do. There is the insecurity of freedom, the responsibilities that many people would gladly do without. Futhermore, economic freedom, though part of our concept of justice, also contradicts equality. The freedom of the marketplace not only allows for but makes inevitable enormous differences in wealth. It makes impossible any governing board that would reward merit, and it is the nature of the free market that hard work and good ideas are not always rewarded. Moreover, there is some question whether economic freedom is in fact that for everyone: For those who are at the subsistence level of the economic ladder, the freedom of the market may mean nothing more than the unavoidable necessity to do whatever they have to do—hardly "freedom" by any definition. The cost of freedom for some, in other words, is the lack of freedom for others.

Justice too is its own reward. It might be argued that a just society is also a prosperous society, but there are poor societies that are nevertheless just, and it is obvious that a very wealthy society (some ancient empires, for example) might be unjust. In fact, one of the costs of justice may be prosperity, as radical free-enterprise theorists have argued. An unbridled economy may be much more efficient, aggressive, and competitive than a regulated economy. But it is important to note that prosperity in itself does not guarantee justice. A nation may be prosperous and at the same time have widespread poverty. Indeed, even if everyone benefits from prosperity, it may still be the case that the difference between the richest and the poorest is more than justice can stand. Enforcing just distribution may well reduce and not just redistribute prosperity. In the same sense, justice may interfere with freedom, in that any attempt to insist on the fair redistribution of goods will inevitably interfere with the freedom of the wealthiest members of society.

The evaluation of capitalism and the modern business world depends on the emphasis we place on these three values—and others, too.

Those who insist on a world in which religious, artistic, and cultural values are primary and supersede all economic considerations will have mixed feelings (at best) about capitalism. Those who emphasize prosperity will tend to be the most uncompromising capitalists, but justice does not thereby cease to be a concern. What if the wealth of the nation could be increased better through a command economy (which is true in many developing nations)? Which would you choose, prosperity or freedom? Those who value freedom will have to accept that freedom also allows one party to take advantage of another, that freedom may not guarantee efficiency and may even minimize the freedom of those whose only free choice is to "work or starve." Those who value justice above all, however, face a difficult dilemma. On the one hand, our sense of justice includes a strong emphasis on freedom and the need to be as prosperous as possible. On the other hand, the core of our sense of justice—the fair distribution of goods to everyone—is not ensured, or even very plausible in our freewheeling business society. At the same time, we have outgrown our peculiarly American faith in the ability of government to ensure fairness. This, I think, is the honest perplexity that most people without ideological blinders feel when they try to think about capitalism and the business world as a whole. It isn't perfect, though we'd like it to be. And it's impossible even to imagine—except in utopian fantasy—anything systematically better. What we can and must do, however, is to correct injustices wherever we can, and not be afraid or embarrassed to do so in the name of "good business."

BEATING THE BOGEYMAN: REGULATION AND BUSINESS RECONSIDERED

"Laissez-faire!" was the cry. "Leave us alone!" Free-enterprise advocates understandably forget or ignore the fact that this familiar slogan was aimed against the national policies of mercantilism—*before*

41,000 PICKLES

There are 41,000 regulations concerning the production, distribution, and sale of hamburgers. For example,

- slices of pickle sold in hamburger sandwiches must be no less than ⅛″ and no more than ⅜″.
- ketchup must flow no more than 9 centimeters in 30 seconds (at 69°F).

Thomas D. Hopkins (Federal Office of Regulatory Affairs)

---

the prominence of free-market capitalism. Moreover, today we have a hard time imagining the brutal regulations *within* the guilds of the precapitalist era, specifying not only maximum and minimum prices but even the exact number of stitches per yard of cloth. Our own current horror stories—41,000 different specifications for a hamburger, for example—at least have a touch of the absurd about them. Nevertheless, such stories are legion and add up to a telling argument against government regulation of business. Regulation is unfair and inefficient, even when it is not downright ridiculous. Let the market take care of itself. That is, after all, what it is designed to do.

The bogeyman of regulation hovers over every discussion of business ethics like a specter, and for good reason. Business ethics is concerned with what is expected from business, what is *demanded* from business. And if business doesn't or won't deliver on its own, someone—namely the government—will step in. If manufacturing won't control its standards, government regulation will set those standards by law. If industry doesn't protect the environment from pollution, then the government will protect the environment from industry. If business won't set fair wages or continues to hire and promote employees on the basis of race or sex, then government bureaus will ensure what business itself will not. Regulation, in other words, is the imposition on business of ethical standards that it is not meeting on its own. But it would be a mistake to think of regulation as the imposition of foreign standards on business. The ethical standards enforced by regulation are, in most cases, just those values that business itself promotes and stands for—prosperity, freedom, and justice, a better life for everyone because of business.

The bogeyman of regulation is one-third myth, one-third misunderstanding and one-third unnecessary. It is a myth because business is not a world unto itself and, indeed, *needs* a power greater than itself to protect its very existence. This is true not only in those transitory and much-debated areas such as protection from low-cost foreign competition, government subsidies for research, and selective tax breaks for certain industries. It is true of the nature of the business game itself. Business could not exist, for example, without respect for and, when necessary, the enforcement of contracts. Government regulation, in this sense, is as basic as the civil law itself. It is not an imposition on business but the foundation that makes business possible.

The bogeyman of regulation is born of confusing stupid and unnecessary regulations—and there are thousands of them—with regulation as such. One part of this misunderstanding has to do with the glib accounting procedures employed where government regulation is concerned. Ronald Reagan's chief economic adviser, Murray Weidenbaum, once made the quick, staggering estimate that the total cost of total compliance with current regulation for American industry would be over $100 billion. But what this assumes is that compliance costs can be simply added onto otherwise completed budgets, that regulation does not in fact stimulate new technologies, new industries, new markets, new jobs, and cut back considerably on energy expenditures, employee illness, and insurance, not to mention the nonbusiness benefits of a cleaner environment, healthier people, and a better climate for doing business. (Ingersoll Rand, for example, found that energy savings in a Massachusetts plant more than equaled the cost of pollution controls forced upon it by regulation.) Regulation is not just a drag on American industry. It is itself an essential part of the market, and though it may force the closing of some plants, it opens up others that are more efficient and more productive, not to mention less embattled.

Regulation is also subject to misunderstanding because we think of it as an industrywide imposition affecting each individual company. But as we have seen, the collective dilemma of many industries is precisely the fact that companies cannot undertake desirable projects themselves, for they would thereby put themselves in a precarious position relative to their competition; nor can they jointly agree with the competition to undertake such projects, because of antitrust laws. So how does an industry ensure that every company will comply with a set of standards that everyone agrees to be necessary? By setting that standard as one of the rules of the game, as a boundary of competition, and enforcing that standard by law. Nor is it the case that all such regulation "corrects" market defects at uniform increased costs to the companies and consumers. The automobile industry in America is possible only because of the most massive single set of regulations in history—the Interstate Highway System. Government "interference" in business does not consist simply of laws saying what business can and must not do; it also sets the stage for the business game itself and makes some industries possible. It is government regulation that defines and protects private property (even if it also takes back a hefty percentage), but without this protection, there could be no business at all. There would be only theft, possession by the strongest, and an unbridled "war of all against all"—which is hardly what we mean by free enterprise.

Regulation makes business possible. But this provides no excuse whatsoever for inefficient or stupid or unnecessary regulation. It does not and should not give support to those who see regulation as a way of "punishing" business. It does not mean that regulation is good in itself. The point is that good regulations are good business, that it is in the interest of business to ensure the right regulations for itself and not to waste its time and credibility complaining about regulation as such.

This brief discussion of the bogeyman leaves out two essential features of regulation, which are so important that they will provide us with an appropriate ending for our study of business ethics. The first is the role of regulation in the pursuit of justice. The second is the importance of a very different kind of regulation, which we might call, somewhat misleadingly, "internal regulation."

Business prospers in our society because, in general, we all prosper. Capitalism is imperfect, but we do believe that it is the best of our alternatives. But it is not enough that it is, in fact, the best of our alternatives. It still requires correction from within, and by its very nature the market is not capable of directed intervention. The familiar argument is that the market will eventually correct injustices, but it surely is one of the premises of ethical sensitivity that "eventually,"

THE LIMITS OF LEGISLATION

More than 4,000 people will go to the emergency room this year because of accidents with pens. Ten thousand Americans were hurt last year by first-aid kits.

Roger McCarthy (president, Failure Analysis Associates)

> ## CAN POLLUTION BE CONTROLLED WITHOUT REGULATION?
>
> In the absence of special government policies, pollution will be excessive. This is because—as economists have known for many decades—pollution constitutes what is known in the jargon as an "externality." That is to say, the costs of pollution are not always borne fully—if at all—by the polluter. . . . Naturally, he has no incentive to economize in the use (of the environment) in the same way that he has for other factors of production that carry a cost, such a labor or capital. . . . This defect of the price mechanism needs to be corrected by governmental action in order to eliminate excessive pollution.
>
> Wilfred Beckerman, *Public Utilities Fortnightly*

though it might be good enough for a historical system, is intolerable to real people who may very well be dead by the time that eventuality takes place. Sometimes, the market must be corrected, and quickly, but without for a moment threatening capitalism or the free market. Indeed, it is one of the travesties of business ethics and free-market rhetoric that every act of government on the behalf of justice is challenged as "blatant socialism." Such nonsense hurts business far more than any socialist argument.

One of the functions of government and of government regulation is to ensure justice. To deny this seems to imply that capitalism is perfect, which is absurd. To insist on this, on the other hand, is not to deny capitalism. It is to protect it, by insisting that it is in fact compatible with and eager to promote justice.

Much if not most regulation is aimed at protecting business, which includes setting up the very conditions for the business world to exist. Regulation assuring justice is not primarily aimed at protecting business—it is aimed at justice—but nevertheless it serves that function, too. The most prevalent attack on business around the world is the accusation that it is blind to justice and concerned only with its own profits. The truth is that there is much in American business that belies that accusation, but the rhetoric of business often encourages it. The free-market system may not include any mechanism to ensure justice, but that does not mean that people in business—who are in fact that system—should not, *as business people,* be concerend with justice. Indeed, if there is one word that would elevate business ethics to a strategic art in business it is "justice." Not "rights," which too often tend to be limited to the rights of business; and certainly not "profits," or even "prosperity." And what business cannot do for itself it should readily welcome on its behalf.

The most important regulations of business are those that are neither imposed nor simply agreed upon but rather define the enterprise of business itself. Some of these are simply inherited from our business traditions. Others have evolved rather quickly in the rapidly changing world of technology—new concerns with information and communication that would have been unimportant, or unimaginable, only a few years ago. These regulations change, not surprisingly, with marketing conditions, the national economy, employment figures, politics, and foreign competition. But what is essential about them is they are *our* rules. They are not just rules that apply to us. They are not just our grudging recognition of the realities of life. They are *our* decisions about how we want to live, what we want to value, how we want to play the game.

What is most important about the rules and regulations that govern business is the fact they are *not,* as in the classic economic rhetoric, mere mechanisms. They are not involuntary, or imposed, or guided from the outside, even by an invisible hand. They are collectively voluntary, willfully accepted by the business community, and the business community can and will be properly praised—or blamed—for them. By the same token, the rules of a game are ultimately sanctioned not by the referee or the audience but by the players themselves, and in business the integrity of the market is the responsibility of the participants too. Unethical practices must be condemned, and condemned loudly and publicly. Unethical players must be expelled and not be allowed to slip back on the field just wearing a different uniform. The traditional faith in the market must be replaced with *confidence in ourselves,* including, especially, confidence in our own ethical and cultural character. If business has a reputation for being culturally without values or taste it is because the people who do business have made much more noise about their profits than about their willing compliance with the laws and mores of the land, their contributions to the well-being of all members of society, and their concern for the consequences of their corporate actions. Adam Smith misled us when he got us thinking about the market as a mechanism, and Milton Friedman threatens us all when he insists on the strict separation of our "fiduciary responsibilities" and all of the other qualities that make us human. In this day of "me-first management," the spray paint is on the corporate wall: Business in America is and must be the home and heart of our ethics. If we can't find ethics there, we might soon not be able to find ethics anywhere.

INTERNATIONAL ETHICS: WHEN IN ROME, OR TOKYO, OR . . .

> *Should I retain any feeling of guilt for having committed a crime in France which is nothing but a virtue in China? Should I make myself miserable about practicing actions in France which would have me burned in Siam?*
>
> *Marquis de Sade,* Justine

Most of what we have written pertains primarily to the ethics of a small number of industrialized societies, essentially business cultures. But with the globalization of business there are other questions that come into play, especially those having to do with a clash of cultures, including a clash of business practices.

Social responsibility is based on the fact that a business is part of a community. The employees of the business live in the community and enjoy its advantages (shops, restaurants, and theaters) and its basic services (roads, sewers, water, electricity). The employees of a business share a life with the other citizens of the community—share needs, values, and interests as well as material and spiritual resources. A business reaps the benefits of its acceptance by society, and its social responsibilities should be viewed as nothing other than giving a fair return for those advantages and fitting into the community that has been so hospitable.

A reasonable rule of thumb, accordingly, is that business should obey the laws and customs of the community. In almost all of the cases we have been considering, this rule is almost trivial, since we can assume that people in business will more or less share the values and beliefs of the community in which they live. A company relocating from Georgia to Connecticut may find a few employees having some difficulty with the transition, but most will find that obeying the local laws and customs in Connecticut will not be much different from obeying the local laws and customs in Georgia. But consider an American company setting up headquarters in South Africa or Saudi Arabia.

One of the most important facts about modern business, from the point of view of social responsibilities, is the rise of the multinational corporation. There have always been comparable problems of cross-cultural commerce, of course. The Greeks had to figure out how to deal with the "barbarians." The mercantile Europeans of precapitalism had to decide how to deal with their colonial subjects—though we can say that in general they did not do well from an ethical point of view. What has changed in the modern age is, first of all, our dramatically improved perspective on the legitimacy of differences among peoples and, from a business perspective, the fact that the multinational corporation is not, like the old colonial empires, a totally asymmetrical relationship between subjects and sovereigns, suppliers, and manufacturers. The multinational corporation situates itself within various cultures. It has a substantial existence in each of them, and it tends to be staffed and energized by the local people in each of its many locations. The rule of thumb, obey the local laws and customs, not only holds as a matter of policy but applies as a matter of fact, since the majority of the employees of the company will in fact be part of the local scene.

"When in Rome, do as the Romans do," goes the old saying. Of course, it is not mentioned that when the Romans went anywhere else, they continued to do as the Romans did—building Roman roads and aqueducts, wearing Roman costumes, and celebrating Roman feasts and holidays. Taking the long view, we should not be too surprised that they were resented and eventually thrown out of most of the far reaches of their empire. Obeying local laws and customs is not just a matter of ethics; it is a prudent policy. When not in Rome, don't do what the Romans did.

What the Romans did is called *imperialism* (Latin for "empire-building"). It was Lenin who later turned the term into a nasty word for international market-grabbing. The problem, of course, is that

"BRIBERY": A QUESTION OF CONTEXT?

The new "business ethics" denies to business the adaptation to cultural mores which has always been considered a moral duty in the traditional approach to ethics. It is now considered "grossly unethical"—indeed it may even be a "questionable practice" if not criminal offense—for an American business operating in Japan to retain as a "counsellor" the distinguished civil servant who retires from his official position in the Japanese government. Yet the business that does not do this is considered in Japan to behave antisocially and to violate its clear ethical duties. Business taking care of retired senior civil servants, the Japanese hold, makes possible two practices they consider essential to the public interest: that a civil servant past age 45 must retire as soon as he is outranked by anyone younger than he; and that governmental salaries and retirement pensions—and with them the burden of the bureaucracy on the taxpayer—be kept low, with the difference between what a first-rate man gets in government service and what he might earn in private employment made up after his retirement through his "counsellor's fees." The Japanese maintain that the expectation of later on being a "counsellor" encourages a civil servant to remain incorruptible, impartial, and objective, and thus to serve only the public good; his counsellorships are obtained for him by his former ministry and its recommendation depends on his rating by his colleagues as a public servant. The Germans, who follow a somewhat similar practice—with senior civil servants expected to be "taken care of" through appointment as industry-association executives—share this conviction. Yet, despite the fact that both the Japanese and the German systems seem to serve their respective societies well and indeed honorably, and even despite the fact that it is considered perfectly "ethical" for American civil servants of equal rank and caliber to move into well-paid executive jobs in business and foundations and into even more lucrative law practices, the American company in Japan that abides by a practice the Japanese consider the very essence of "social responsibility" is pilloried in the present discussion of "business ethics" as a horrible example of "unethical practices."

Peter Drucker, "Business Ethics," *Public Interest*

THE EMERGING TEN

Here are ten countries that have strong potential to affect world markets in the new millennium: Argentina, Brazil, China, India, Indonesia, Mexico, Poland, South Africa, South Korea, Turkey.

—*The Big Ten,* Jeffrey E. Garten (Basic Books, 1997)

CREATING MISERY

BSR: What of the charge that American corporations disrupt cultures of developing nations through their promotion of products and advertising?

Mead: What this advertising does is make people believe that we live in a way in which we don't, that we all have Cadillacs and they ought to have them, too. American movies and American advertising both give a very distorted picture of American life. Just as the notion spreads to every poor home in this country that everyone except they themselves has a $20,000 bathroom, the same thing is even worse overseas.

BSR: Might not this spur rising expectations, rising hopes, and make ultimately for more productive societies?

Mead: No, it makes societies more miserable. The developing society does not yet have the resources in labor or technology to produce an airline—one of the first things they always want is an airline—which is very expensive—or a city with tall buildings. So a very small segment of the population gets "show" things, such as Cadillacs, and the rest stay poor. In fact, the problem is getting worse. Populations are increasing rapidly as modern medicine spreads and fewer babies die. There are more children and fewer people to look after them. People are miserable, and they feel that they're being deprived. . . .

From an interview with anthropologist Margaret Mead, *Business and Society Review*

American business is often accused of "imperialism" when there is no question of "force" at all. Some Third World critics have trouble acknowledging that the American way of life, made possible by the American way of doing business, is extremely attractive and seductive. But the line between offering a product—or way of life—to a free people who have a choice in the matter and essentially seducing a captive audience who lose much more than they gain is absolutely critical here—and it is not always easy to discern. What we consider an investment some people consider an intrusion. What we consider a necessity of life some people consider a frivolous and perhaps degrading luxury. What we consider freedom to choose some people consider the destruction of their way of life.

International markets and multinational corporations are the mainstream of business today (unlike the enclosed economic worlds envisioned by Adam Smith). The essence of international business ethics is just the same as the essence of local business ethics—respect for the freedom and well-being of others—consumers, suppliers, employees, and the community at large. The complication is cultural diversity. International business assumes and appeals to freedom of choice. Imperialism substitutes force for freedom and has nothing to do with free markets. Ethically speaking—and in the not very long run, too— imperialism is bad business.

"When in Rome. . . ." But this rule of thumb is not always workable in international business. A business is a business, and sometimes the demands of good business contradict local practices. It is hard to do business in a culture that imposes heavy penalties on what we consider ordinary business transactions, in a culture that considers working more than a three-hour day unreasonable, in a culture that has no decent (by our standards) communication or transportation system. It is hard to do business in a culture that is wholly unfamiliar not only with the products one produces but with the whole system of practices that support them. In such cases, the business in question seems to have two choices: Change the society or abandon the business. The first is usually possible, but sometimes the second preferable. The first rule of international business ethics is recognizing that not everyone has or wants to have a consumer and profit-minded society.

Sometimes, of course, the changes that are necessary to render a society fit for doing business are very much to the advantage of everyone involved. No open society suffers when there is an improvement in education, transportation, communication, and financial resources. But it is not always clear how "open" a society is—whether or not we approve of societies that "turn their backs on the world and progress." The magic of the market is, in some cultures, a very black magic indeed, totally destroying everything people live for and putting nothing of value (to them) in its place. Our society worries inordinately about the extinction of an unremarkable species of fish, but it often seems indifferent to the destruction of other human modes of existence.

Even societies that are open to change from outside have limits; a culture may benefit from improved roads and a railroad but be severely damaged by the international travel that an airport brings in. (The island of Bali comes to mind.) A culture may benefit greatly from increased literacy but suffer from the subsequent "brain drain" of its most talented youth to more developed career markets elsewhere. Indeed, the painful fact seems to be that every bit of progress has consequences that are destructive of some tradition or other, and the central question of international business ethics must always be "What

---

U.S. INVESTMENT AND HUMAN RIGHTS

[A coalition of labor unions, opponents of child labor, and human-rights groups in the United States and Canada] has seized on recent allegations of mistreatment of workers in Vietnam and Central America to pressure U.S. companies to allow independent non-governmental organizations to freely visit offshore plants and inform U.S. consumers of their findings. Corporate behavior overseas "has become the most popular human-rights issue of the day in this country," said Richard Dicker, who tracks U.S. corporations for Human Rights Watch. . . . In January, Dicker wrote a critical report about a Philips-Van Heusen Corp. plant in Guatemala that led that company to begin collective bargaining with a Guatemalan union that had been illegally suppressed. . . . [A non-governmental human rights organization] in El Salvador has been monitoring a Taiwanese-owned supplier for Gap Inc. . . . A similar group in Honduras will . . . monitor suppliers that export to the United States. . . . But [the challenge to open foreign plants to these human rights organizations has been resisted by the business community] and has become a dividing point inside the anti-sweatshop task force appointed by President Clinton. . . . Still, some cracks are appearing in the corporate opposition to independent monitoring. . . . Nike Inc., which has been one of the chief targets of the labor-rights movement, hired civil-rights activist Andrew Young to review its code of conduct. The company has been criticized . . . for hiring contractors that physically punished their employees.

—*Journal of Commerce,* April 8, 1997

---

are we destroying?" as well as the altruistic "What can we do for them?" and the self-interested "What can we do for ourselves?"

Changing a culture to make it fertile for business is not in itself unethical. One can look around the world and show—as Milton Friedman is so fond of doing—just how much business and free enterprise have helped nations that were impoverished and miserable. (Chile is one of his favorite and more unfortunate examples.) But changing a nation to make it ripe for business is one thing; trying to turn it into another American consumer society is something else. Some multinational corporations too readily use their power to change customs and beliefs that do not interfere or help with business but simply seem distasteful or strange. Enforcing dress codes or changing business hours just to conform to American habits—and putting locals "out of synch" with everyone else—is not essential for business. Introducing foreign entertainments into a society where they are taboo or offensive inevitably breeds dangerous resentment. More attacks on American imperialism are based on such unwanted cultural transformations than on any economic considerations of justice. Iran, most famously, did not so much object to the money and industry we were pouring into the country as to the unnecessary "Western" changes that we were initiating at the same time, so contradictory to their religious and ethical beliefs. Few of these had to do with business or, for that matter, with the political contingencies of the times.

The ethical problem of imperialism is a problem of freedom and responsibility. The assumption of the free-market system is informed and responsible consumer choice. (We don't let children buy razor blades.) If natives can be seduced into buying products, that does not necessarily imply a "free" market. The marketing of baby formula in Africa is an apt if unfortunate illustration. Nestlé (Abbott Laboratories, American Home Products, and Bristol-Myers) engaged in a number of marketing practices that would be considered entirely ethical and ordinary here: having the products endorsed and distributed by people in white coats, giving the impression of medical approval. Nestlé gave out free samples and made the product readily available to any mother who asked for it. It was simply assumed that the mothers knew what they wanted and could read and understand the directions. It was not anticipated that the mothers would make the formula with contaminated water. Knowledge that use of the formula diminished the mother's capacity for breast feeding was assumed to be a familiar natural consequence of any substitution of a manufactured product for nature. But the fact was that these common marketing assumptions were inapplicable in that market, and the result was tragic. Thousands of babies became ill and died. Nestlé had to spend years and millions of dollars defending itself and only now has corrected its tarnished name in the business world. No one questions the ability of the major corporations to create international markets. The question is when and whether one should, whether one is complying with local customs as well as international codes of ethics, whether one's contributions to other societies do in fact outweigh the harmful consequences.

Imperialism is imposing unwanted values on other people, even if not by physical force, even in the guise of free-market choices. But the problem of imperialism is coupled with an equally troublesome ethical dilemma: the problem of *paternalism*. It was wrong for Nestlé to assume that the African mothers knew what they wanted and what was good for them and their babies. But what should they have done? Who

---

THIRD-WORLD ECONOMICS

"People's movements" reject the established development game and its dogmas, putting local reality and practice in their place. They spend no time "brainstorming," or playing other parlor games about "developmental issues" because one of the most precious resources of poor people is time itself. The hungry and sick cannot wait. They cannot afford interminable debates about the relative merits of Keynesianism and monetarism, "top down" and "bottom up" development. To hell in a handbasket, they say, with all the high-sounding tag-lines of the development set.

Varinda Tarzie Vittachi, *Newsweek*

---

are they to decide what mothers and babies in Africa need? The double bind can become a real dilemma for powerful companies: On the one hand, they are wrong to assume that consumers know what they want. On the other hand, they can be and often are accused of interfering with other people's freedom by imposing their values and their sense of "what's good for them." There is no easy formula for treading the treacherous path between imperialism and paternalism, but knowing that the path is there, and watching out for the dangers on both sides, is the key to international business ethics.

It is not always the case that one should conform to the Romans, even in Rome. The continuing example is South Africa, even with the formal end of apartheid and although there are thousands of less controversial cases throughout the business world (not all of them outside the United States). The facts of the case are well known: Black workers in South Africa cannot buy property or enter into collective bargaining—when they can find work at all. They are paid grossly inferior wages and are still subject to abuse, arrest, and imprisonment without recourse to law. This policy continues to be enforced. Accordingly, many international groups (and local groups too) still urge divestment of business in South Africa, thus depriving that segregated society of its financial support.

The problem is that, first of all, it is not clear that American divestment would bring about any beneficial political change. On the other hand, the American presence in South Africa has been a considerable force for reform and improvement, and at least those black workers who are employed by American firms have benefited greatly.

BEYOND THE MULTINATIONAL

The global corporation thinks in terms of the world as being one single market. . . . The global corporation operates at low relative costs and sells the same things in the same way everywhere.

There are some parts of the world that have not yielded, but the globalization of taste preferences is increasing. McDonald's on the Ginza (Tokyo), for example, is the company's most productive store in the world.

Theodore Levitt (Harvard Business School)

American companies have improved black schools, provided decent housing, better transportation, health care, and recreational facilities. But those benefits for some must be weighed against the immoral situation of the whole. Doing business in South Africa supports and implies acceptance of the situation, with whatever intentions or qualifications. Not doing business in South Africa deprives many people of reforms and benefits. But whatever one decides on this difficult problem, one thing is clear: One should *not* do in Johannesburg as the Jo'bergers do. Morality transcends not only markets but cultural boundaries too. And, of course, South Africa is simply the most familiar example among thousands around the world.

There is some talk today of the global corporation whose primary "virtue" is the final breaking down of all cultural differences and the creation of a true "world" market. No idea in American business has ever been more dangerous. The assumption that all people are basically the same in regard to their tastes as consumers has always been the primary ethical liability of American corporations abroad and one of the reasons that we are often hated in places where we are only trying to make a buck and do some good. To elevate this assumption to an institution would be the final disaster. Individual differences and free choices are what make business successful here. It is the same internationally. Tastes and desires are not the same. Of course, we can force others to take our products and supply us, but let's not fool ourselves into thinking that this is business or free enterprise.

CONCLUSION: WHAT DO WE STAND FOR? PEOPLE OR PROFITS?

What do we stand for—people or profits? Ultimately, this is not a choice but a matter of emphasis. Paying attention to people and what they need and want is the best way to bring in the profits. But does this basic principle hold in the expanding and now global world of business? Can we use the precepts of business ethics in a global economy, or are these limited in application? In light of the North American Free Trade Agreement, which effectively opens the borders among the United States, Canada, and Mexico, no one needs to be convinced of the urgency of this topic, or of the enormous difficulties it presents to the ethicist or to the international business person. Particularly with reference to the United States and Mexico, the problems of fair as well as free trade are a matter of considerable controversy. The two nations have very different standards of living and, consequently, very different expectations. Unemployment in the United States is a serious problem, but the number of unemployed in Mexico, many of whom would like to come to the United States for work, is devastating.

As difficult as questions of justice and fairness may be at the national level, at the international level they are all but mind numbing. It is one thing to issue the challenge, how can we train and provide possibilities for millions of unemployed and underemployed American workers. But when we open up the question to the global market and ask the same question of hundreds of millions of workers, what are we to do? How do you so extend what is already a serious challenge to a world filled with cruel dictatorships, civil wars, starving millions, and more millions of homeless refugees? Indeed, even the more modest question—how does one act when one sets up shop elsewhere?—finds itself caught in a tangle of cross-cultural differences and inequities. What are the constraints on international business, and what are the rights of others that we must respect and cannot deny?

There are no easy answers to such questions, and the usual dogmatisms get stretched thin indeed when the global economy comes into question. Yet the situation is not so hopeless as many commentators suppose, and there is a good bit of space between amoral opportunism on the one hand and resolute insistence on one's own, perhaps paro-

TWO RUNS, THREE FUMBLES, AND LOVE-FORTY

The bottom line of any formalized standard of world-wide ethics is to attach a structured code of oscillating principles. It's as if we were to apply football rules to the games of tennis, soccer, and baseball and hope there wouldn't be any confusion.

William Mackie (Ingersoll-Rand Corporation)

chial, principles on the other. Take, for example, one of the most common applications of the "When in Rome, do as the Romans do" philosophy, the justification of facilitating payments and favors that in this country would clearly count as "bribes." Some companies, Lockheed notoriously, insist that it is simply the cost of doing business in another country; while others, Procter and Gamble, for example, hold themselves up as paragons of virtue, refuse to pay the amounts demanded, and hold out until they can gain entry into the market in some other, less compromising way. But over and above the arguments to the effect of "that's the way they do business over there" and "we refuse to compromise our principles," there is a broader set of considerations that are more at home in the ethics of free enterprise as such. One way to put it would be: can "corruption" be a legitimate way of doing business anywhere?

Our answer depends upon what we mean by "doing business," and here the whole argument of this book comes back as a reply. Insofar as business is (wrongly) conceived as a self-enclosed game or a simple search for profits, then, yes, payoffs can simply be made part of the game strategy or, perhaps, even considered part of the ground rules. But insofar as business has larger ambitions and responsibilities, to the freedom of the free market and the prosperity and well-being of the community it serves, then corrupt practices obviously hurt not only the legitimate businesses trying to enter the market but everyone involved or impacted by the market. Prices go up; quality suffers. Supply is compromised; demand is manipulated or distorted. But what such an argument presupposes is that the market is in fact such a social enterprise, that it is a very general and not carefully circumscribed way of satisfying the needs of the human condition, and though culture may bend and shape these needs in some interestingly different ways in different societies, we all recognize the basic essentials without which any social or economic system must be judged to be a failure.

It is my belief that the free-enterprise system can and will supply those basic needs and transform the world as it does so. But this does not mean denying the dangers, overlooking abuses, or destroying other cultures and other values than narrowly circumscribed business values, and it does not license the socially irresponsible pursuit of profits that too many people confuse with the free-enterprise system. Adam Smith was making an extremely important point when he defended the virtues of self-interest and the ability of properly directed self-interest to produce prosperity for all. But Adam Smith never believed and never suggested that unrestricted self-interest was a good thing, and despite his much-abused "invisible hand" comment he never implied that free enterprise devoid of a sense of human sympathy and solidarity would have but the most horrible consequences. Free enterprise presumes a sense of community and social responsibility, a strong sense of *noblesse oblige* on the part of those of us who succeed and a strong sense of sympathy and benevolence for those who do not or have not yet had the chance. What free enterprise does not need and can no longer tolerate are those proud new millionaires who proclaim their virtue instead of expressing their gratitude and turn their considerable resources to the sole purpose of self-protection, shutting out those who have no such resources at all.

What the new world of business requires is not something radically new so much as a return to some very old traditional values, a sense of community, an insistence on integrity, a recognition that we are all part of a larger world and that it is our responsibility—because it is in our power—to change it for the better as we improve ourselves. We need, in other words, to stand for something, and not just the market itself. The new world of business may thus turn out not to be so new at all. But it might be a good deal better.

INDEX

ABOUT THE AUTHOR

ROBERT C. SOLOMON is Quincy Lee Centennial Professor of Philosophy and Business and Distinguished Teaching Professor at the University of Texas at Austin. He is the author of several other books about business ethics, including *Above the Bottom Line* and *Ethics and Excellence*. He is also the author of *The Passions, In the Spirit of Hegel, About Love, A Passion for Justice,* and *The Bully Culture*. With Kathleen Higgins, he is coauthor of *A Short History of Philosophy* and *A Passion for Wisdom* and coeditor of *From Africa to Zen*. He regularly consults and designs programs for a variety of corporations and organizations concerned about business ethics in the United States and abroad.